T0354270

Easily Slip
into
Another World

Easily Slip into Another World

A LIFE IN MUSIC

Henry Threadgill
and Brent Hayes Edwards

Alfred A. Knopf

New York *2024*

THIS IS A BORZOI BOOK
PUBLISHED BY ALFRED A. KNOPF

www.aaknopf.com

Knopf, Borzoi Books, and the colophon are registered trademarks
of Penguin Random House LLC.

Grateful acknowledgment is made to Blank Forms, Inc., for permission
to reprint excerpts from *Nothing But the Music* by Thulani Davis.
Originally published by Blank Forms, Brooklyn, New York, in 2020.

Library of Congress Cataloging-in-Publication Data
Names: Threadgill, Henry, author. | Edwards, Brent Hayes, author.
Title: Easily slip into another world: a life in music / Henry Threadgill with
Brent Hayes Edwards.
Description: New York: Alfred A. Knopf, 2023. |
Identifiers: LCCN 2022038295 (print) | LCCN 2022038296 (ebook) |
ISBN 9781524749071 (hardcover) | ISBN 9781524749088 (ebook)
Subjects: LCSH: Threadgill, Henry. | Composers—United States—
Biography. | Saxophonists—United States—Biography. | Jazz musicians—
United States—Biography. | LCGFT: Autobiographies.
Classification: LCC ML410.T4534 A3 2023 (print) | LCC ML410.T4534 (ebook) |
DDC 781.65092 [B]—dc23/eng/20220810
LC record available at https://lccn.loc.gov/2022038295
LC ebook record available at https://lccn.loc.gov/2022038296

Jacket photograph by Jules Allen Photography
Jacket design by Linda Huang

Manufactured in the United States of America
Published May 16, 2023
Second Printing, March 2024

For my mother, Lillian Threadgill,
who put me on this road

Contents

Easily Slip
into
Another World

———————

1.

Too Much Sugar

No matter the season, Peyton Robinson always wore the same thing. Whether it was 110 degrees or 10 below zero, my great-grandfather used to walk around Chicago in a three-piece wool suit with long underwear beneath it, high lace-up leather shoes with wool socks up to his knees, an overcoat, and a top hat. His body temperature never changed. I used to watch the way he would sweat. It would be mid-August and he would be sitting there calmly with the sweat running down his neck in rivulets. He'd eat spicy food, too—he especially loved wild game: bear meat and raccoons and snakes and all kinds of rustic stuff. I figured that all these peculiar habits were the reason he lived so long and never seemed to catch a cold.

Peyton Robinson didn't live with us. When I was young, I lived in a big and noisy apartment on 33rd and Cottage Grove near Groveland Park with my grandparents, my mother, my younger sister, and a number of my aunts, uncles, and cousins. But my great-grandfather lived in a rough neighborhood way out on the West Side. As I got older, I came to see Peyton Robinson as something approaching a creature of legend, the protagonist of a trove of family lore. It thrilled me when he came to visit, like some apparition from another century, or another planet. And I loved to think I came from such a singularity—from an ancestor who seemed to move through the world entirely on his own terms.

The stories were riveting. Years later my mother told me that once Peyton Robinson got into some trouble with a gang over on the West Side. One evening somebody said something rude to him and he said, "Fuck you." The person was associated with the gang, and they conveyed a message that my great-grandfather had better watch his mouth if he didn't want anything to happen to him.

Peyton Robinson went out at three a.m. with a shotgun and just started shooting up into the air, bellowing in the middle of the night. "Come on out in the street, motherfuckers, here I am!" he yelled. "I'm right here!"

It woke up the whole neighborhood. People were peeping out from behind their curtains at this crazy man screaming in the alley. But nobody ventured out to meet his challenge. And after that, people gave him a wide berth in the street.

Even the meanest dogs knew better, somehow. Often he would come to visit us early in the morning, arriving while everyone was still asleep. He would walk down the back alleys with his three-piece suit and a cane. Usually dogs would bark and growl and rush at the fences when people came down the alleys. But when Peyton Robinson strode by, the German shepherds and bulldogs were quiet.

I live in sound.

All my references go back to sound. I go back in my memory and I don't see: I hear. The first thing I remember is the sound of the streetcar that went by our apartment building. This was before I started kindergarten. I must have been about three years old. There was a hospital nearby, and all these people would get off at 33rd Street. As the streetcar came in, the first thing you would hear is the carriage bell, announcing its arrival with a *cling cling.* The carriage bell was made out of brass and sterling silver and built into the floor of the streetcar. It worked with a foot pedal, and the driver would pump it as he pulled in. You find carriage bells in the Caribbean, too, in Jamaica and Ber-

muda and other places. When I heard that sound, I would run
to the window. A few of the young grandchildren stayed home
with my grandmother Gertrude during the day while my mother
and my grandfather went to work and my aunts and uncles went
to school.

The radio was on all day long. My grandmother would listen
to shows like *Arthur Godfrey Time* and Art Linkletter's *House
Party*. Art Linkletter had a house band that featured an accordion
player. I still remember that in particular because I wasn't crazy
about accordion at that time, and I thought the band sounded
strange. After their shows finished, sometimes my grandmother
would switch to another station where they were playing classical music. My sister and my cousins would get impatient and run
off and play, but I would sit and listen and daydream on it. And
then it might go from that to Serbian music, because Chicago
had the biggest Serbian community in the country, the largest
outside Yugoslavia. There was a Serbian radio station, a Serbian
newspaper. And there was also a large Polish population, mostly
living in an area behind the Stock Yards. So that music would
come on, too.

In those days radio was more or less a hodgepodge. I remember Mexican music, country music (which people used to call
"hillbilly" back then), jazz, rhythm and blues, boogie-woogie,
plus regular programming including radio plays, detective
shows, and science fiction. On Sundays my grandfather would
put on a gospel station and listen to Mahalia Jackson, James
Cleveland, Clay Evans, and the Pilgrim Travelers. There was a
little of everything. In a way, you could say that the programmers
didn't have any idea what they were doing—which is the way it
really should be. It was uncontrolled, untamed by the forces of
commercialism. A lot of it was improvised. Television was like
that in the beginning, too: Ted Mack's *Original Amateur Hour,
Arthur Godfrey and His Friends,* the *General Electric Theater*
on CBS hosted by Ronald Reagan, the *Ford Star Jubilee* with
live stagings of scripts by Noël Coward and Herman Wouk, *The
Nat King Cole Show, The Kate Smith Hour* on NBC. But radio

was the main thing then: the same way kids sit for hours in front of the television or the computer now, back then we would sit in front of the radio and skip from station to station. And it was amazing, the amount of music there was.

By the time I hit high school, Studs Terkel had started hosting his radio show on WFMT, and I was enthralled by how wide and eclectic he made the world sound. He would play everything from blues and Mexican *son jarocho* to Central African music, Indian classical music, and flamenco, and he interspersed the music with interviews of all sorts of people—film and theater directors, actors, poets, blues singers, architects and industrial designers, orchestra conductors, folklore collectors, choreographers. Decades later, Studs Terkel's program might have been called a "world music" show, but he did it without the label, before it was a marketing category, and that made it more thrilling: your ears could roam, and you heard unexpected echoes between far-flung corners of the globe.

When I was young, boogie-woogie was the music that caught my attention. Before it did, I wasn't even aware that there was a piano in the house. It was in the hallway: a player piano, the kind you stick rolls in. When I started hearing boogie-woogie—it was popular then: Albert Ammons, Pete Johnson, Meade Lux Lewis, and people like that—I was just swept off. I was determined to learn how to play it myself, and when I was in elementary school I started pecking at the piano. I didn't take formal lessons, but I was able to figure out some things by ear. I would sit there engrossed, trying to replicate a riff I heard on the radio or on a record, straining to stretch my little hands to fit those piston-like left-hand rhythms. Sometimes I'd put on a piano roll and then I could see where the keys were depressed and follow the patterns. I lost track of time. I could sit and play the piano for hours and no one would say anything because they knew where I was and I wasn't getting into trouble. I was like a cow with a bell around its neck.

On Sundays generally we would go to my grandmother Gertrude's church, the Church of God in Christ, which was a

I could sit and play the piano for hours . . .

Holiness-Pentecostal denomination, or what people called a "sanctified" church, on Indiana Avenue around 32nd Street. There was a famous minister there, Reverend Charles, and they would always have these assistant ministers and visiting preachers coming in. The "singing preacher" was always a big thing there. I remember one in particular at that church named Sammy Lewis. My sister and my cousins and my youngest uncle and I would go to church and get knocked out by the music, and we'd come back home and put on our own little show. We would fight over who was going to be Singing Sammy Lewis. It became a whole ritual: we put all sorts of gunk in our hair, dressed up in our aunts' and uncles' clothes, and set up a stage in the house.

Occasionally we would go to my other grandmother's church. My father's mother, Helen Threadgill, belonged to a more traditional house of worship, the Olivet Baptist Church on 31st and South Park, or what is now Martin Luther King Jr. Drive. It was more "sophisticated," you could say, than the Church of God in Christ. The minister of Olivet Baptist Church was Joseph Jackson, the head of the Southern Baptist Convention, who was very influential in terms of drumming up votes for city hall downtown. It was the biggest church on the South Side of Chicago, a beautiful stone building with fabulous rugs and a balcony. At the Baptist church they sang arrangements out of the hymnal. It sounded good, but it was more restrained. At the Church of God in Christ, though, they would just *sing*. They would go off: people would speak in tongues and fall on the floor, kicking and screaming. So Reverend Charles's church was the one that grabbed my attention. The whole thing was like a ritual of theater and movement and sound and drama. And it wasn't planned. Each week the service would follow a similar layout or template, but it was unpredictable. Things could take off in any direction.

The Church of God in Christ also had regular visiting preachers and singers like Mahalia Jackson and James Cleveland. When Mahalia Jackson would come there to sing Sunday afternoons—most of the time they'd have these afternoon concerts—the entire neighborhood would be out in front of the church, including people who had no interest at all in religion. The church would be jam-packed, so they had to put speakers outside when she sang. I remember being overwhelmed by her and the other singers who used to come through there.

Early Sunday mornings my grandfather, Luther Pierce, would sometimes take me with him to the Maxwell Street Market, what people used to call Jew Town. It was a big outdoor market, and blues musicians would be on the sidewalk playing. My grandfather wouldn't really listen to blues on the radio at home. But at Maxwell Street I got to hear it. On Sunday morning at six o'clock in the morning they'd be out there on a little platform less than a foot high playing guitars hooked up to portable amplifiers. Muddy Waters, Arvella Gray. The one who really mesmerized me was Howlin' Wolf—the *power* of his sound almost had me frozen in my footsteps.

My mother was the person who was responsible for taking me to hear concerts when I was a kid. She did various things for work while I was growing up. Eventually she worked as an accountant at a bank downtown, but I remember that for a while when I was little, she did a bunch of small jobs at home: she would bake cakes for people in the neighborhood, for example, and she also made lampshades on commission. There would be dozens of frames all around the apartment, and she'd painstakingly cut silk or other fabric and stretch it onto the shades. But my mother also liked music, and it turns out she had studied the piano. I always thought the piano in our hallway was my aunt's piano— that my grandparents had bought it for my aunt who had gone off to study voice and opera in college. I didn't find out until years later that it was actually my mother's piano. When I was a child, I never knew that she had studied piano at all. She never told me.

At that time, you could go to the big movie houses and see a film, and then there would be a stage show. I went to see so much live music that way. I was still a toddler, maybe only two and a half or three, when my mother took me to see Sugar Chile

. . . my mother also liked music . . .

Robinson, the "child wonder" from Harlem who played piano and organ. We went to see Sugar Chile and people like Lucky Millinder and Louis Jordan multiple times before I started elementary school. Louis Jordan was a great entertainer, and his music was joyous and loose-limbed. I liked the way he played the saxophone. What he played was kind of a mix of jazz and rhythm and blues, and the lyrics had these double meanings. I remember people around us in the audience would be cracking up. I didn't get it—I was too young to understand—but I would look over and see people laughing. I'd say to myself, I wonder what they're laughing at.

These concerts were mostly at the Regal, which was on the South Side and had a history of stage shows. Or downtown in the Loop, at the Chicago Theater, or at the State-Lake. I can remember sitting back in the balcony at the Regal. My mother used to take my sister, too, but my sister would sleep through it half the time—she wasn't interested. I was entranced, though. I remember that I was particularly fascinated with Sugar Chile. I couldn't get that kid out of my mind. It was astonishing and intimidating to see the way this kid up there in a white tuxedo would come on stage and play like that. We'd be so far back that I couldn't tell exactly what age he was, but I could tell he was a little boy. He was bigger than me, but he was still young. I just couldn't believe that kid.

In 1951, when I was in elementary school (I started at Doolittle and then switched to Douglass Grammar School a year later), we moved to 31st Street. My parents were separated, and every week my father would come and pick up my sister, Carol, and me. He would be sharp, he'd come by and pick us up in his big car. My father ran a sort of gambling house. He would pick us up in the morning and take us to his casino. And he would bring us in and turn on the lights and open the place up, taking the covers off the beautiful green felt tables, which later in the evening would be bustling with games of craps, blackjack, poker, and baccarat.

*. . . every week my father would come and
pick up my sister, Carol, and me.*

Once we were there, just the three of us, my father would give me money and tell me to go and play the jukebox. There was no pop music. It was nothing but jazz artists: all the records were by big names like Count Basie, Duke Ellington, and Benny Goodman. He would say, "Here, Moon"—he'd always call me Moon, joking that with my big head I looked like Moon Mullins, the character in the syndicated cartoon strip—"you go play some music." And he'd give me a handful of nickels. I would go and put on record after record. I remember I used to love to sit there. He would get out his whisk broom and clean off the tables, and as he worked he would sing along a little bit to the tunes I put on. He knew most of them by heart, because he loved the great swing bands, Woody Herman and all of them. My sister didn't pay much attention to the jukebox but, again, I would get transported. I would lose all sense of my surroundings: I wouldn't even be there, I would be gone. I remember trying to understand the songs I was listening to. And not only the lyrics—something in me was curious to decipher the secrets of the songs' pulsating architecture. Sometimes it seemed the spell could be sustained indefinitely: one tune would end, but the beat continued in the gentle rasp of the whisk broom on the felt, and then the jukebox arm would deliver the next disc into position. So easy to slip into another world.

There was a Leader Cleaners on 31st and Cottage Grove, and there were a lot of businesses on 33rd Street. My two youngest aunts were young women by then, maybe eighteen years old or so, and boys were coming by to see them. And they had clothes in the cleaners. Often they would ask one of the young kids to go and pick up their dresses. The task usually fell to me or my cousin Michael, who was a year older. A lot of the time, they'd offer us a nickel or something to go get it. But I would offer to get it for free, because next to the Leader Cleaners there was a record shop. In those days the music they were playing was always piped through speakers outside. That's when I became aware of Gene Ammons, because that's where I heard "Street of Dreams" and "Red Top." I used to hope that somebody had something at the cleaners so that I could go over there and stand outside of the record shop and hear "Street of Dreams."

And then one of my aunts, who was precociously hip, started going out to the clubs. It was an incredible era: people like Billie Holiday and Bird and Lester Young were coming through town. So then I started hearing these names and associating them with the music coming out of the record store. This was before fourth grade, so I was still young. I was indoctrinated early on with Jazz at the Philharmonic and Gene Ammons. And I started noticing Sarah Vaughan, too, because she had a hit I used to hear at the record store. At three or four o'clock on Friday, the street was bustling. That's when the store would be pushing these records, too. It was the end of the week, and people would have just gotten paid. The record store would put on the hits, hoping to get people to come in and buy them. Saturday it was the same way.

In 1954 we moved from 31st Street to Sangamon Street between 59th and 60th in Englewood, where my grandparents and my mother bought a house. My aunt got the first Admiral console television/radio/record player. It was a three-piece unit. You opened one door and there the television was. You opened another door on the right and the turntable would slide out, with a radio built into the receiver. And then down below that there was a cabinet where you could store your records. I remember the first 33⅓ album we had: *Jazz at the Philharmonic* with Lionel Hampton, Willie Smith, Charlie Shavers, and a bunch of other people playing. One of the pieces was "Stardust," and that one got me. I would put it on all the time. Through *Jazz at the Philharmonic* I discovered Flip Phillips, too. And Slam Stewart, the bass player, who used to sing when he played the bass: "Give me more money!" Nat King Cole entered the picture around the same time, because both of my aunts were enthralled with his debonair singing. They had his records, too: "I'm Never Satisfied." A lot of records started turning up in the house because we had this new unit.

In Englewood I went to Beale School, just a block away from home, from the fourth grade to the eighth grade. When I got to seventh grade in 1956–57 I had a teacher named Mr. Zimmerman who used to wear these blue serge suits all the time. He was a very quiet man. Not that we were bad, but he really controlled the class without hardly saying anything. I think the kids might have been a little bit afraid of him. Mr. Zimmerman would make us take a nap in the afternoon, which was unusual in seventh grade. But in fact it was very important to me, because I was always daydreaming. It didn't take much to set my imagination off, and I couldn't wait. The year before, I used to walk past his classroom, I remember, and wish I were in his class. I couldn't wait to get to seventh grade because I knew that they took a nap, and I saw that nap as their dream time.

But the important thing was, he would play classical music during our nap period. For almost forty-five minutes in the afternoon. Mr. Zimmerman would tell the kids to put their heads down and rest, and he would go and stand at the window and stare out the window as if he were remembering something. I think he was a veteran, maybe from the Korean War. There was something about him. After becoming a veteran myself I can kind of spot certain things in people, especially people that have been in war zones. I can't tell from people who've never been in a war zone—they don't have any of the little signature kinds of things I can pick up on—but with people that have been in those kinds of dynamic situations, there are telltale signs. I'm sure there was something like that going on with Mr. Zimmerman, because he would use that period for some type of reflection and meditation. And he was a good teacher. He explained things well.

Mr. Zimmerman loved Tchaikovsky. At the time, I didn't know who Tchaikovsky was. I didn't know who he was even after seventh grade, to be honest, even if we were listening to him during nap time. I didn't find out until I was in high school playing in the band and we were performing Tchaikovsky. And I realized that his Fifth Symphony had been one of Mr. Zimmerman's favorites. I was crazy about that thing. It was just like Howlin' Wolf—it would take me off. Every afternoon after lunch, I couldn't wait to run to class to get ready for nap time so that I could listen to Tchaikovsky and daydream. And basically he would only play Tchaikovsky: *The Nutcracker,* the *Capriccio Italien,* all these different pieces that I ended up finding out the names of only much later. He put music on every day. I wasn't aware of any other kids being affected by it, though, at least not the way I was. Sometimes he would look back and he would see me, because I wouldn't have my head down. I would forget the posture I was supposed to be in. Instead I would sit up, listening and dreaming.

Moving to Englewood meant moving to a racially mixed neighborhood. A couple of years after we moved there, I started getting in some trouble with some friends of mine. We weren't robbing anybody. We tried to break into a few places and find something to steal. Sometimes we came close to getting caught by the police. What shocked me was that the cops didn't simply try to apprehend us; they would shoot at us, Black children, barely teenagers—and I mean shoot to kill.

It's hard to explain what that's like, being ten or eleven years old and having the police chase you in a squad car and shoot at you. People talk about being scared—they don't know what being scared is. I was running for my motherfucking life. Once I remember we got away from them by running up an alley and jumping over a fence. There were these narrow gangways between buildings, and you could jump down into one and get away that way. There were these gangways everywhere, so the police wouldn't know which one you went into.

The cops were shooting at us as we ran across the street, hopped the fence, and leapt down into a gangway. Once we were sure we'd lost them, we stopped to catch our breath. And my friend Billy showed us a hole in his shoe: one of the bullets had gone clean through the heel!

That was too close for comfort. When I realized that the police wouldn't think twice about killing us, I stopped fooling around with that. In that neighborhood there were Jewish kids, Polish kids, Greek kids. All my white friends were annoyed that I stopped taking part in their escapades. They did the same stuff the Black kids were doing, and even worse. But the police never pulled out their guns and shot at the white children for some minor nonsense. It made me face the fact that I had experiences a white kid would never have.

In 1969, after I returned from Vietnam, I went to visit my maternal grandmother in the house in Englewood. A couple of young thugs had been trying to coerce her into letting them stash some stolen goods in her backyard. Grandma Gertrude stood up to them. "Get out of my yard," she said. Totally calm. But the way she said things, you could tell she was not ever going to back down. Still they tried to intimidate her. I remember that while I was visiting, they actually fired a couple of gunshots through the window. No one had told me about the whole situation, so I was startled when it happened. I thought I'd survived my days of dodging gunfire in the war. We were sitting there at the kitchen table, and suddenly the window shattered. The bullet passed right over my head and lodged in the wall. I reflexively dove under the table. But my grandmother didn't even move. She just sat there, looking at them out the window. I think they must have gotten the message, because they didn't come back after that. She was like her father, Peyton Robinson: unbreakable.

I started taking piano lessons when we moved to Englewood. A lady called Ms. Holmes used to come and give me and my sister lessons. My mother had gotten a piano from Lyon & Healy. I kept that piano for years, until I gave it away when I came to New York.

This lady would come to the house. But my sister and I didn't like her at all. Every week, rather than coming home for my piano lesson, I would stay out and play ball and stuff and get into trouble. Ms. Holmes would beat you on the knuckles with a ruler when you were playing wrong. So you were constantly afraid of making a mistake. And when you're starting out, all you're going to do is make mistakes. She didn't know how to teach music. That's the case with most people, really. That's why you hear people say, "I just couldn't learn music": it's because their teachers didn't know what they were doing. You have to understand it properly to teach it. I know that now, in retrospect.

If Ms. Holmes had been a good teacher she could have explained it to me, because it was simpler than anything that I was learning in school. Certainly it was much simpler than the science and mathematics that we were learning in fourth grade. It was much simpler. The only thing was that you had to physically execute something. But we didn't really understand music notation properly. She didn't get that across. Still, I kept fooling around with the piano on my own until I got to high school, and that's when my mother got me a tenor saxophone, when I was about fifteen.

Those thugs who tried to hassle my grandmother were lucky Peyton Robinson wasn't there. He was the one who brought my mother's family up to Chicago. I heard whispers about the reason they left the South: my great-grandfather and his twin brother had shot and killed a bunch of white people in Alabama. The whites tried to take their land—tried to swindle them out of their property. It was the best land in the region: rolling pastures right next to the river. And Peyton Robinson wasn't having it. When the white folks tried to force the issue, he shot them dead. That's why he had to get the family out of there. They hit the road and spent some time in Mississippi, where my grandmother was born, before they came up to Chicago.

———

My mother had eight brothers and sisters, and my aunt Evelyn was the middle sister. She was the first one to go to college and she decided to study opera, which was fairly unusual. We didn't even know what the word meant. I was about three when she met a bass player named Nevin Wilson, who was playing with Ahmad Jamal. Nevin was the first real musician in my life. They got married and moved to Rockford, Illinois, and over the years I would sometimes go to stay with them. So I was exposed to some of the music that they were doing. I wanted to play bass because my uncle played bass. But when I got up on a chair to play it, it hurt my fingers. I asked him why I was having all these problems, and he told me I was going to have to wait to grow up to play bass. I said, "I guess I won't play the bass if I have to wait to grow up to do it."

I didn't have any intentions at that point in terms of becoming a musician. I just knew I liked music a lot and I wanted to play it. I kept noodling at the keyboard, learning things by ear.

Nevin was playing with Ahmad Jamal in Chicago. Ahmad had a solo piano gig, and Nevin used to go down and help him out sometimes, because it was a big deal. Years later Ahmad told me, "I'd never have made it if it hadn't been for Nevin coming and helping me out." I heard them play a couple of times. Nevin used to talk about Ahmad all the time and play the records too. Even though I was young, I could tell that what he was doing was different. The distribution of space, the assignment of pitches and stuff to the drums—it was the first time I heard drums playing all of these pitches. And also his attitude: Ahmad Jamal would do whatever *he* wanted to do. He would stop the band right in the middle of a song. Or stretch it out—he'd play something as long as he wanted to play it. It didn't necessarily do what it was "supposed" to do. *He* decided what it was going to do. Many years later, reading Miles Davis's autobiography, I understood how great his influence was. Miles would bring his whole band to listen to Ahmad Jamal. And you started hearing the difference in Miles's band too, with Red Garland and Coltrane, how that space started opening up.

I had never really known fear as a young child living in a Black community in the first years of my life. Once we moved to Englewood, two things happened that gave me nightmares. It was like an inauguration.

The first was the lynching of Emmett Till—when we saw those pictures of his mutilated body in *Jet* in September 1955. Our parents reacted to it, but they didn't realize their children looked at those photos, too. The worst part was, I knew him. I used to go to the same barbershop as Emmett Till in Chicago. The barbershop was owned by Mr. Parker, the father of my friend Donald. There were always a lot of kids coming and going in that place. But I remember seeing Emmett Till there. His father would bring him in. My own parents didn't know about this, because it wouldn't have occurred to them that I would be in the barbershop with this kid. But we knew him, and then we saw those photos. How can you think that I could grow up and handle that on my own? What was I supposed to do with that? Where was I supposed to tuck that away?

Around the same time, I almost got killed myself. One day my friend Milton Chapman and I walked across 59th Street to a wood factory at the corner of Peoria, by the Blue Island railroad tracks. The factory took all the wood scraps they weren't going to use and put them in a bin in the back. So we went across to get a few pieces to make toys. We made almost all our own toys, scooters and stilts and stuff like that. The next thing I knew, I heard people down the block yelling, "Kill him!" It was white women, mothers—women holding babies, yelling to anybody in earshot. "Kill him!" I looked over my shoulder, confused. I didn't know what they were talking about. "Kill him!" And then bricks and rocks started raining down on me. I turned around and started running as fast as I could.

We didn't know that you're not supposed to cross 59th Street.

Englewood was an integrated neighborhood, but it was all white on the other side of that street, and there was some sort of invisible line. Coming from a Black community, we didn't pay any attention to that. I knew there was a white neighborhood over there, but I didn't think anything of it.

When it happened, Milton and I had gone maybe a fifth of the way down the block to the factory yard, just past the railroad tracks. We had grabbed a few pieces of wood and were coming back with them. The white people came out like hunting dogs. It was like they smelled us or something. Like a siren went off. This wasn't other kids attacking us: it was a pack of grown-ups screaming as they rushed down the street, throwing bricks at us. And as I ran away, I was trying to figure out, What did we do? This was about a few pieces of wood? What did we do? We knew that other kids went and took wood scraps from the factory yard. Did they think we were stealing it?

Milton and I ran across 59th Street into an alley and hid in somebody's basement. We sat there for a long time, making sure we hadn't been followed, drenched in sweat, our chests heaving. We just sat there looking at each other. We didn't even say anything. They had stoned us! We were both sitting there stunned, trying to figure it out. Finally we both cleaned ourselves up and went home. That much was clear: I've got to go home and you've got to go home. We both knew that nobody else could know about it. We were afraid to tell our parents, because we thought we had done something wrong. We were afraid they would say, "What have you been doing? What did you go down there upsetting white people for?" We simply couldn't understand it. And we knew, without even discussing it, that there was no one we could talk to.

I was still just a kid when I first heard Charlie Parker. I was listening to all these different kinds of music. When I heard Bird, I didn't know what it was about, but I was just crazy about it.

And by the time I turned fourteen or fifteen years old, I

knew I had to play the saxophone. It wasn't that I decided to abandon the piano—it was simply that I was captivated by Bird. I still appreciated the locomotive thrust of boogie-woogie. But I fell in love with Charlie Parker's dazzlingly quick-witted improvisations.

There was something about the reality of what he was playing, in terms of the time I was living in. It felt modern—emphatically up-to-date. *Now's the time.* I could feel an association between the music and the social events of the moment. Charlie Parker was a new sort of virtuoso, too. We had come out of the swing era, which was dominated by big bands. By the mid-1940s, the advent of bebop contracted everything down to these small ensembles featuring players graced with astounding technical mastery. It wasn't just a matter of their virtuosity, though; they also extended their musical concept from the rhythmic and harmonic points of view. When Parker took the saxophone out of the big band context and reframed it in a smaller context, he magnified it. He heard it much more critically because it wasn't simply playing a part—it wasn't a part of a chorus anymore. It had to stand alone.

When I first heard Charlie Parker on record, I said, "That's it!" On that exact day I told myself, "This is the door." And it was a door to other doors. Before I heard Bird, I had a concept of what jazz was, and I thought I had an idea of how wide it was or how big it was. And then all of a sudden a door opened into a new sound—and that meant there were other thresholds to cross.

I made myself a saxophone out of wire hangers and stuff. It didn't play—it was just something to mime playing with. I learned all this music and I would pretend to play it on my toy saxophone. I memorized entire arrangements from records, and I could sing all the parts on the records. Everybody I knew could do that. My friends and I listened to everybody's part on every record: the drum part, the bass part, the piano part, every soloist. We could sing every note. All the kids I was around knew everyone in all the bands, including the famous white groups like the Glenn Miller Orchestra and Paul Whiteman and His Orchestra. All the West Coast groups, too. We knew every song and could sing every part—that's what we would do for entertainment. We'd get together and say, "You do the bass, you do drums, I'll do piano, you do the lead."

By the time I was in seventh grade or eighth grade, there were Friday-night dances at people's houses: boys and girls packed into the basement dancing, squeezing up against each other in the dark. Around that time, I started singing a little, doing some doo-wop stuff with quartets.

After I graduated from Beale in 1958, I went to Englewood High School. A lot of people I knew there ended up becoming musicians, including the drummers Ajaramu, Arlington Davis Jr., and Steve McCall, and the horn players Louis Satterfield and Don Myrick. My friend Milton was an aspiring musician, too—he wanted to play trumpet—and he started Englewood High the year before me. In the spring of 1958, Milton took me to hear Stan Getz and Chet Baker in concert in the high-school auditorium. Musicians would come to Chicago for a main gig at a nightclub, and they'd sometimes do things like a high-school concert as a side job.

At that time there were these mail-in record clubs that would send you records. My friends and I couldn't afford to buy them, so we'd order records under the names of people in the neighborhood. Then we'd sit next door and wait for the mailman. We knew the people wouldn't be home, because it was during the afternoon when they were at work. I remember there were albums by Dakota Staton, Dave Brubeck, Don Ellis, Paul Gonsalves, Paul Quinichette . . . And the very first records we got that way were by Stan Getz and Chet Baker. So between the concert and their records, I started to understand who they were.

There were a lot of concerts like that in the schools around Chicago. Bands and ensembles would come and play. And even the school dances were all live music, not recorded music. That was true anyplace people went to dance. The skating rink, too,

VOL. 20 - NO. 2   WILLIAM G. BEALE SCHOOL, CHICAGO, ILLINOIS   JANUARY, 1958   10¢

BEALE GRADUATION CLASS

Top, left to right: Michael West, Dolores Poree, Fred Kurgan, Sam White, Victoria Davis, Kenneth Pugh, Eugene Ringo, Donald Randall, Jim Murray, Mayor Ardella Mosley, Henry Threadgill.

Center: Mr. Burke, Beverly DeLeigh, Willie Hairston, Clyde Topps, Reid Alexander, Norman Fuller, Christine Lukesh, Douglas Ichihashi, Willie Ritchie, Prince Humphries, Mr. Johnston, Principal.

First Row: Barbara Preston, Caroline Adams, Geraldine Smith, City Clerk Joyce Foster, Meredith Wilson, Bonnie Reynolds, Sharon Chisum, Marquetta Person.

Not photographed: Betty Isby, James Lewis.

. . . after I graduated from Beale in 1958 . . .

for instance—I loved to go skating at Park City Roller Rink. I remember my mother bought me skates so that I could go. It was a famous place, and they would have big dance concerts there, too, on the holidays. Once we went to Park City and heard Muddy Waters and Howlin' Wolf and a bunch of other blues bands. But that day a big fight broke out between rival gangs, and we had to leave.

When I was about fifteen, I finally convinced my mother to buy me a tenor saxophone. I found out later that my grandmother paid for it—not my grandmother Gertrude, but my father's mother. My mother didn't have enough money. But Grandma Threadgill didn't want it to be known that she had paid for it. I went with my mother down to the Lyon & Healy music store and she signed me up for free lessons. It was a group class every Saturday morning where people were playing all sorts of different instruments. It culminated in a little recital after a few weeks. It was nonsense: you can't teach that way. Everyone got a little attention, but there were too many people with too many different instruments, trumpets and violins and clarinets all going at the same time.

So that was brief. I started going downtown to the Chicago School of Music, and that's where I got my first real serious saxophone teacher, Jack Gell. I don't know how my mother found out about the Chicago School of Music, but that was a hugely important thing in my life in terms of my development. Jack Gell was already famous. He played tenor in Les Brown's Band of Renown, and he performed with Woody Herman, too. He took me through the saxophone instruction books, the etudes and rhythm books, and taught me scales and how to read music. The rhythm books had syncopated rhythms and shifting time signatures to teach you how to read rhythm in different meters— how to go from 4/4 time to cut time to 3/4 time, and things like that.

One of Gell's other students was a kid about a year younger

than me named Anthony Braxton. We were each taking private lessons, but Gell introduced us in the hallway at the Chicago School of Music. It turned out that Braxton lived down the street from my aunt at 61st and Wabash. Mr. Gell used to play us off against one another. He would tell Braxton that he needed to pay better attention and play "more like Threadgill." And he'd be simultaneously telling me the same thing, admonishing me to emulate Braxton. Sometimes we'd be sitting there together in the hallway and one of us would go in while the other waited his turn. But more often than not, there'd be two or three hours between my lesson and Braxton's, so we didn't hear what the other one was doing.

At Englewood High School I was in the school band, which was directed by Dieter Kolber. It was a great ensemble. We played concert band music: Wagner, Tchaikovsky, Sousa marches—the classical literature. We won the state championship one year. And the choir won, too. This was considered a great feat. And then I went to the yearly state competition for instrumental soloists and came in second on tenor saxophone playing a piece called "Cypress Song" for tenor saxophone and piano.

But in school I was a mess. My freshman and sophomore years at Englewood, I started to get in serious trouble. In junior high school I had been upstanding—I even found an after-school job resetting pins at Queens Recreation, a whites-only bowling alley, pool hall, and ballroom on South Ashland. But by the time I started high school, I fell in with a crowd of dedicated miscreants. I was smoking, dabbling in petty crime (minor burglary, pickpocketing), drinking 50-cent pints of cheap wine, and experimenting with "goofballs" (what we used to call barbiturates). I regularly skipped class, or showed up drunk or high. I broadcast my delinquency in my changing coiffures. First I dyed my hair red and had it cut into a ducktail. Then I straightened it and let it stick out every which way like an agitated porcupine. Then I went orange. And once I'd exhausted the rainbow,

I showed up one day completely bald. In 1958 or 1959, people hadn't seen shit like that.

I was drunk at eight o'clock in the morning, before I even arrived at school. I have a vivid memory of rushing in one day, and skipping into the basement where the chemistry and physics classes were. The building furnace was down there, too, so it was always hot. I was so high that I got halfway down the hall and I passed out—*boom!* I just keeled over on the floor. I can see it to this very day. The next thing I knew, somebody was helping me up and carrying me down the hall. And then it was straight to the principal: "Threadgill, drunk again. Up to my office!" He shot me a disgusted look. "We have to stop this," he declared. I think he was mainly worried that other students might be inspired by my ignominious example. So he expelled me right then and there. I got kicked out of school for drunkenness.

I didn't know what to do. I tried going to DuSable High School and speaking with Captain Walter Dyett, the famous musical director there. That was the first place I ran to. There were a number of places I might have been able to transfer, but I wasn't interested in going anyplace else, because I knew about the reputation of DuSable and all the famous musicians who had gone there: Nat King Cole, Johnny Griffin, Dinah Washington, Gene Ammons, Wilbur Ware. The list was endless—everybody had come out of that place. I told myself that's the place to go. I wasn't supposed to be able to attend DuSable because it was in a different school district, but I used my aunt's address so I could try to get in.

Captain Dyett looked at my transcript. I think Mr. Kolber, the Englewood band director, wrote a letter on my behalf. Dyett said, "They speak very highly of you as a musician, but when I look at your other records, you look like you're incorrigible. And I don't think I want anything to do with that." And he turned me down. I thought, Oh no, where does that leave me? "Incorrigible!" Eventually I went back to Englewood and they let me back in. I made a kind of plea bargain and promised to behave, and I got back in.

That's when I made up my mind to be a musician. I knew I had to get my life straightened out. I changed all my ways, I started fixing all of my mistakes. It took me a minute to recover, too, because I had really screwed up. Those years have almost become a blur. Eventually I got myself together, though.

I was friends with some girls at school. I remember they got so mad at me one day: this other girl kept staring at me all googly-eyed, trying to flirt with me, but I just ignored her.

"You didn't even notice!" they said. "You were just walking down the hallway with your head down carrying that saxophone and you didn't even look! The girl was tripping over herself right in front of you and you didn't do anything!"

"I apologize," I said sheepishly. "You all just don't understand, see."

These girls were the most brilliant girls in school. I don't know why they liked me. But what they didn't understand was that I had screwed up. I really had to clean up my act. I knew that high school wasn't the end of it. I had to study. You can't go out, you can't party, Henry, I told myself. You have to focus on your schoolwork, night and day, all year round. It took almost two years to get back on track. But I made it.

During the period when I was getting in trouble, my mother would send me to my father's house. That's when I got into my father's record collection. Bebop wasn't really his thing, but he had a lot of big band stuff and progressive West Coast bands. I would just sit there on the weekends and my father would say, "If you're going to drink, Moon, you can drink something here in the house. But you can't go out." I was drinking cheap stuff out in the street. When I got a taste of all the expensive liquor he had at his house—vodka, whiskey, cognac—I said to myself, "I don't even want to drink this stuff." So I would just play records. He would tell me, "Okay, I'm going out, I'll be back later." He'd come back hours later and I'd still be sitting there listening to music. I remember him saying, "Did you play this record?" and

That's when I got into my father's record collection.

bringing out a special one: it looked like it was made of steel. It was Woody Herman's big band with Gene Ammons. And he pulled it out and played it for me.

Chicago had a wealth of tenor saxophone players then. It was very difficult not to fall under the spell of Chicago tenors, because they were powerful musicians, innovative players: John Gilmore, Eddie Williams, Eddie Harris, Clifford Jordan, Von Freeman, Gene Ammons, Jay Peters. There was a list of them that just went on and on. Gene Ammons was already one of my favorites, and later I got into Eddie Williams, Von Freeman, and Clifford Jordan. I started trying to go see Gene Ammons play live, too. I'd always turn up if I could, and I used to try to position myself near him while he was playing. I'd watch him and listen very closely to how he would produce his sound. He had a way of putting air through the instrument that was important for the production of the type of massive sound that he had. It wasn't so much loud as it was *big*: an expansive outpouring that would permeate everything. He would play in a room without a microphone and fill up the entire room with sound.

John Coltrane didn't really grab me at first, but I was obsessed with Sonny Rollins. He was my main man. I wanted to play like him. I loved his sound. When you're aspiring to become an artist, living out of your imagination in a realm of fantasy, you need something to hold on to. You're out there floating in the middle of nothing—you're totally ungrounded.

So it helps to have a hero: something to aim for, a strong figure to worship. A role model is a belief system, something that takes you where you want to go. Sonny Rollins was that for me. He was my ship. For me it wasn't Charlie Parker, it wasn't Coltrane. It was Sonny who took me through. I wasn't just aiming for his sound, I was also aiming for everything he represented as an artist: his level of expertise, his level of dedication. I owe him so much. He was the musical giant I latched on to, and I found that I could sail off what he was doing.

As it turned out, Sonny Rollins's niece went to Englewood High School. She was about two years ahead of me. I remember she was a hall monitor, and I used to cut class to try to hit on her. I wasn't really interested in her, though; I was interested in trying to find Sonny Rollins. I wanted to know when he was coming to town. He used to stay on 58th Street where his relatives lived.

I used to go up to Sonny's niece and say, "Why don't you come out with me" and stuff like that, and she'd tell me, "Oh, you silly little boy. I'm not interested in you, Henry. You're too young." She'd admonish me: "You need to be in class. Did you cut class?"

"Um, I've got an excuse," I'd say—I was lying—and then ask my real question: "So when is your uncle coming to town? When is he going to be at your house?" I was planning to camp out in front of her house to wait on him, because I had read in *Metronome* or another jazz magazine about the way he'd camped out on Coleman Hawkins. So, I told myself, if Sonny Rollins camped out on Coleman Hawkins, then I'm camping out on him. I didn't know how you were supposed to go about meeting these great people and learning something from them. I would surmise things from what I was reading or from gossip I heard. When I read that, I thought, Okay, I'll be waiting for him.

He never showed up. I only realized much later that she was just telling me something to get rid of me because I was bugging her. "Sonny's coming on Friday," she said. And I cut school and went and sat on her porch all day, all up into the night, waiting for Sonny Rollins, and he didn't show. The next Monday morning, I went up to her at school. She said, "I don't know what happened." I said, "Okay." But I never did give up. It never did occur to me that she was lying to me. I told myself, Sonny has *got* to show up. This is his family, he's got to show up. And furthermore, I'm waiting for him—that's why he's got to show up, too.

I did go to see the Sonny Rollins Quartet once at McKie's in the Strand Hotel one time when Gene Ammons sat in with the band. It was incredible. You can often hear things live that will never get on record. I remember it was the last night of the week they were there, Sunday night. McKie's locked the doors of the club around two thirty or three a.m. and they wouldn't let anybody else in. They played until the next morning. And Gene Ammons was playing up in the higher harmonics of the saxophone, the altissimo range, and he never played below that. Very high notes. He played all the melodies an octave higher than Sonny Rollins. It was impressive. I had no idea he could play like that—I didn't even know you could play that high on the saxophone. It was quite a lesson.

When I say I fell under the spell of Chicago tenors, I don't mean that I wanted to play someone else's solo. I would pick up little things, licks and stuff, but I didn't spend time trying to transcribe a solo so I could play the exact same thing. At least not after one time when I bought the sheet music for Coleman Hawkins's solo on "Body and Soul." I took it right back to the store. I said, "I can't play this! I don't know how anybody could play this! I don't know how he plays this!" When I was listening to all these saxophonists, I more or less listened to how they negotiated things—not so much *what* they did, exactly, but *how* they went about it.

I started playing music with some friends from school—guys who wanted to play jazz. We would practice in the hall or behind the auditorium, or at somebody's house. Eventually we tried to get little gigs now and then. Not so much to make money. We just wanted to play somewhere, to see what we could do. There were eight or nine of us in all: the saxophonist Virgil Pumphrey, who later took the name Abshalom Ben Shlomo; the bass player Allen Joyner, who took the name M'Chaka Uba; the drummer Arlington Davis Jr., whose nickname was Butch; the Pulliam family—Pat played piccolo and John played tuba in the school band, and their older brother Bob played alto sax. We would go over to the Pulliam house, and Bob and a friend of his who was a trumpet player would play pieces by Bird and Diz like it was nothing. You would have thought they wrote this music, the way they were playing it. It would be just the two of them. No basses, no drums. And you could hear everything. The melody, where they'd start to improvise. These guys were on top of it. Sometimes I'd play part of the head with them, but when I couldn't keep up I'd drop out and listen. Now and then, Bob Pulliam would say to me, "Henry, get on the piano." I knew how to play chords, so I learned to comp behind them. Bob would write out the chord changes for me and put them on the piano. By accompanying them, I learned how the piece went and got familiar with how the harmony sounded and moved.

Even after I had straightened myself up, I was still having trouble in school academically because I was out in the street every night. I'd go out after everybody went to sleep at my house. I'd climb out the window with my saxophone and then go walk to the end of the Englewood train line at 63rd and Loomis, where it was easy to sneak through the rail yard and clamber up to the El tracks with my saxophone on my back in a hard case. You can imagine how much I weighed at the time, climbing up through the train tracks. I loved Rollins so much that I got a stencil and put "SONNY ROLLINS" in big black capital letters on my saxophone case. When I climbed up to the El, I'd push my case up through in front of me and then wriggle through after it, so every night I'd see Sonny's name stenciled there, like a beacon I was pulling myself up to.

I would take that train up to 58th Street to transfer to the Jackson Park train and go to the East Side, to 63rd and Cottage Grove, where everything was jumping. It was like Fifty-second Street in New York. Every single night. I wasn't sitting in with the bands, but I took my horn because you never knew what was going to happen. Somebody might show you something. And that's how I got into all the places. I was going to places where kids couldn't get in. They said, "That's young Threadgill; he's going to be all right. He's trying to play." The waitresses and bartenders said, "Okay, just sit down here. Order a Coca-Cola."

And some of the musicians would bring me in. I knew a lot

of musicians by then. Eddie Williams and Earl Ezell and these different people. Lewis Taylor. Sleepy Anderson. When I got a chance to talk to them, I'd ask them what show they were working on or something. You just kind of played it by ear. Sometimes some of the cats would be down on their luck, and they tried to borrow my horn.

"I don't mind," I'd tell them, "but you have to see my grandmother about that." And they'd have to come to my house. Grandma Gertrude would make me go to the gig with them. "The only way you can borrow Henry's horn is, he's got to go with you." She added: "If you don't come back here with my grandson and his saxophone, I *will* find you. There's no place that you'll be able to hide."

They knew that she meant it. That wasn't just any woman who was talking. They could tell that that they were looking at someone who could go ballistic. When she'd lose her temper, we used to jump out the window and run out of the house. It was dangerous. You could get seriously hurt. This was Peyton Robinson's daughter, after all. She didn't even know what she was doing— when she lost her temper, she kicked everybody's ass within kicking distance. It didn't matter whether you were involved or not. You might be an innocent bystander. But if you were in the area where she exploded, too bad. You shouldn't have been there.

I'd go out with my buddy Butch Davis. We might go to see one band play at nine o'clock at night and stay until midnight. Then we'd move on to another club, and that set would be over at three or four o'clock in the morning. We'd often end up staying up drinking coffee until five, talking to one of the musicians or something. Then, to make my way back home, when I came back to 63rd I'd have to walk farther east to Woodlawn or Stony Island at the end of the Jackson Park line, where I knew I could climb up to the platform without getting caught. And then I'd ride back to 58th Street and transfer again to the Englewood train to go back to 63rd and Halsted. Finally I'd walk from there to my mother's house.

By the time I slipped back in through the window at home,

it would often be an hour or two before I needed to wake up for school. My family would call me and I wouldn't be able to get up because I'd just gone to bed! I couldn't keep my eyes open. So I ended up having to go to summer school and even to night school to catch up.

The Pulliam family and Abshalom Ben Shlomo lived on the same block as the bassist Ronnie Boykins. This was at 64th and Carpenter. It was only two blocks from where Boykins was rehearsing with Sun Ra and the Arkestra at the corner of 63rd and Morgan. The Arkestra rehearsed at night in a wild-game market. They sold deer, raccoons, possums, and bear. There weren't too many Black people in Englewood. We were only the second Black family on the block where I lived. There were a lot of Greeks as well as some Poles and Italians and Jews. The wild-game market was owned by a Greek man, as a matter of fact, and was one of a number of Greek-owned businesses in the area. This Greek guy liked Sun Ra for some reason, and he let him use the place at night.

While we were in high school, Abshalom and I got in the habit of going there to sit and listen to them rehearse. They played in the back of the market, in a sort of storage area. You'd go through the store and walk past these bears and wild boar, hooked by their feet with their heads hanging down. I think that Ronnie Boykins must have invited us the first time, although I did have a couple of other connections to the band. I had another friend in school, Harry Pryor, who played trombone, and his older brothers were both musicians: Henry Pryor was a trumpeter who played with Dizzy Gillespie's big band, and Nate Pryor was a trombonist with the Sun Ra Arkestra at the time.

We didn't come with our horns. We knew better than that. Not with what Sun Ra was doing. We weren't that advanced. Our whole musical package was still too uneven then. But Sun Ra let the two of us sit there and listen. He didn't say anything. They were too busy working on their music.

*While we were in high school,
Abshalom and I got in the habit . . .*

Sun Ra's thing was very personal. I considered it far more personal and far more esoteric and complex than other stuff I was hearing. Compared to the more conventional orchestras, this was a whole other world. It wasn't something you could just walk into, the way you might be able to step into a band down-town if you possessed enough skill. Sun Ra's music was struc-tured in a completely different way. So I would listen and try to figure it out: What is this stuff doing? How is it moving harmoni-cally? We would get our lesson by being there, by watching, by listening to the conversation, occasionally by getting a look at the scores, and mainly by hearing the music that was coming out.

I did eventually get to talk with a few of the members of the Arkestra, like John Gilmore. He was playing some very advanced harmonic and rhythmic information on the saxophone. His rhythmic approach was amazing. John used to tell me about practicing out of drum books, working on rhythmic patterns. So I went out and bought a whole bunch of drum books, and I'd play with different drummers. My friend Butch and I used to practice together, and we'd only practice out of drum books. It gives you a grounding in rhythmic patterns that you wouldn't ordinarily have, playing a melodic instrument. Gilmore's playing was *very* rhythmic playing. I don't mean that it was necessarily always busy, even if at times it was. It's more that there were very unusual rhythmic patterns in his playing. A lot of people knew about his musical thinking; Coltrane used to come and listen to him play. Gilmore was a highly sophisticated player, and totally original.

Another crucial figure in my early musical education during high school was John Hauser. In terms of music education, he was arguably the most influential figure in Chicago aside from Captain Dyett at DuSable High School. He was a great saxo-phone and clarinet player who had been in the Earl "Fatha" Hines orchestra, and he had a studio where he put together these small ensembles. He taught us how to read stock arrangements. They were simple, but it gave us our first experience of reading arrangements and the rhythms, the syncopation, in big-band writing—they were pretty square but they served to get us prepared. He was also a talented composer himself, and wrote concertos for saxophone and orchestra. Hauser taught us a new standard of excellence. As musicians, we had to come up to that level. The fact was, there weren't any jazz ensembles where you could go and do this kind of thing in the area. So Hauser started his studio to give young Black musicians on the South Side a place to start learning something about it.

At the same time, I was still taking lessons from Jack Gell, and he got me into another group, George Hunter's big band. It was the big band at the Chicago School of Music. They rehearsed there on Monday nights. They were crack studio musicians, all professional and semiprofessional—and they were all white. They did the rehearsals for their own enjoyment when they were in town. And Mr. Hunter had an impressive book with about nine hundred pieces of music. Mr. Gell was preparing me by having me practice out of these rhythm books and books for Broadway shows, things that force you to switch from one time signature to another. He noticed how I was working on my solo-ing. And because Mr. Gell thought I had the ability to solo, he asked Mr. Hunter to let me into his band. I was just a sixteen-year-old kid, but everyone else there was an adult—guys with families, homes, yachts, everything, professional musicians trav-eling all over the world.

When I first went in there, I was scared to death. I went in there the first day and the guys were going to the back room to pick up the music. They came out with suitcases! These were not stock arrangements. These were orchestrations by the great arrangers of the day: people who were arranging for Count Basie, people who were arranging for Maynard Ferguson. This is where I really began to learn something, where I really started to learn how to play in a big band. But it was a trying experience, because these guys were way ahead of me. I'd been in a concert band at high school and then in Hauser's band, but this was a whole other level of organization. And this music was all written out by hand, not printed scores. I'd never seen music laid out that way.

The first time I played with the Hunter band, I failed miserably. I sat down and Mr. Hunter called off the names of the pieces. He'd call off pieces of music five or six at a time. He said, "152, 818, 17, 516, 344"—and everybody would go digging in their suitcases for the scores. The very first piece, he counted out a fast tempo: "one-two, one-two-three-four" and *bam!* I played the first note and that was it—I had no idea where they were! The notes were flying all over the place!

I took my failure personally. After about three or four pieces, I just took my horn apart and put it in the case. I stood up and walked out, and as I walked out I slammed the door as hard as I could. The band stopped abruptly and the whole place got quiet; at first they thought I'd shattered the glass.

I was so mad and upset that I convinced myself it was racism, that they did it *to* me—that they scrubbed me out—because they didn't want to have me in there. It's because I'm Black, I told myself. But the real truth was, I couldn't keep up with them. I didn't know enough to keep up with them.

Mr. Gell heard about it, of course. When I came back for my next lesson, he just said, "I heard about your *exit*."

It happened around the beginning of June. I was so upset with myself. It made me doubt my abilities as a musician. I had been staying at my mother's house on the second floor, and I moved into the basement. I took all my things down to the basement and I didn't come out again until school started back up in the fall.

My friends came by and asked, "What's wrong with Henry? Doesn't he want to come out and play ball?" They'd sit on the porch and hear me downstairs and ask my mother and grandmother, "Is he ever going to come out?" My family told them, "We don't know."

"Is that all he does?" my friends said. "Does he eat?"

And in fact, I didn't even come upstairs for meals; my family just put plates of food outside the basement door for me.

I pulled all the shades down and kept them closed. I was going through a sort of dramatic madness. I wasn't going to come out until it was time to go back down to the Chicago School of Music and face those people again. Because I knew I had to face them. The Hunter band went on hiatus over the summer because the guys had constant employment all season. So I had until September. I worked hard, day and night.

The only thing I'd come out to do was take my weekly lesson with Mr. Gell. When September rolled around, Mr. Gell asked me, "So, what are you going to do? Are you going to let them wash you out?" He offered to tell Mr. Hunter that I was hoping to go back. And so I went back.

When I went into the rehearsal room, I was embarrassed, thinking of how I'd stomped out in June. But there were a lot of new guys in the room, and Hunter acted as if it had never happened. I sat down and he called five or six pieces and hit the tempo. And I was hanging in there. I was missing some stuff, but I'd learned how to stick with it in spite of what you miss, and keep things moving. When you make a mistake you have to keep going: don't flinch, because when you flinch, you pause, and the moment has passed. If you pay attention, you can catch up—I learned how to keep an eye out for where they were, and when I missed something I could get back in. You just keep up and catch it in the next spot. Once I started doing that, it was all about filling in the spaces. You simply looked at what you couldn't do and tried to figure out what you were having trouble with; I analyzed it that way, and every week those gaps got smaller and smaller. I also started learning about the intricacy of section playing: I figured out what role the fourth tenor had in relation to the second tenor and in relation to the second alto. They weren't just playing parts: there was a sort of support and color that you were supposed to add to the music from your particular chair.

I kept going to the Hunter band rehearsals every week, all the way through the rest of high school and into my first year of college. It was extraordinary; nobody I knew my age had that kind of experience. They even let me start taking a solo here and there, and I was stumbling around, but they seemed to appreciate that I had a sound—they could hear what I was trying to do. I got lost, but I could hear certain things and get in little things now and then. The other musicians would kind of look back at me as if to say, "Look at what the kid's doing!"

Sometimes a work of art has a shadow title: a provisional nickname or draft label—something you call it as you're making it, but that doesn't end up being the final title when it matures. It's as though the work sloughs them off as it grows the way a snake sheds its skin. I thought of calling this book *Failure Is Everything.* As much as any other phrase, it's my first tenet: a fundamental truth that sums up what I've learned through experience. Maybe it should be my epitaph: "Henry Threadgill: Failure is Everything." I don't mean to be fatalistic—it's simply a fact. Failure is the greatest motivator of all. When you fail at something, there are only three things that can happen. You can give up—drop it completely and go in a different direction—or let it shut you down. You can lose your moral bearings and become a cheat or a fraud. Or else you get highly motivated to fix whatever went wrong. It heightens your determination: now you have something to prove.

My father wasn't especially talkative. He was a man of action. No fooling around. He must have gotten it from his own father, who drove liquor for the mob all across the country, from Alabama all the way to Canada. That's the way my father grew up: in the car with my grandfather, running hooch, a .45 on the seat. Not exactly the usual family-car-trip vacation, and not an occasion for light banter. But my father did have a way with words, and he had these pithy, enigmatic phrases he'd drop from time to time. One thing he'd say was: "Too much sugar." He'd hear a story about somebody getting a break, and that would be his sole comment, accompanied by a chuckle: "Too much sugar." It meant that the person was getting more than he deserved for once after getting shortchanged all the time. But it was double-edged, because that "too much" also implied that, on some level, you *need* some deprivation in life. You can get too much of a good thing.

In life, however much progress you make, you're always going to hit a wall. And walls are good for you, because they're challenging. You have to figure out how to climb over or dig under or detour your way around. Otherwise, you stay where you're at. And I realized early on that I wasn't going to be content to stay where I was.

I started composing around my senior year in high school. At first I was just making up music at the piano. Then I started writing it down. And I realized how complex composition was. I hadn't developed any skills in that area. I didn't know anything about orchestration—the range of various instruments, for example. These were mostly things that would come once I got to college. At the same time, I already understood a lot about harmony, from playing piano at the Pulliams' house. And at home I would sometimes get out hymnals and sight-read chorales and things of that sort. So I had a basic understanding of voice leading and harmonic progressions. But I didn't really know what I was doing. I was just swimming around, trying to figure out how things operated.

Another musician who had a big impact on me was Ornette Coleman. I must have been about fifteen or sixteen when I turned on the radio and heard "Lonely Woman" for the first time. For me and my little group of friends who were starting to play music, that record was like an alarm clock going off. We all heard it, like a call in the wilderness or something. "Did you hear that music?" we said to each other. "We got to get to that." We had been practicing things like "Daahoud," the Clifford Brown tune, and we knew in our hearts that we weren't going anywhere with it. There were musicians like Frank Strozier and Booker Little who came in the wake of that and inherited that approach, but we were too young. So the emergence of Ornette—and then,

a few years afterwards, late-period Coltrane and Albert Ayler—
was a big thing for us. "Man, there it *is*," we told each other.
There's the voice of new possibility.

We didn't know what it meant. It was a sound that said
"This is the way"—but which way is that? We just knew it was
something new, and something we could invest ourselves in
completely. In the arts, you keep making replicas and variations
of the same thing. And for a young musician, that repetition is
only enforced by the people who teach you and the people who
hire you to play, almost all of whom want you to do the same
old thing. It can destroy your development—it can take years to
find yourself. But you've got to fight your way through all that
mess. Kids spend hours practicing and learning a Coltrane solo.
What do you want to learn Coltrane's solo on "Giant Steps" for?
What are you trying to find out? To engage with it and look at
it and study it, yes—but to engage in it physically, to learn it by
heart, is only to contaminate yourself. You might check it out a
little and try to figure it out. But don't steal that stuff, because
it's powerful. When you're an artist, you've got to be careful in
your training. Practice doesn't make perfect; practice makes permanent. When you start putting things in yourself, it's going to
take time to get them out. You might need a big aesthetic enema.

My first composition was called "Ornette." Even then, I
wasn't trying to write so-called European classical music. At
the same time, I wasn't necessarily trying to compose something
with the earmarks of jazz, either. My thoughts went beyond the
confines of bebop—of the whole jazz tradition, to be honest. I
had friends who only concentrated on bop, but I just couldn't do
it. My interests were too broad; nothing was too far away. When
I first heard Schoenberg's *Pierrot Lunaire,* I couldn't even talk.
So many things had a deep impact on my ears, from polka and
gospel on the radio to Hindemith and Bartók. So when I started
to write my own compositions, it wasn't that I was trying to fit
into a particular corner of the landscape. There were just things
I was trying to do, things I was trying to say in sound. And even
then, I didn't think they had to be called anything.

2

Satellites

My first day at Wilson Junior College in the fall of 1962, I went to campus with my friend the trumpeter Milton Chapman, who'd been a year ahead of me in high school. We still never talked about the time we almost got ourselves killed wandering to the wood factory on the wrong side of the tracks. But we'd stayed friends and had both gotten consumed with music. Wilson (which is now called Kennedy-King College) was right in Englewood, at 69th and Normal, so I wasn't going far. But since Milton had already been there a year, he knew the lay of the land.

On the way over, he told me, "There's somebody I want you to meet as soon as we get there." We walked into the cafeteria and I noticed a guy sitting alone at a table by the wall with a big briefcase planted on the floor next to him. He was wearing a navy turtleneck sweater, a charcoal sport coat, black pants, and a pair of well-worn high-tops. Seeing his frugal lunch—just a bowl of soup with a roll—my first thought was that he clearly didn't have much money. Even before Milton said anything, somehow I knew this was the guy he wanted me to meet.

I felt even more certain when I saw that what I initially took to be a briefcase was actually a Selmer saxophone case. And I was right: Milton took me straight over to him and introduced us. The student's name was Joseph Jarman.

We became close almost immediately. Jarman was almost

seven years older than me and had been through a lot more than
I had. He'd attended DuSable High School and studied under
Captain Walter Dyett, starting on the drums because his family couldn't afford a saxophone. Joseph had already been in the
service—he'd been a paratrooper, I found out much later (he
never spoke about it), before finally getting to play saxophone
in the 11th Airborne Division Band in Germany. Now, back in
Chicago, he was stuck in a miserable marriage, I soon learned,
and in addition to going to school he was working as a door-
to-door Fuller Brush salesman to make ends meet. Despite our
differences, we quickly realized that we had very similar tastes in
music and shared a burning desire to learn the trade.

We took lots of classes together and played in the concert
band and other ensembles on campus. I was a liberal arts major,
so I was taking a wide variety of subjects: not only music but
also math, physics, humanities, phys ed. To avoid the draft and
maintain your 2-S status as a full-time college student, you had
to be enrolled in sixteen to eighteen credit hours a semester. So I
was taking everything.

Different subjects would launch me into the throes of temporary obsession: existentialist philosophy one month, abstract
expressionist painting the next. I fell in love with literature: I
read *The Brothers Karamazov* for a class and it catapulted me
into the universe of great Russian fiction. Jarman was intro-
verted—he was a deeply spiritual cat, even then—but he wrote
poetry compulsively and loved theater, so he got me interested
in that as well. I even started writing some poetry myself and
hanging out with some Chicago figures like the legendary David
Moore (who later called himself Amus Mor). I heard him read
his electric "Poem to the Hip Generation": "Who are we? Where
are we going? What are we here for?" Moore was something
else: in his work, the music wasn't just accompaniment or an
object of emulation; instead it was right up inside the words.
He had a mesmerizing delivery. A girlfriend of mine took some
of my stuff and showed it to another aspiring poet, Don L. Lee
(who subsequently changed his name to Haki Madhubuti), who

was a year or two ahead of me at Wilson. I don't remember my poems, but I recall that she was very critical of them. I should be paying more attention to what Lee and LeRoi Jones were doing, she told me.

But music was the center of our world. And there was an astonishing confluence at Wilson in those years, especially of musicians who would soon become deeply involved in the Association for the Advancement of Creative Musicians and the Chicago scene in general. In the early 1960s, our fellow students at Wilson included Malachi Favors, Eddie Williams, Louis Hall, Jack DeJohnette, Roscoe Mitchell, and Anthony Braxton. Wilson shared its cafeteria with Chicago Teachers College across the street, and Bunky Green and Eddie Harris went there, so they were around, too. We had extraordinary teachers: we studied piano with Lela Hanmer, conducting and arranging with Otto Jelinek, and theory and counterpoint with Richard Wang. We studied strings with Mr. Carruthers; I played viola.

It gave us a solid foundation in Western classical music and composition. Wang led the dance ensemble, an octet that mainly played things like Woody Herman arrangements. But most of what we were learning wasn't jazz—jazz was what we did on the side, when I practiced rhythmic patterns out of drum books with Butch Davis, or when a friend like the alto player Sonny Greer Jr. (the son of Duke Ellington's great drummer) would teach me a few bebop licks. The stuff we were learning from teachers like Richard Wang was the core of the classical tradition. And we went all in. We worked so hard in those classes that we wore the teachers out. Mr. Wang would give us an assignment— say, to harmonize the melody of a chorale. Rather than just do one version, we'd come in the next day with five or ten different versions! Milton Chapman lived only one block away from my mother, and he had a blackboard and a piano in the basement of his house. We'd habitually stay up late working on our homework, drinking coffee and taking NoDoz.

It was the first time I had met so many musicians of that caliber, many of whom were more advanced than I was. I was around some great musicians when I was in high school, but Wilson was another level. A lot of these guys had been living abroad in the service, like Joseph Jarman, or had been freelancing out in the street. They were professionalized in a way I hadn't seen up close before. And then there was the practical instruction in the courses, from species counterpoint to orchestral arranging and conducting.

I learned just as much in our extracurricular activities as I did at Wilson. Joseph had a loose-knit group of musicians who would get together at his place at 43rd and State, in a sort of community center in the housing project where he was living. Different people came through, including the tenor saxophonist Fred Anderson, the flutist Joel Brandon, the bassist Eddie Chappell, the drummer Arthur Reed, and the trumpeter Billy Brimfield. (Over the next few years Jarman would also start working with the pianist Christopher Gaddy and the drummer Thurman Barker, younger musicians who, along with Clark, formed the core of his working band by the middle of the decade.) Joseph invited me over and I started playing with them. We would play Joseph's music, and we started doing some Ornette Coleman compositions, "Lonely Woman" and things of that sort, and some Eric Dolphy, too. I also brought in some of my own tunes.

I was also still going regularly to the bebop jam sessions on weekends at the Pulliam house with friends from high school, including Butch Davis and Abshalom Ben Shlomo. One Sunday, a wiry guy with an intense gaze showed up. He had an alto saxophone case, but he didn't take out his horn. He just stood there and checked us out. It was Roscoe Mitchell, and he had just returned from a stint in the US Army Band in Heidelberg, Germany. (He told me later that while he was there he periodically went to jam sessions in Berlin, where once he heard a young tenor saxophonist named Albert Ayler, whose sound was uniquely ferocious.) It turned out that Roscoe had been two years ahead of me at Englewood High School; we knew some people in common, like Don Myrick, but I hadn't met him before. Now Roscoe was also starting college at Wilson.

I introduced Roscoe to Joseph Jarman, and the three of us started playing together. Joseph and I used to head over to Roscoe's place on the South Side every Saturday morning at eight to play with yet another changing cast of talented musicians, including the drummer Richard Drahseer Smith, the bassists Malachi Favors and Walter Chapel, and the pianist Louis Hall. Sometimes Jack DeJohnette was there, too, or another young pianist, named Byron. We'd practice for hours and then listen to records together, classic Blue Note albums by Art Blakey or Horace Silver. Roscoe was a huge Wayne Shorter fan, so we played his compositions as well. Roscoe came back from the service with a pile of transcriptions of that post-bebop repertoire, and we played through his stockpile of charts. I'd be on tenor, with Roscoe and Joseph on alto.

We had a music club at Wilson, and we invited the pianist Muhal Richard Abrams to come and give a concert. Muhal was starting to attract some attention for the sessions he led every Monday night at the C&C Lounge on 64th Street and Cottage Grove with a unit he called the Experimental Band. There was another scene emerging around these sessions. Part of what was special about it was that Muhal encouraged people to bring their own compositions and have them played by the ensemble. I knew a few of the people who regularly played in the Experimental Band, including Eddie Harris and Don Myrick. Most of the young musicians around Wilson eventually passed through Muhal's orbit.

After the concert at Wilson, Muhal invited me to come down to the C&C Lounge the following week, and I went to a few sessions of the Experimental Band. It was thrilling to play the brand-new charts, which felt, yes, experimental—you never knew what somebody might show up with. After a while I got up the nerve to bring in an arrangement of one of my own compositions. But the guys who were there that evening couldn't play it. One of them made a condescending comment implying that there was a problem with the way I'd written it out—that I hadn't mastered the principles of orchestration. But I knew how to write music correctly. Whether you liked it was another matter, of course. The fact was, they were just having trouble sight-reading it.

I didn't go back to the Experimental Band after that experience. But I did start to spend time with Muhal. Initially I was planning to study the Schillinger System of music theory with him, but when we started, I found that I understood enough of what it was about on a certain level that it didn't seem necessary to me. I had enough skill on the piano that I could go back and forth with him and work out some of the harmonic stuff he started to show me.

"Where did you get that from?" he'd say, surprised.

Still, Muhal was far more advanced. He treated me as an equal but he was way beyond me. Beyond his sharp intellect and musical talent, Muhal was one of the most highly disciplined people I'd ever met. He'd pick up a book on any topic—electronics, say—and go through it systematically and teach himself the entire field out of the book. He gobbled up whole areas of knowledge: a book on advanced mathematics, a book on plumbing, a book on industrial design, a book on computer programming. At his house, you couldn't even see most of his library because he had bookshelves in front of bookshelves. The whole place represented an incredible track record of self-instruction. Muhal was a very pragmatic thinker. He'd just pick up a book and start on the first page.

I'd say, "You completed the whole thing, man?"

Muhal would peer back at me matter-of-factly. "Yes. Don't you understand it, Henry?" And he'd break it down for me in plain language.

I just couldn't proceed that way. Reading a book in an unfamiliar field, I'd get to a point where the language gets too convoluted—too abstruse, too technical. I'd bail on it. Who needs the hassle? But I've learned a lot just from observing somebody like Muhal, who was able to drive all the way through and master so much through sheer determination. It stimulated me to push myself farther.

It did make me realize that in the end, all of us were teaching ourselves. All my years of going to school, I basically didn't learn anything. You put on a record of Varèse or Beethoven or Ellington: how could anybody teach you what they're doing? I spent almost all my time trying to take music apart and understand it. But months into college, although I knew the principles of orchestration I was still trying to figure out what it meant to find my own voice as a composer. I knew one thing for sure: you had to know far more than what the teachers were telling you. If you wanted to figure out how Beethoven had composed a given piece, clearly it went way beyond any technique or procedure you could learn in a class. It became obvious to me that you have to take over as your own instructor to find your own way. We had courses with titles like Form and Analysis, and we'd carefully unpack what was going on in the development section of a composition. But doing that doesn't make you a composer.

The thing was, even if it had been possible, I wasn't interested in going back and writing in those historical styles. From my earliest years in school, I already knew I wanted to do something different from traditional European composition as it was being taught. I didn't want to be bogged down by the rules and regulations of diatonic harmony. I didn't want to follow the sonata form—I didn't want to buy those same familiar patterns and make the same familiar clothes.

Even in Western classical music, by the time you get to Schoenberg the formulaic approach to composition in so much music instruction falls apart. At that point in the history of European composition, the problem became figuring out a way to let listeners know where they were if you weren't going to give them the usual landmarks or send them down the same old paths. From this perspective, twelve-tone or serial composition was an attempt to differentiate and segregate the elements of the musical fabric in order to give it structure, to make it navigable.

How can you give music a different sort of formal integrity, one that wouldn't rely on the old systems of harmonic structure? I didn't want to become Schoenberg or Webern, but I was faced with this same kind of question. If I wasn't going to use the classical model, then what was I going to use?

Not that you're ever in complete control. You don't simply choose your own path. So many other voices, other currents, other influences go into shaping your sensibility—and in ways beyond your knowing.

I discovered a couple of composers around this time that helped me see a way ahead. When I first heard the music of Edgard Varèse, I didn't know what to make of it, because it was so unlike anything else. It wasn't behaving. It wasn't doing what music is supposed to be doing. And then I started to like it precisely because of its unique behavior. It impressed me because of the way it was put together. I couldn't figure out how it was made. I understood each of the individual elements, but I couldn't get the whole picture. And I appreciated that. Varèse wasn't following any of the classical methods of organization, including what Schoenberg was doing. And he was *intent* on not doing what everyone else had done; Varèse was obsessed with not doing things the way other European composers had. I was able to hold on to that determination, that obstinacy, as a sort of model of what I wanted to obtain. It provided me with a line of development: it gave me an image of how I should be operating in whatever music I was trying to write.

Debussy's music is an entirely different world, of course, but he also came to represent a kind of model for me. In any artistic milieu, there's always a prescribed way: the official version, the way things must be done. They're all shuffling the same deck of cards. But Debussy said, Forget it. Everything is supposed to be based in some discernible logic? Every note I use, every gesture, is supposed to have an explanation? In Debussy's music, it's as though he's saying: No. I don't have to explain anything. This was a new approach—just do what you feel, whether or not it holds up in terms of some sort of formal analysis. The point he was making is that music is ultimately beyond anything one can say about it analytically. The art skips that. And this was what I learned from Debussy: to dare, to go ahead and take the leap. Don't reject something simply because you can't explain it.

So Debussy and Varèse have remained important models for me not because I'm trying in any way to imitate what they were doing or to sound like them, but because of the way they found their place and their music in a rugged individual way. When I heard them, I said to myself, I can do the same thing over here in my world.

Whether you look at Varèse or Ellington, Bud Powell or Maria Callas, Beethoven or Liszt or Ali Akbar Khan: the content of their art is intimately linked to their being born in history at a particular time. This is why you can't simply reproduce it. Young people studying jazz these days are deluded if they think they're learning to play the way Dizzy Gillespie played, or the way Bill Evans played. You can't do it the way they did it. Any art is tied to its historical moment. And tied to the life of the artist, and all the social, psychological, and spiritual content that molded that life. Music is everything that makes the musician: family, friends, hardships, joys, the sounds on the street, how tight you buckle your belt, the person who happens to be sitting across from you in the subway car, what you ate for breakfast—all of it.

Muhal is in the same category as Varèse or Debussy for me. With him, it was not just a matter of his nonconformity as a composer—his insistence on making his own way. It was also his drive. And it was also crucial that this was a model that was out there in the community. It was right there to be grasped. It wasn't a product of a distant tradition or an elite institution: it didn't require the validation of the American Conservatory or the University of Chicago. Anything Muhal wanted to go after, he would just go after it. Nothing was off-limits, nothing was beyond him. It was frankly mind-boggling, watching how broad his musical journey became. And his mind was unpredictable, too. I never knew what he was going to get into next. He refused to be constrained by expectations or conventions of any sort. Muhal was as elusive as a rabbit—you might think you had him cornered in his burrow, but he always seemed to have another exit ready.

Muhal's breadth—his unboundedness—taught me something about my own capabilities. It was amazing to meet someone like that, who was older than I was and who pushed himself that way. It set me on fire. Watching his example, you see what you have to do. It puts you on notice. And so you show up at the session with five or six new arrangements. No slacking allowed here. No coasting on your talent. You've got to bring it, *your* thing, right now.

The stories my mother and aunts would occasionally tell me about my great-grandfather almost sounded like myths. But they were true. He had been born in the early 1870s in Mississippi during Reconstruction. Somehow, in the midst of organized racial terror, he decided he wasn't going to take any shit from any man. When they moved to Alabama and bought property, he and his twin brother walked around with guns on their hips. Nobody dared mess with them. Black people were scared of them, and white people were scared of them. They didn't call nobody "Sir," and they expected to be addressed as "Mister." And they didn't pay for anything. They'd just walk into the store and take whatever they wanted. My great-grandfather simply refused to play by the rules. "Fuck the rules"—that was his attitude: "*I* make the rules."

Peyton Robinson married a woman named Phoebe who was at least part Native American; although I never met her, apparently my great-grandmother was just as much of a badass as he and his brother were. When my cousins and I marveled at

Peyton Robinson in the late 1950s

how tough my grandmother Gertrude was, my mother just said, "You should have seen *her* mama."

My great-grandfather was still alive when I was a child, so I knew the stories about him weren't just tall tales. When I was still young, his twin brother got killed in Chicago. A group of people attacked him. My great-grandfather was an old man, but just as fierce as ever: I remember he said to me, "I just wish I'd been there."

I was taken aback. "But Papa, what could you have done if there were so many of them?" I asked him.

His gaze was stone cold and distant, like he was envisioning the wrath he would have rendered. "They ain't seen nothing. I wish I'd been there. Then they would've seen something."

Sometimes I wonder where my own resilience and determination come from. Not from a classroom, that's for sure.

When I was a teenager, I was a scaredy-cat. Even if I was acting out for a while in high school, still I was this scrawny dude, and I certainly wasn't getting into fights with anyone. My cousin Michael was liable to get into a scrape from time to time. But not me. Anytime I found myself in a dicey situation, I used to try to talk myself out of it.

My strategy involved deflection and misdirection. When a bully got up in my face, ready to kick my ass, I'd say, "You should have heard what so-and-so said about your mama."

"What?" the guy would blurt, momentarily distracted by the phantom secondary target. "You best not be fooling. What did he say about my mama?" And as soon as he turned his head, I'd jet. *Vroom!*

But somewhere along the way I developed an attitude. Not arrogance, but resilience. Don't tread on me.

I think my great-grandfather especially liked me because I would antagonize him. I used to get on his nerves. I would hassle him and badger him with questions because it was the only way

I could get him to tell me anything about his life. I wanted to know everything about him. He fascinated me.

So I'd find ways to get him talking. I'd happen by him while carrying a book and he'd say, "What's that you're reading?" "Oh, let me show you, Papa," I'd answer. And he'd tell me, "Go get my glasses." He had a cigar box full of old glasses. He had gone to the Jew Town market and bought a box of twenty-five or thirty used prescription eyeglasses. He'd pull out the box and try on one pair after another. "Okay, these work," he'd finally proclaim when he came across a pair that helped him read the print. And he'd squint at the book I was reading and ask me questions about it.

Other times I'd walk over to him while I was eating a snack. He'd ask, "What's that you're eating?"

"Peanut butter," I'd answer, grinning at him. "You want some, Papa?"

"I can't eat that!" he'd exclaim gruffly. "Go get my tooth-es." He wouldn't say "*teeth*." He always said "*tooth-es*," with two syllables.

He had another cigar box full of false teeth—he'd paid another fifty cents or a dollar for a whole box of teeth! I'd run off and fetch the box. And again he'd try them on for size, putting one set after another in his gums. "That don't work, no. That don't work neither. . . . *There* you go." He was eminently practical in everything he did.

It may have been my youngest uncle Joseph who brought a copy of Miles Davis's *'Round About Midnight* to the house on 59th Street. He had these hip friends, and he started bringing records home. When I heard John Coltrane on that record, it had the same effect as when I heard Howlin' Wolf and Tchaikovsky. I said, "Who is *that*?" It wasn't just that Coltrane had a different sound. It was the *geometry* of how he was playing. If you drew a picture of what his solos sounded like, the lines would be like graph lines, systematic and precise. Like someone drawing a picture of something accelerating from zero to fifteen and then shooting up to a plateau at forty. The organization was so immediately clear. What struck me was something like the physicalization of that geometry; you could hear the shapes in his playing.

Coltrane was the first person that made me aware that sound could have geometry. It was even more striking to me than Gene Ammons, although I'd say that Ammons had a greater impact on me. With Gene Ammons, it was that his playing didn't move the way everybody else was moving. It felt like watching a crowd rush down the street, feeling impressed at their speed and fluidity. A crowd of people as smooth as Jesse Owens: everybody's just sailing along. In the midst of it, you notice, here comes this one guy—crawling! And somehow he's outpacing everyone else, even though they're all running and he's crawling. That's what Gene Ammons sounded like.

I got to talk to Coltrane once. I was still in high school, so it must have been around 1961. (Later, when I was in college, I saw his great quartet with McCoy Tyner, Jimmy Garrison, and Elvin Jones a number of times.) Between sets, I tried to ask Coltrane for some tips, but I couldn't get any information—he was too busy asking *me* questions! He started asking me, "What are you listening to?" and "What are you practicing?" and stuff like that. I was trying to figure out: what is with this guy? You're *John Coltrane*, I thought. I'm a no-shit saxophone player named Henry Threadgill. And you keep asking *me* what I'm working on?

Coltrane said to me: "So, who are you listening to right now?"

"Ornette," I answered.

"Oh, you like Ornette? What pieces?"

I thought, Oh, man, come on. Give me a break here.

Then I said something about using a thesaurus and Coltrane exclaimed, "Oh, you've been using a thesaurus?" as though it was the most inspired suggestion he'd ever heard.

It was sweet, in retrospect. It just shows you how humble a person he was. That he could be open to a young person my age, at my level of development. It was totally genuine interest.

We were talking in a folding-door telephone booth in the hallway for about forty-five minutes. For his entire break between sets. They couldn't find him! He was smoking cigarettes as he talked to me and the air in the booth got thick with smoke, to the point that you could hardly see we were in there. The next set was supposed to be starting, and John Coltrane was still with me in the telephone booth asking me questions about music.

I recently found a program for a concert I'd totally forgotten about: in April 1964, I wrote a piece for the Wilson concert band directed by Lela Hanmer and Otto Jelinek. The program featured works by Gounod, Holst, Mozart, Humperdinck, Verdi, and other classical composers; Joseph and Roscoe played in the band with me, but my piece, "Scenes," was the only work by a Wilson student included. The program notes made it clear that my teachers had high hopes for me: they described "Scenes" as "a most promising first work by this young composer." Unfortunately I no longer have the score. I can't recall whether I copied out all the parts by myself—I have no recollection of doing so, but somebody must have done it. I don't remember rehearsing the piece, either, or what it sounded like. It's possible that the school kept the score; at that point it wouldn't have occurred to me to make a second copy.

It's hard to describe your own development in retrospect. How do you "become" a composer? What are the steps along the way? How do you learn the ropes? It's like you're a snowball rolling down a hill. A snowball doesn't roll in an even fashion. It might pick up more snow on one side than the other. It's lumpy, it's uneven. That's how it is as you're learning an art. You don't have a sense of what's at the bottom of the hill. You're just picking

CHICAGO CITY JUNIOR COLLEGE

WOODROW WILSON BRANCH

CHARLES R. MONROE, *Dean*

CONCERT

Thirtieth Annual Music Festival

under the direction of

LELA HANMER
OTTO JELINEK

COLLEGE AUDITORIUM   6800 SOUTH STEWART AVENUE
FRIDAY   APRIL 17, 1964   8:00 P.M.

WILSON CONCERT BAND

OTTO JELINEK, *Conductor*

Frank J. Abraham	Robert L. Parker
Eugenia D. Bouchee	Wardell R. Peel
Charles D. Buchler	John E. Powell
William Caldwell	Brooks R. Rettker
Walter N. Chepulis	Leonard H. Smith
Garland M. Cleggett	Paul E. Sobanski
Andrew N. Davare	Robert Streich
Jon L. Hawkins	Charles R. Taylor
Jerold H. Hopkins	Ira L. Thigpen
Joseph Jarman	Willis Thigpen Jr.
Herbert Jenkins	Robert P. Thorton
Melvin L. Jones	Henry L. Threadgill
Clark Jordan	Leslie B. Turner
Roscoe Mitchell	Julius L. Walker
Brian C. Munch	James Whitfield
Dennis J. Opalinski	

☆ ☆ ☆

Program

Spirit of Music ....David Bennett
Choir and Band
Andre Morrison, Katherine Paynter,
Phyllis Washington, Ruth Young, *soloists*

Gallia ....Charles Gounod (1818-1893)
Choir
Vera Carpenter, *Soprano*   College String Quartet

First Suite in E flat ....Gustav Holst (1874-1934)
Chaconne   Intermezzo   March
Concert Band

Alleluia ....Randall Thompson
Every Night When The Sun Goes In ....arr. Stanley Sheppard
Choir

— INTERMISSION —

Tampico Overture ....Forest Buchtel
Scenes (first performance) ....Henry Threadgill
Concert Band

Il Mio Tesoro Intanto (from "Don Giovanni") ....W. A. Mozart (1756-91)
Robert Ingram Jr., *tenor*

Spinning Wheel Quartet (from "Martha") .....Frederick Von Flotow (1812-83)
Elaine Wallace, *soprano*   Robert Ingram Jr., *tenor*
Cordelia Harris, *alto*   Theodore McEwing, *baritone*

Eri Tu ....Guiseppi Verdi (1913-1901)
Theodore McEwing, *baritone*

Hansel and Gretel selections ....Humperdinck-Fitzgerald (1854-1921)
Die Meistersinger excerpts ....Wagner-Osterling (1813-83)
Concert Band

The Merry Widow selections ....Lehar-Bennett
Choir and Band
Hazel Glover, Theodore McEwing, *soloists*

Smoking in Lower Lobby only — Near Exits

things up, figuring it out as best you can as you hurtle along. It's an accumulation of information and the gradual attainment of skill and control. You don't have time to set a target, or even to control your course. I did see other people coming up at the same time I did who seemed to attain a level of polish in terms of the music that they were striving to play or write. They'd get to a point where they'd met the requirements and perfected their art to a very high level. But my own interests were so broad that I knew I wasn't going to be satisfied by achieving proficiency in one domain. I was never aiming simply to attain the status quo, whether that meant Coltrane or Varèse. So it made my path to self-invention much more uncertain.

Wilson only lasted two years, and almost as soon as I got there I was considering what my next step would be. I knew I needed more: more instruction, more exposure. I decided to transition to the American Conservatory of Music, which was in another part of the city, on South Michigan across the street from the Art Institute of Chicago. Founded in 1886, it was the oldest degree-granting music school in the Midwest. I liked the idea of a conservatory, with the tutorial type of one-on-one teaching. You could move at your own pace. I started taking classes there while I was still in my second year at Wilson. This was a big change in a lot of ways, not least because Wilson was a city college with a majority Black student population; the American Conservatory was a private school and mostly white. I finished my liberal arts degree at Wilson in 1964 and started taking the prerequisites (literature, psychology, sociology) I would need in order to matriculate formally at the American Conservatory. I took the prerequisite courses gradually over the next couple of years as I could afford them, some at the Conservatory and some at the University of Chicago.

My second year at Wilson, I remember, I showed up the first day and ran into my friend Anthony Braxton. He had already been in the military, and when he came back he had a part-time job working in registration. I borrowed fifteen dollars from my mother to pay the registration fee.

I was still living with my mother during this period, but I started to take on various part-time jobs to support myself. I'd help people clean out an apartment building, or I'd help to gather clinker, the coal left over from furnaces. The University of Chicago had a Sleep Center where you could get paid to spend the night sleeping hooked up to electrodes. I also worked at Orchestra Hall as an usher, and at McCormick Place as a waiter. Orchestra Hall was a great gig, because I got to see Fritz Reiner conduct the Chicago Symphony Orchestra. My teacher Otto Jelinek would also sometimes get us tickets to see the orchestra at the Edgewater Beach Hotel ballroom on Sundays, in concerts that were broadcast on television. Mr. Jelinek got us front-row seats where we could follow the music on a score during the performance. I started to see other performances that blew me away, too: the Kabuki theater, Cambodian music, the Nikolais Dance Theatre, the Negro Ensemble Company doing Douglas Turner Ward's *Day of Absence* in Hyde Park, Beckett's *Waiting for Godot.*

Not long after I started taking classes at the American Conservatory, I had an assignment where I had to go to a live concert and write up a report about it. Any classical music. I went down to Roosevelt University, where they had concerts at one o'clock on Friday afternoons. I didn't know who was playing or anything. I just had to write the report. I was running late that day, and I couldn't find the concert hall. I started to panic—you can't just sneak in after the show has started.

In addition to my occasional nights at the Sleep Center, I also found a job at the University of Chicago hospital in the spring of 1965. I was a lab technician. I would monitor various tests they were running on people, collecting samples and taking them to the appropriate lab. It was a great job because I got to a place where nobody knew how to do it but me. I had inherited the position from a guy who was going to work on his doctorate, and he told me never to divulge how I did the work. "That way," he told me, "they'll be totally dependent on you."

My bosses thought it took all day to collect and deliver the samples. But I had the routing figured out so that it took no time at all. I would do the rounds in about an hour and a half at the hospital in the morning, go to the library and study music, then come back in the afternoon and do the rounds again. It was simple. Basically I worked for about two to two and a half hours. When I had a day off and someone else had to take it over, which happened occasionally, it would take them two days to figure it out because no one knew where anything went but me. It was an entire system you had to memorize: the hemoglobin test had to go to some particular room in basement of the Fermi Institute, for example.

I had a good friend in the hospital. There were students who lived there. I had two composer friends, white guys, who were paying their way through their doctoral programs by working as guinea pigs for medical research. I would go periodically and collect samples from them: blood, urine, and feces. I was close to one of them, who I thought was particularly talented. We'd meet in a cafeteria on campus, but he wasn't allowed to have anything to eat or drink outside; they controlled his diet and gave him all his meals. I always wondered what they were giving him; clearly that was part of the experiment. He was studying for his PhD in composition with Easley Blackwood Jr. and Ralph Shapey, the founder of the University of Chicago Contemporary Chamber Players. I used to look at my friend's compositions—he was working on these big orchestral scores—and talk to him about what it was like to study with Blackwood. We regularly went to hear the Contemporary Chamber Players, which was a particularly cutting-edge group: I heard Berio and Schoenberg and Hindemith and a whole range of modern music at their concerts.

———

I asked a little old man in a rumpled suit how to get to the concert. He gave me the once-over and said calmly, "I think I know where you want to go. Follow me." And he took me to the side of this big building to an entrance that led to what seemed to be a deserted hallway. I started wondering if he was pulling my leg.

"Wow," I said, in a slightly dubious tone, "you really know your way around here."

"Yes, I do," the man answered. "I've been here before."

He led me to a door that we reached by going up three stairs, and we walked through the door and emerged at the side of the stage of a large auditorium. The hall was full and a large audience was sitting there looking at us expectantly. He pointed me to a seat toward the side of the front row.

"Go on down, have a seat."

I was about to say, "Well, aren't you going to come, too?" when I saw him turn and stride confidently up onto the stage and sit down at the piano. I stared at him, my mouth agape. As he sat down, he looked back over at me and winked. There was nothing to do but take my seat. As the man started to play a Chopin waltz, I caught a glance of the program of the person sitting next to me: the little old man at the piano was none other than Arthur Rubinstein.

My great-grandfather passed away in 1962. I know it was a few years after Sputnik, because I'll never forget his reaction to that event. My aunt had bought the Admiral TV console a few years earlier, and so in October 1957 all the neighbors came over to our place to see the news coverage. Everybody was crowded around the set, and I noticed that Papa was sitting alone in another room. I wondered why he hadn't joined us. So I went over to him and said, "Papa, don't you want to come and see the rocket—"

"That ain't shit," he interrupted me brusquely. But he didn't seem to be in a bad mood or anything.

"What do you mean, Papa?" I asked.

He said, "Let me tell you something. I started out with a mule and a plow. Then there was a horse and buggy. Then along came the bicycle."

I stared at him, genuinely puzzled.

"Then the train came along, and then the car. And then the airplane came along." He paused. "And this here?" he added. "This here ain't shit."

He meant that he'd already seen all those great technological revolutions within his lifetime. This was just another advance. He'd lived through the others, and he'd live through this one.

"So, what, now I'm supposed to jump up in awe? There's going to be another one coming—what about the next one? Naw. I'm just keeping my seat." He gave me an obstinate look. And he ended the discussion with his ultimate verdict on the practical implications of satellite technology: "It ain't gonna make me have no good shit, is it?"

In the same period when I was making the transition from Wilson to the American Conservatory, I found myself pulled into the orbit of an entirely different kind of musical scene. I'd stayed in touch with Joan Cox, the pianist who accompanied me for my performance of "Cypress Song" at the state competition back in high school. She ended up going to Teachers College right across the street from Wilson, and so we kept hanging out. We had a mutual infatuation going on, and one thing led to another. She was also extremely talented; she could have been a great musician if she'd pursued it.

Joan was a devout churchgoer. And I was infatuated: so I started going to church with her at the Langley Church of God on 62nd and South Langley, right around the corner from all the nightclubs at 63rd and Cottage Grove. The pastor at Langley was a charismatic man named Reverend Morris. It had been a long time since I'd been in a church like that. It reminded me of Reverend Charles's church, the church I had gone to as a young child with my maternal grandmother. That had been a Church of God in Christ. This new one was a Church of God. They're different denominations, but both sanctified—and there was the same lightning in the air at the services.

Reverend Morris would sometimes turn over the pulpit to his assistant pastors or to various visiting preachers. One of the other ministers at the Langley Church of God was famous in his own right: a Reverend Hines, who came from somewhere in the Caribbean. He was a brilliant intellectual and a mesmerizing speaker. His sermons had a level of erudition and an exegetical power that went much farther than your run-of-the-mill Sunday-morning brimstone. I remember being intrigued by other kinds of intellectuals around the same time. For a little while I was attracted to Elijah Muhammad, for example, although only from a distance. (I was always suspicious of the hyperventilating tone of most of the articles about the Nation of Islam in the newspapers; Elijah Muhammad was strident and uncompromising, but he and his followers seemed disciplined and respectful, unlike many of their critics.) But in the end it was Reverend Hines who captivated me with the force of his vision.

Every summer when I was little, I had to go to Bible class at the Olivet Baptist Church, Grandma Threadgill's church. It was one of the ways people kept their kids occupied once school let out in the summer. If you didn't go to camp, you went to Bible class. It made for long days, because the Bible-study classes were strict and tedious, but just outside on 31st Street the evangelists would set up their tents and hold revival meetings. And I couldn't help getting intrigued by the more boisterous activities going on there. I saw a phenomenal preacher there named Horace Sheppard, who was renowned all over the country. He was based in Philadelphia but he would regularly travel to give guest sermons at other churches and to lead revival meetings in other cities. He had started preaching as a teenager, and even a few years later, when I first saw him, people still called him the Boy Wonder or the Atomic Bomb.

Soon I was a regular at Langley. I started doing some arrangements for the medium-sized unit, which usually included saxes, trumpet, trombone, piano, organ, bass, and drums. They had some fabulous musicians there. As at other churches in Chicago, you'd see some of the same faces playing in a church Sunday morning that you might have seen playing in a nightclub Saturday night; one of the bassists at the church played regularly with Gene Ammons, for instance. I liked the challenge of trying to adapt what I was learning at the conservatory to the functional context of a worship service.

Around the beginning of 1965, something momentous happened at the Langley Church of God. By then I was spending a lot of time there and serving as a de facto music director, although I didn't always play with the band myself. I was there one Saturday afternoon and Reverend Morris asked me to take a solo. He called me up and asked me to do "His Eye Is on the Sparrow." All the pillars of the church were there: the deacons and deaconesses, sitting up in the front pews. I moistened the reed on my tenor and began to play the melody, and the strangest thing happened: there was hardly any reaction at all. The matronly church ladies sat there watching me blow my heart out, and they barely stirred. There were a few little murmurs of polite encouragement. A few desultory words of approval—"yes . . . yes." It was almost patronizing. Respectful, sure, but blatantly unmoved.

I was shocked. This was a sanctified church; usually when the music started people were falling out on the floor and exploding down the aisles!

Reverend Morris had an exceptional ear. He was savvy, too. After the service he came up to me and told me, "You know, Henry, I have an old saxophone up under the pulpit. It's a little smaller than the one you were playing today." He went and pulled it out; it was an old Martin alto sax.

"It probably needs some work," the reverend said. "Could you get it fixed for me? Whatever it costs, get it fixed and bring me the bill."

So I took the horn to get repaired and brought it back a few days later. When I showed it to Reverend Morris, he said, "I'd like you to play again for Sunday service. Why don't you play the same piece you were playing the other day. But would you mind trying it on this other horn?"

I wasn't sure what the point was, but I agreed. And so that Sunday, I played "His Eye Is on the Sparrow" again, this time on alto. And this time, the response was completely different. The congregation was buzzing: you know it's going well when people start commenting while you're playing. Not just a few half-hearted notes of assent, but unrestrained interjections of spontaneous approval. A rippling cascade of Amens as I reached the bridge. And outbursts of commentary as I got farther into my solo. "Play your instrument, young man!" People were clearly following the well-known lyrics behind my flourishes on the melody, because a few of them started speaking out the words for emphasis, as though to second what I was "saying" on the saxophone. "Because I'm *happy*," one woman emphasized. "I sing because I'm *free* . . ."

After the service, Reverend Morris came up to me with a sly smile. "I knew it," he said. "You just didn't have the right horn."

What Reverend Morris had realized—and what I understood only after I witnessed the change in the congregation's reaction— was that the tenor saxophone didn't register in this music. The tenor is a blues horn. A rhythm-and-blues horn. It's got that Saturday-night, big-bellied heft to its sound. But the people at church just didn't hear the tenor. There's something about the similarity between the range and timbre of the alto and the human voice—that was what seemed to work for the church situation. After that experience I stopped playing the tenor at the Langley Church of God. It was only alto and occasionally a little clarinet. And soon the alto came to be at the center of my musical world. I used it for solos with the band at church, and I also started performing concerts with some of the other Langley musicians, above all Reverend Morris's daughter Jo Jo, who was a music major in college, studying to be an opera singer. Sometimes it was for services at Langley, but Jo Jo and I started doing small concerts of religious music elsewhere, too.

It was the first time I'd sensed the potential of the horn. I had fooled around with it a little bit, and of course I'd been playing for years with Joseph and Roscoe, who were alto players. But I had never thought I would play it myself.

It was partly that my primary influences had been tenor players: Gene Ammons, Sonny Rollins, Eddie Williams, John Coltrane . . . I didn't have a comparable list in terms of the alto. It was Ornette Coleman and Eric Dolphy, and it pretty much ended there. It took me a long time to appreciate great alto players like Johnny Hodges, Marshal Royal, and Willie Smith. I was certainly struck by Charlie Parker, but with him it wasn't so much about his sound on the horn as it was a matter of the level of expression—the torrent of ideas that seemed to be coming out for the first time in his music. The harmonic sophistication, the intricate organization of the musical information into elegant arcs, even if they were coming out at a blistering pace.

It's difficult in hindsight to convey the impact of a truly revolutionary development. You have to be there in the moment when something comes along to get a sense of its effect. Twenty or forty years later, listening to a Charlie Parker record, it might not seem like such a big deal. But it *was* a big deal. Hearing Charlie Parker for the first time felt like watching someone leap off a cliff and take flight.

To my mind, most of the great alto players after Bird seemed to emerge directly from his music. Obviously Cannonball Adderley and Sonny Stitt were phenomenal players, but to me their language was an elaboration on the bebop aesthetic Parker had established: the next rung in the ladder. On alto, only Ornette and Dolphy seemed to introduce an entirely original *sound*. In contrast, the diversity of the tenor players of that era was astounding: Chu Berry didn't sound like Lester Young, who didn't sound like Coleman Hawkins, who didn't sound like Don Byas. John Gilmore didn't sound like Johnny Griffin. Von Freeman didn't sound like Frank Wess.

After the fact, it's also hard to comprehend the brilliance of Charlie Parker's closest contemporaries, especially the ones who *weren't* just mimicking his advances. Bud Powell? It was frightening the way these people executed music. Listen to Bud Powell on that famous live album at Massey Hall in 1953. He's not just playing Charlie Parker lines on the piano. Powell is doing so much more *in the company of* Parker: he's playing so many lead-ins and chordal variations on every beat that it's dizzying. It's hard to believe, the sheer velocity of his intellect. And then there are Bud's own solos! It felt like they were pouring out of an inexhaustible well of melodic invention. Looking back, it's hard to explain what a quantum leap it felt like at the time. It was as though the race everyone was running—the only race anyone knew—was the sixty-yard dash, and suddenly Bud Powell showed us how to run a marathon. Endurance, intensity, pacing: all the basic rules of engagement were redefined.

Or think of Miles Davis. This teenager steps up next to Charlie Parker and Dizzy Gillespie, strides into this arena bursting with pyrotechnics. And what did Miles do? He looked for contrast. He went for minimalism: an economy of expression that was all the more stunning in those surroundings. I once read something Miles said. "There were a lot of guys who could have been in my position with Charlie Parker," he admitted. "But would they have learned what I learned?" That was the whole thing. Miles didn't come away from the experience playing like Bird in any kind of way. For most musicians, it would have been almost impossible to evade that influence—to keep from being infected by Parker's lines, to avoid picking up bits of his phrasing. But Miles figured out how to get something from Bird almost through a kind of parallel thinking. He propelled himself into another world and took that information into another dimension. To me, *that* was true brilliance.

———

One Sunday I went to the Langley Church of God and the guest was none other than Horace Sheppard, the traveling evangelical preacher I'd seen on 31st Street as a child. Reverend Morris asked me to play. So I got to meet Sheppard and perform during the service.

Sheppard was just as much of a firebrand as when I'd seen him on 31st Street years before. He was still one of the most devastating speakers I'd ever seen, capable of an almost unbelievable range of nuance. And his message was powerful: he would talk about freedom in a way that people weren't used to hearing in church—in a way that, even if it was infused with the stories and cadences of the Bible, was as timely and political as anything going on in the civil rights movement. But it was above all the significance and the power of his *sound* that nabbed me. His voice was like somebody blowing a horn. He had the dynamic range and timbral subtlety of an instrumentalist. Whoa! I said to myself the first time I heard him.

He was one of those preachers who would vocalize, whose voice would take on distinct tonal contours, especially as his sermons gradually built up to a pulsating intensity. He would start by reading from the Scripture, his voice almost flat and pedantic: "Let us turn now to the first verse of the Book of Revelation . . ." But then, as he started recounting the vision John was granted on the island of Patmos, his voice would swell and transform: "I am Alpha and Omega, the first and the last . . ." Sheppard could change keys as he shifted gears; he added a tonal layer to his language to give a dynamic quality to what he was saying. "I'll *tell* you about a dream . . ." He wasn't just moaning; Sheppard had precise control over the pitch of his words. It would go to another harmonic plateau. He could also do something almost like ventriloquism: he could suddenly seem to be projecting sound from a different part of his body, as though his lungs grew three times bigger, or he somehow opened up a new cavity in his chest. The words would take on an entirely different volume.

There was a physicality to his sermons, too. He was a short guy, but extremely athletic and surprisingly agile. He would turn sideways to the microphone for dramatic effect, peering out at the congregation and whispering, before abruptly turning to the front and letting his voice boom. Sometimes it was almost like James Brown: he would come flying out from behind the pulpit down right in front of the pews and land doing the splits—right in the middle of the sermon!

Horace Sheppard was a recruiter as well. He was always on the lookout for talent. Like Billy Graham or Charles Harrison Mason, he would travel the country to put on these crusades or revivals with an enormous entourage. It was basically a professional troupe. There was a virtuosic pianist named Alan Turner, who had started out as a classical concert soloist before joining Sheppard's outfit. Sheppard had hired multiple members of the Simpson family, who seemed to be able to play every instrument under the sun. The youngest daughter had perfect pitch and amazing recall, and she would do this number with the pianist where he would sit there and improvise a passage, and she would play it all back on the organ, almost like an echo in another voice.

After hearing me in church that day, Sheppard invited me to join his troupe. How could I say no? From my perspective, it represented a gig as a professional musician: the commitment to the art form, the itinerant life, the excitement of seeing new places and playing before new audiences. And he took me everywhere. Sheppard's home base was his church in Philadelphia, the High Street Church of God in Germantown. Sometimes I would go there. I would stay with the Simpson family while I was in town. But I didn't move from Chicago; I'd just go to meet Sheppard whenever he needed me. It was often when he took the show on the road: he would just call me and tell me to go to the airport. And there'd be a plane ticket there waiting for me. First class. I'd land in Los Angeles or Detroit or Pittsburgh and head to the hotel where a room was already reserved in my name. And we'd do camp meetings and revivals, sometimes all-day or all-night affairs. I saw what America looked like outside of a geography book.

The main attraction was Sheppard himself, of course. But it was structured as a sort of revue in which every member of the troupe had a role to play. It was modular in that there was some room for improvisation; you had a sense of the kind of number you might be featuring in, but not necessarily exactly when it would take place during the series of events, or how long it might run. He would call on us when he needed us. In the middle of a long sermon, the pace might shift and he'd look over to me sitting with the other musicians. "Henry, play 'In the Upper Room' for the people," Sheppard would request. And we would go right into it—when I was featured, it was usually me with a single accompanist on piano or organ.

Sometimes he had clear instructions with regard to the role I was supposed to play in the orchestration of the service. "Start at the back of the nave," he'd direct me before we started. Or if we were in a tent at a camp meeting, he might have me waiting outside. "When I call on you, I want you to walk through the congregation playing 'We'll Understand It Better By and By.' Start it out simple and sweet. But by the time you get to the altar, I want this place torn down." So I would build up to an emotional crescendo as I played and made my way to the front. And once I got there, it would segue directly into the next segment—I'd take it up a level and the next person would take it up *another* level. *Zoom!* And then Sheppard himself might come leaping out from behind the pulpit and launch back into the course of his sermon. As I walked slowly by, he'd pop out behind me and jump down into the splits, his voice resounding out of the mike. The audience was astounded: they were completely blown away. And what a rush, to be at the center of such a whirlpool of spiritual power—I loved it!

The tunes I would perform were almost like wordless arias—but of course everyone knew the lyrics, because these were the most recognizable classics of the gospel tradition. So I had to play the melodies in a way that wouldn't stray too far from the

words, but that conveyed them with a sort of straining or aspiration that seemed to go beyond language. "Precious Lord,"
"Amazing Grace," "How Great Thou Art," "The Lord Has
Been a Shelter" (which both Mahalia Jackson and Sam Cooke
had recorded), "How I Got Over": the song might have started
out as a hymn or a spiritual, but in Reverend Sheppard's revivals
everything we touched ended up being a gospel.

When I started traveling with Sheppard in 1965, I stopped hanging out as much with my old friends like Joseph and Roscoe.
So I wasn't around for the founding of the Association for the
Advancement of Creative Musicians that May. I mainly kept in
touch with that world through another scene that had started
up the year before, at the Avon Hotel. The Avon Hotel was
down the street from the University of Chicago hospital, where
I kept working as a lab technician even as I became increasingly
involved with Sheppard. Located at 61st Street and Stony Island
Avenue, the Avon was an offshoot of the university's International House. At first it was one of the places that took the over-
flow population of foreign students when International House
filled up. But it became the informal headquarters of a sort of
university counterculture. Some of the far-out students and pro-
fessors took apartments there, too, and there was some of the
experimentation with drugs and "alternative lifestyles" that was
very much of the moment. Artists were attracted to that atmosphere, and it ended up serving as a sort of long-term residency
hotel for a number of people who had no connection to the
university. Joseph Jarman lived there for a time, as did a number of other musicians including Wilbur Ware, Leonard Jones,
Charles Clark, Christopher Gaddy, Butch Davis, and Abshalom
Ben Shlomo. I would often go by the Avon in the afternoon and
practice with some of them when I had a break in my rounds at
the hospital.

   People knew I had gotten involved with the church. Not surprisingly, they were skeptical. I remember that once in the spring

of 1965 I gave a concert at a church around 55th Street and I invited a friend of mine, the bass player M'chaka Uba (formerly Allen Joyner). The concert took place at night and the church was illuminated only by candlelight. It spooked him. He went back and told everybody at the Avon that I had gone off the deep end. "Henry's gone *way* out," I heard he said. "He's playing with these sanctified people in churches—in the dark, with people shouting and praying in funny languages. It's like some kind of strange ritualistic stuff. Damn. I don't know what happened to him."

At that point I was a believer, of course. I was deep into the doctrine. I was into the philosophical aspects of the theology as well. I thought a lot about the interpretation of the symbolic registers of evangelical Christianity. There were things that were very interesting to me and yet befuddling at the same time: Nebuchadnezzar's dream . . . the Four Horsemen of the Apocalypse. How numbers and symbols are interpreted in such different ways by different denominations and different religions. And how the entire worldview tended to see things in terms of millennia.

I still very much saw myself as a composer, and in the music I was writing I was trying to find a middle ground between what I considered to be religious or spiritual music—not just liturgical music for a service, but in a broader sense—and the sort of experimentation I had been starting to do at Wilson and more recently at the American Conservatory. If I was making music within the world of the Church of God, still I was thinking about music devoted to worship in a way that wasn't restricted to the gospel tradition. I considered myself to be taking into account the entire pan-European lineage at the same time, so I was drawing on what I knew about Palestrina and Allegri's *Miserere* and Bach's *Passions* and Mendelssohn's biblical oratorios and many other works that had germinated in various Christian traditions.

It was certainly true that some heavy stuff went down at the Sheppard revivals. And there was a point beyond which I found

myself unable to go. There were sessions that were basically exor-
cisms. They were casting out demons. Sometimes they'd take the
afflicted person into a sort of back room. They'd close the door
and only certain people had the right to be there. "That woman
is possessed by the devil, Henry," they explained. "You can't
come in here. It's too dangerous." I would hear all this violent
thrashing and screaming and stomping—it sounded like a fight.
Are they praying in there, I wondered, or beating her up? Everyone would wait outside as we all listened to these horrible noises,
imagining the desperate battle behind the door. These sessions
could go on for quite some time. Finally the person would come
out, sobbing quietly, propped up by the reverend and the faith
healers, all of them sweating profusely and looking disheveled.
It was a mystery. And mysteries do draw me in. I said to myself,
I've got to get into that room!

But I never did.

They kept talking about a "higher commitment." But I didn't
see how I could go any farther. I felt like I had already committed as much as I could commit. And I started to be bothered by
some of the contradictions—if not hypocrisies—in the way the
whole situation was set up. They were happy to proclaim the
greatness of the musicians who were playing for the church. But
they didn't have any sense of the practical necessities of everyday life, much less any sense of what it meant to choose to be
an artist. Everything was for the glory of God, and that was
all fine and everything—but who's going to take care of me?
Who's going to put food on my table? I remember being struck
by it. I'd write some music, rehearse the group, and perform it
in the church. Nobody got paid. When I toured with Horace
Sheppard, my expenses were covered, but I got nothing for my
artistic contribution or my time—it was somehow taken for
granted that that was purely a donation, supposedly given out of
my undying commitment to the cause. Over time, as it happened
again and again, this became an issue in the back of my mind.
I didn't ever confront anyone about it. But it became a nagging
concern. I couldn't figure out how to make them see me not just

as a believer with a talent, but as a professional musician. They simply didn't understand music in the same way people did in the secular world. And gradually this tiny crack in my dedication to their world grew bigger and bigger, to the point where I couldn't stay.

When Malcolm X was shot in the Audubon Ballroom in February 1965, Reverend Morris stood up before the congregation at the Langley Church of God and asked us to mourn his loss. "He was a great man," Morris declared. I remember being taken aback. In that climate, it seemed like a big leap. I assumed that for people in the church, the Nation of Islam represented a completely different world—not only because of religion, but because the evangelical milieu was so far away from the mundane concerns of the material world. For people so single-minded in their focus on salvation, I thought, it would be considered folly to advocate for political justice or social revolution.

At the church, I was careful never to mention that I was an admirer of Malcolm and everything he stood for. But given where I had grown up and what I had seen—given the path my life was taking in the early 1960s—I found it impossible not to be impressed by Malcolm. Like Muhal Richard Abrams or the poet Amus Mor, for me Malcolm was one of the main models, a figure whose example defined the times. I remember watching Malcolm on these talk shows on TV. They didn't have anybody who could handle him. It would always be two or three or four white intellectuals up against Malcolm, as though one antagonist wasn't sufficient. How is that fair? I wondered. And then he would demolish every argument they came up with. What he said was bold, but he never advanced opinions that he couldn't back up with facts. And the country had never seen anything like that before. They'd never seen a Black man on TV who could battle intellectually like that, who had the arsenal of facts and the rhetorical agility to dominate any debate. It was the most sophisticated thing that young Black men in my generation had ever seen.

I was surprised when Reverend Morris spoke of Malcolm—he

had the entire congregation stand for a moment of silence in his honor—but maybe I shouldn't have been. The Church of God wasn't a middle-of-the-road Baptist or Methodist institution, after all. This was an extremist church. They really started to get out there into some dark stuff. So for them to recognize Malcolm, maybe it wasn't only a nod to the persuasiveness of his message in the political environment that surrounded us. Maybe it was also one extremism acknowledging another. Game recognize game. That's why I got pulled into the church in the first place, to be honest. If the Church of God hadn't been way out, I wouldn't have been there.

My mother always used to accuse me of being an extremist. She'd say, "Henry, why do you always have to take the most radical option? Why do you have to fall in with extremism?" I would always object—"Come on now, you know that's not fair," I'd respond, laughing off the charge—but it was absolutely true when I look at it in retrospect.

3

Democratic Vistas

—When did you first become aware of its presence?
—I'm not even sure how to answer that. Is the field mouse aware of the presence of the hawk? It wasn't a state I was familiar with; it's not a sensation I was prepared to recognize. How would I have ever imagined that I would be stalked?

Toward the end of the spring of 1966, my draft board officer warned me that they were about to call my number. I was still working at the University of Chicago hospital in order to make money to pay for my classes at the conservatory. The problem was that I was only going to school part-time. I thought I was flying under the radar. But the draft board found out and they took away my three-year deferment status.

There were three options open to me: I could join, I could wait to be drafted, or I could volunteer for the draft. If you were a professional in a given trade, volunteering for the draft meant that you agreed to sign a contract with the military to provide whatever happened to be your professional expertise. If you were drafted, on the other hand, all bets were off. You might be a brain surgeon, but if the army decided they needed you to dig holes, your expertise didn't matter: you were going to dig holes. If you volunteered for the draft, however, the military had to honor that contract and employ you in your professional capacity.

"Henry, you've got enough experience as a musician to be considered a professional," my draft officer told me. "You should volunteer for the draft. That way you can keep playing music."

There were implications for how long you had to serve as well. If you joined, your term was three years, while if you were drafted it was two years. But if you volunteered for the draft, it meant you would serve two and a half years rather than three, provided that you could get a letter from an employer demonstrating that you were going to return to your previous area of professional activity.

I volunteered for the draft as a musician and signed a contract with the US Army in August 1966.

I ended up enlisting with my old friend Milton Chapman. We took the train down from Chicago together. The first place they sent us was Fort Knox in Kentucky. Just as we were going in, we saw a group of soldiers marching out of the compound. Watching them file by, I was surprised to see a familiar face: Fred Whalum, another friend from Chicago. There wasn't even time to say hello—he just gave me a quick, surreptitious wave when he noticed me. Later I found out that he had somehow been discharged even before he started basic training. But at the time I wasn't sure what was going on.

As it turned out, Milton and I weren't there long either. We walked in and walked right back out. Right after we arrived, there was an outbreak of spinal meningitis. The entire fort was evacuated. They burned all the clothes and bedding and rushed everybody out with nothing more than the clothes on their backs. We had to sit by the side of the road for hours and hours until they finally started taking a head count and figuring out what to do. Eventually we set up camp in tents in a field nearby until they shipped us to other places.

Milton and I ended up getting sent to do our basic training

in Fort Campbell, Tennessee. "Take the last train to Clarksville and I'll meet you at the station . . .": that was the soundtrack to basic training for me—the first big hit by the Monkees. When I think of that time, that's the sound that comes back. Clarksville was the closest city to the fort. And in basic training, after a few weeks they give you a weekend pass to have some fun in town. That was where we all went. "We'll have one more night together": those lyrics seemed like an uncanny description of our situation—the fatalism, the longing, the foreboding. "And I don't know if I'm ever coming home": the refrain of young men living in the knowledge that soon they were going off to war.

Milton was in a different situation because he had joined the army. He was still playing trumpet, and he was hoping to end up in a military band. But it wasn't up to him. After basic training they sent him to the Naval School of Music in Virginia Beach. We kept in touch, writing each other letters. The Naval School was well regarded, and a number of prominent jazz musicians went through there. But nothing was guaranteed. Milton was anxious: he told me that it felt like being in college again, but with much higher stakes. If he failed the tests, if his playing wasn't up to par, then he might not be assigned to a band. You had to earn your way in. And if you didn't, you'd end up being a grunt in the infantry.

In the end Milton did make it, and was stationed with a band somewhere in Georgia. Ironically, he never saw action in the war, while I was the one who got sent over.

After basic training I went straight to an assignment with the 437th Army Band, stationed at Fort Riley outside of Junction City, Kansas. There were fantastic musicians in that band. There was a talented bassist who had toured with Johnny Mathis for years. A clarinetist named William Broadnax, a Mexican-American trumpeter named Loreago. The piano player, Jack Davis, had been with Anthony Braxton in Korea. He was always talking about how eccentric Braxton was. Apparently Braxton

Standing in the middle of a group of colleagues from
the Fort Riley band, including clarinetist William Broadnax (right) and
pianist Jack Davis (second from right), May 1967

used to drive everybody there crazy playing his Coltrane and
Cecil Taylor records loud all night long in the barracks.

There were other bands at Fort Riley attached to the army
divisions based there: the 9th Division Band, the 1st Division
Band. The 437th wasn't attached to a particular division, so we
played for various functions around the fort. We had plenty of
free time, and some of the guys in the band started working on
things in the evenings. I was studying Ornette's music, transcribing his tunes and trying to figure out how they worked harmoni-
cally. We had a dedicated space, a rehearsal hall, and we could
just go in there and play all night if we wanted to. Aside from the
official events, we were also playing informal gigs on the side:
sometimes we would go to Kansas City and play for officers'
club parties and things like that.

As part of my contract as a professional musician, the military also agreed to pay for continuing education: I took some
classes at Kansas State University in Manhattan. It was a fun
place to hang out near the base: a little college town with a
bookstore and a restaurant. I started playing with some other
groups in the music scene around campus. I also found a couple
of jobs on the side. Although I had left Horace Sheppard, I still
gravitated to that evangelical milieu, and I started working as
the choral director and band arranger for a Church of God in
Junction City. Manhattan was also the headquarters of the Stan
Kenton Foundation. Some of us were hired to go out on a picnic
boat moored on the Kansas River to work for the foundation
grading big-band material. We would sight-read the charts and
determine what level they were right for: one arrangement might
be appropriate for high schoolers, for example, while another
might require more expertise.

I found that being in Kansas provided other sorts of extracurricular education as well. Growing up in Chicago with such a
hodgepodge of sounds on the radio, I was pretty indiscriminate
in my listening: I took it all in. But if there was one kind of music
I was never drawn to, it was country music. I just couldn't abide
all that twangy guitar and lonesome-cowboy warbling. "Did

you ever see a robin weep?" Oh, enough with the ranch-hand laments, I'd think.

So it was a culture shock to be stationed in Kansas, where sometimes I got the impression that the entire musical universe had been reduced to country and western. That was all you heard on every radio station; that was all there was on every jukebox in every bar. It felt like a devious form of torture invented specifically to drive me crazy, tune by tune.

Being sequestered in that sonic environment taught me that I had to kill my limitations. Get over it. I learned that it was a mistake to close the door completely. Otherwise I might shut out something—the eerie vocalizations of a steel guitar—that might prove valuable for my own music, that might direct me to a sound or a technique or a strategy that I could use. I learned to hear the brilliance in a singer like Hank Williams, which resides in the small things. Now when one of his tunes comes on the radio, I warble along: "The silence of a falling star lights up a purple sky . . ."

> —How long did it take you to notice it?
> —It was a gradual realization—a slow dawning, only slightly quicker to arrive than the dawn itself. That's what made it so terrifying in the end: how drawn out it was. It was just a feeling at first, a faint perturbation, and then there was what I thought I saw, and then there was doubt, and calm, until the unease came again—the weird conviction that I was being watched—until it dissipated again, and that cycle went on and on and on, my anxiety ratcheted up a tiny bit each time. Until I knew what I saw, and knew it was coming closer. By then I was panicked. But it took hours.

After a couple of months with the 437th, I got transferred and promoted to become the head arranger for the top band at Fort Riley, the Post Band, which was also known as the general's band. When I won the Pulitzer Prize for Music in 2016, I found out that the band had had a designated arranger at least once before: the composer Robert Ward, a World War II veteran who also won the Pulitzer (in 1962). But when I was appointed to be the band arranger at the end of the fall of 1966, I was under the impression that I had inaugurated the position. I ended up eradicating it, too.

The general's band performed for special events around the fort. We played for visiting dignitaries, for officers' parties and dances, for parades. There were the martial standards, of course—"Colonel Bogey," "The Stars and Stripes Forever"—but we would also sometimes be asked to do covers of popular hits by Herb Albert or Dionne Warwick. Sometimes there would be quixotic requests: on the general's birthday, we got up at six a.m. and surprised him with a dawn fanfare of his favorite Irish and English folk classics: "When Irish Eyes Are Smiling," "Green Grow the Rushes."

One of our main assignments was to play at the highly formalized departures of various units and divisions that were being sent to Southeast Asia. In the winter of 1967 there were thousands of troops being sent over to the war, and sometimes it seemed like all of them came through Fort Riley. The logistics took an enormous amount of coordination: there were train schedules to coordinate, supplies and belongings to transport. Armored vehicle units, paratrooper units, engineer units: each group would march by in formation. The post commanders and company commanders were positioned on a grandstand reviewing the troops as they filed past, and the Post Band stood and played song after song to send the guys off with a hero's farewell.

This went on for days and days. There was so much traffic that we hardly ever got a break. Sometimes these departure ceremonies would take place at the fort, but the band was also dispatched to other locations around the area—wherever the troops were based before they left. We would catch a few hours of sleep on the floor of a depot by the railhead with our instruments lying next to us. Sometimes there wasn't even time for a proper meal; they had doughnut dollies—young women who would come around with coffee and doughnuts to keep us going.

Years later in New York, I met the trumpeter Ted Daniel and realized that I must have played him off from Fort Riley when he was mobilized with the 9th Division that winter. It was so damn cold; I remember thinking my fingers were going to fall off as I played the same tunes over and over again and watched the endless lines of soldiers march by us on the bandstand. Ted started in the infantry but he took his trumpet with him to Vietnam and was able to get himself transferred into the band once he was there. He was lucky, he told me: just after he got switched over to the band, his company was almost wiped out in battle.

In the summer of 1967, I was asked to arrange a medley of the great American national songs: "America the Beautiful," "The Star-Spangled Banner," "America (My Country 'Tis of Thee)," "God Bless America." I put a lot of time into it: I'd been listening to a lot of Thelonious Monk and Stravinsky, and my arrangement had some of the same kinds of angularity and dissonance. (I was also listening to Cecil Taylor, but at that time I found I wasn't able to do much with Cecil's music in terms of integrating it into an orchestration for a concert band.)

The bandleader was away, so he never heard the music before we performed it. I did the arrangement and a sergeant named Marcato was leading the rehearsals in the absence of the band director. The guys in the band were knocked out. "Damn, Henry," they told me, "this is really sophisticated stuff!"

We went to play the medley in Kansas City. We knew the premiere would be a big ceremonial occasion, but we didn't know who would be there. It turned out to be a gathering of all the big military brass—the generals, the colonels, the majors from all the divisions stationed in the region—as well as political leaders, including the governor and state legislators, the mayor and the city council, and religious dignitaries from the Catholic Church and various Protestant denominations. They were all seated up on a platform in front of a large audience.

The band director showed up just in time for the concert. He hadn't even had a chance to look over the score, much less approve it. The plan was for him to conduct it on the fly and hope for the best. We launched into the arrangement and didn't get more than eight bars into it before the Catholic archbishop stood up and yelled at us: "Blasphemy!" He was furious. The pristine white and crimson of his chasuble and his ornate pointy miter only made his outburst all the more shocking. "This is an outrage!" he thundered. "Pure blasphemy!" The conductor, unsure what to do, signaled to the band to stop.

I was standing in the wings. Once I was promoted to arranger, I didn't even have to play in the band myself anymore. I was just along for the ride. I figured I'd hear my arrangement and then hang out in Kansas City.

The crowd murmured in confusion as the archbishop glared at the governor and the other politicians. Flustered, they turned to the clutch of generals. "Who's responsible for this travesty?" the politicians demanded. The generals jumped to their feet. They were certainly not going to be called on the carpet over this mess. They looked over to the band director, and he looked at Sergeant Marcato. And Marcato pointed at me and said, "Threadgill's the one who did it! He wrote the music."

I peered out from the wings. "Um, what's the problem?" I asked.

They stopped the entire event right there. As the audience shuffled out, there was a sort of huddle around the archbishop with the band director and the army officers. I didn't know what was going on. Blasphemy? A piece of music? What did that even mean? How could an arrangement be blasphemous?

The band was herded back into the bus to return to Fort Riley. The band director informed me: "Threadgill, you're back in the band tomorrow. Report for band in the morning."

"What? Back in uniform?" I was confused. As the arranger, I didn't even need to wear my military dress. I had been dressing in civilian clothes for months.

"Yes," he answered in a severe tone. "You're in the second clarinet section, in uniform, tomorrow."

I tried to engage him in a civil conversation. "What is this about? What's going on?" He refused to discuss it further. I wasn't sure what was up, but I knew I was in trouble. I knew how the chain of command works. These people kick spit on asses. When the archbishop jumped on the generals, they had to find somebody to take the blame.

We got back to the fort in the early evening. I remember that even the sunset looked ominous that day. The next morning, I scrambled to get ready for band rehearsal, trying to get my fatigues on straight, looking for a reed that would work for my clarinet. We started at nine o'clock and rehearsed until noon, when we had a lunch break.

The rehearsal studio was a big, beautiful room, and by midday the sunlight was streaming in through the windows. As we sat back down for the afternoon session, I was thinking that despite the abrupt reversal of fortune, it was actually a pleasure to play in the group again, to rediscover the reflexes of section playing in a large ensemble.

The band director taps on the podium and we sit up attentively as he raises his baton. Just as he is about to give the downbeat, the door opens and there's a messenger in full dress carrying a dispatch bag. "At ease and attention," the band director tells us. We place our instruments down to listen to the messenger.

He opens his leather dispatch bag, pulls a number of documents out of an official-looking envelope, and starts reading. There's a laundry list of orders. "According to so-and-so . . . The 5th Army such-and-such . . . In accordance with the . . ." It went on and on. And then: ". . . According to the Military Code of Justice, Private Henry Threadgill—"

I look up, surprised to hear my name. "Who? What did he say?"

"Be quiet and listen," the band director reprimands me.

"—has been assigned to the 4th Infantry Division in Pleiku."

"Pleiku?" I sputter.

The director snaps: "Shut up and listen!"

I have thirty days to get my life together, the order continues, and then I have to report to Oakland, California, on a particular date.

"Wait one second!" I say. "Listen—" The bandleader tells me again to close my mouth, but I ignore him. "—I play clarinet. This is a high-priority instrument. In a concert band, this is the highest-priority instrument there is. It's like the violin in an orchestra."

The band director gives me an icy stare. "We know what you play."

"What do you mean, I'm being transferred? I applied to be stationed abroad, either in France or in Panama. I was told I couldn't join those bands because there was a shortage of capable clarinet players here. Now you're letting me go?!"

"I've got nothing to do with this," the band director says.

I'm completely numb. The guys in the band sit there in complete silence, trying not to look at me. I know what I want to say: "What in the world is going on? My arrangement was just a piece of music! Doesn't anyone have a sense of humor here? You're telling me that you're shipping me off to war because of a piece of music?"

But there's no one to say it to.

And that's it. They order me to get up right there and leave the rehearsal hall, go back and clear out my bunk, turn in my clothes, go to the quartermaster, stop by the finance office, get all my papers. And I'm on my way back to Chicago for thirty days to arrange my affairs before I'm deployed to Vietnam.

—Where were you physically at the time of the incident?
—On the perimeter. Same setup as always. Night guard

duty is a team of two. My usual partner Coleman was already gone, so that night I'd been paired with some guy I hardly knew. We were in a little structure on the side of the road that runs around the 4th Infantry base camp. Lookout posts every few hundred yards. I was in a sandbag bunker with a Quonset roof of corrugated galvanized steel, sitting at a machine gun and peering out a loophole at the surrounding area. My partner was on a covered wooden platform with sandbag walls, elevated about thirty feet in the air, with a klieg light. So we were right next to each other, but not close enough to talk.

—Where were you geographically at the time of the incident?

—Latitude 13° 52′ 37.2″ N, longitude 108° 1′12″ E.

—Where were you morally at the time of the incident?

—A nervous wreck. I was ready to go home. My last sixty days. My short time—or at least it should have been. But my papers had been lost. I didn't think I was ever going to get out.

In the Church of God, we considered the Catholic Church to be an institution of the devil. The mark of the beast of the false prophet. Not that the Protestant church was much better. From that perspective it was no surprise that it was the archbishop who jumped up and started the ruckus. It wasn't the politicians or the military brass; they had just been listening politely. The trouble started in the quarters of theology. And it was such a drastic reaction—to shut down the entire ceremony! All for the supposed blasphemy of a few bars of music. My arrangement was an attempt to do something different, to find other musical possibilities in those old familiar songs, but in no way was it an attempt to mock the national anthem. It was outrageous: first the idea that a few bars of music could be construed as blasphemy; and then the utterly disproportionate response. As though a musical peccadillo could merit the death sentence.

On my bike at 53rd and Blackstone between Claude Lawrence
and Abshalom Ben Shlomo in Chicago during the month before I was
deployed to Vietnam, August 1967

I went back to Chicago in August 1967 feeling like a condemned man. I spent time with my family and hung out with old friends like Abshalom Ben Shlomo. I also saw my girlfriend, Joan. There wasn't much to say.

"I'll be here waiting for you to get back," she told me. I looked at her in silence. Yeah, *right*, I thought. Sure you will.

When I went out to Oakland to prepare for my deployment, I heard that the very next day she found a new boyfriend. The very next day! I didn't expect her to wait for me. But I would have appreciated a little bit of communication—a modest gesture of concern. I wrote her letters from California and then once I got to Southeast Asia, and she never wrote me back. And she was supposedly so devout! I couldn't believe it—Throw me a line, I was thinking. Just write me a letter, goddamn!

Doing drills in basic training, we all learned to chant those classic call-and-response cadences:

Ain't no need of writing home
Jody's got your girl and gone.

There were a hundred variations of the "jody call," some more wistful, some more vulgar.

Ain't no use in looking back
Jody's got your Cadillac.

Jody was the recurring figure in almost all of them: it was a generic name for that no-count snake at home who would filch our stuff while we were risking our lives halfway around the world. The cadences put a name on the indistinct fear of young men facing the unknown, in an attempt to make a joke out of the prospect of facing death: we laughed about little losses to assuage our anxiety at the prospect of that ultimate loss. But sometimes the jodies masked and deflected the real deprivations we were going through—the ways many of us were being ripped away from what we knew and what we loved.

Your girl as lonely as can be
Till Jody provided the company.
Sound off one, two, sound off three, four . . .

The jodies were the rhythm we stepped to—they synchro-
nized our anxieties and kept our feet moving. More than anything else, they were the playlist of our departure.

In September 1967 I was sent to join the 4th Infantry Division in
Pleiku in the Central Highlands of Vietnam. I was designated a
member of the 4th Infantry Band. It functioned as both a concert
band for seated concerts and as a marching band for parades.
The double duty required some versatility: the tuba player in
the marching band would have to be able to play contrabass for
the concert band. The pianist would play glockenspiel when we
were doing parades. I played both clarinet and alto saxophone,
depending on the circumstances.

But in terms of my situation, the key word was "infantry."
There were all sorts of jobs in any given infantry division: there
were infantry cooks, infantry ophthalmologists, infantry sup-
ply clerks, infantry orderlies, infantry radio operators, infantry
truck mechanics. But the common denominator was that infantry status. If there was an attack or a sudden mobilization to the
front lines, if they needed troops to go out on a scouting mission,
you reverted to that infantry status. At any moment, you had to
be ready to drop your clarinet or your monkey wrench and grab
your M-16.

So that was how they got me. I was technically still operating under the terms of my contract with the US Army. But the
terms of that contract had been broadened, as it were. Little did
I know—it must have been somewhere in the small print.

I was in a company in the 4th Division that was comprised of the
band and a decontamination group trained to deal with hazard-

ous chemicals like napalm. We were all infantry grunts at the end of the day, but everybody in the band also had a secondary occupation aside from playing music. Some of my bandmates were trained to serve as what we called "alerts," which meant a kind of long-distance scout. They would go out by themselves into the jungle to try to sniff out enemy positions. Some of the guys liked the chance to get away from the drudgery of the base camp. But it was inherently dangerous, because you were on your own. Some guys just never came back. Being a mailman entailed the same sort of risk. They would get killed all the time, trying to deliver letters and care packages from one camp to another. The jungle had an insatiable appetite for mailmen.

I was designated to be a "shotgun." In a convoy, I would be the one seated with a weapon next to the driver. If anything broke out, it was my job to cover him and to try to defend the vehicle. Just like the dude with a shotgun next to the stagecoach driver in a cowboy movie. Convoys weren't exactly tranquil duty, either. Anytime you were moving from one place to another you put yourself in a vulnerable position. There were land mines, ambushes, snipers perched along known transport routes—everything you could imagine.

When the band traveled to play in other areas, we carried our sheet music in shoulder bags emblazoned with the signature "ivy" badge of the 4th, with four green leaves against a diamond-shaped background. We played for ceremonies and picnics and barbecues at the base camp, which was huge, sprawled out across a red-earth expanse in the highlands, and sometimes we went out and played concerts for platoons that needed entertainment in camps around the region. We also played concerts for the local population and for South Vietnamese government ceremonies in Pleiku and the surrounding towns.

There were a bunch of good musicians, and just as I had in Kansas, I got in the habit of playing at night with some of the

With Ray Heckman and the French horn player we called Dirty Red
at the 4th Infantry base camp

guys. There was another alto player, named Bob Haub; a pianist
named Pete Martin Malijewski; a *bad* tenor player out of Cincin-
nati named Ray Heckman; and my main man, a young drummer
named Napoli who hailed from the East Village in New York.
Napoli was a scrawny little dude, but he could really play. After
we finished band rehearsal, we'd meet up in the evening in the
camp's music hall to practice Ornette and Coltrane tunes. I had
a cassette player and a few of us had tapes we'd brought from
home. We'd transcribe tunes like "Dahomey Dance" and "Ram-
blin'" and work on them all night, smoking in the rehearsal hall.
As long as there wasn't anything going on, we could play as late
as we wanted.

> *—What was the first thing you saw?*
> *—It was only an inkling at first. Being on guard duty
> is all about thinking you might have seen or heard some-
> thing and then realizing that you didn't. Your senses are
> primed. It's hard to describe how exhausting it is to main-
> tain that state of awareness for such a long time. You can
> see a little bit, depending on how much moonlight there is
> and what the weather's like. But even then, it's a constant
> straining against the limits of your senses. Our position is
> set overlooking a ravine filled with thick vegetation. You
> can't make out the ground and you can't always tell how
> deep the brush is. So you're staring at the gentle perturba-
> tions of the canopy of leaves and vines in an inky green
> mass that stands out in contrast to the night sky only in
> that it seems darker and denser.*
> *—But what was the first thing you saw?*
> *—It was first of all the vague feeling that something was
> looking at me. Then, slowly, it was as though I started
> to localize where that gaze was coming from: a particu-
> lar point in the ravine. At first I couldn't see anything at
> all, but I stared at it and stared at it and then I thought I
> saw something. Two tiny points reflecting the moonlight.
> Not flickering matches. Not the dull glow of a cigarette*

tip. No. Something subtler. Then the chilling realization: I
was looking at two eyes, looking at me.

The band director was a no-nonsense type. And the company
commander was a straight-out infantryman. But there were tensions with some of the officers. Some of them were flush with
pretension about following protocol and respecting military
hierarchy. All this bullshit about bars. But they quickly learned
that this war was complete insanity. And then they would be the
first to disregard the rules when it was a matter of saving their
own asses. They had to learn to take off their insignias and to
avoid certain gestures of deference. If a sniper is watching and
he sees one guy wearing bars, or one guy saluting another—well,
he immediately knows who to shoot first. Kill the head and the
body goes with it.

Occasionally we would have to perform with replacement
conductors, and some of them were real pieces of work. Once we
did a concert with this fool who was a total greenhorn in terms
of the realities of combat in Vietnam. He was some ROTC hack
who was book learned but field ignorant. He was insufferably
arrogant, spouting army bromides without any sense of where
he was.

This hack was scheduled to conduct the band for a ceremony
in a village. It was a festive affair with a bunch of local offi-
cials and Buddhist priests in attendance. When we arrived, we
noticed that the bandstand had been erected in the middle of a
sort of corral. We looked at it and said, "What the hell is this?"
Why would he want to put us up on a stage in a big, fenced-in
arena? We'd be sitting ducks for an ambush.

The conductor ignored our warnings and ordered us up onto
the bandstand. And then he had the nerve to tell us that he didn't
want us to take our weapons onto the platform with us. We
looked at him like he was crazy. As a rule, when we played concerts in a village or in a jungle camp, we would have our rifles
just in case. But this fool was concerned about appearances.

Some of us had been in the Central Highlands for months

at that point. We weren't about to take any shit. The pressures of living constantly with mortal risk in a bewildering and alien environment—the insanity of the entire war, which made no sense at all to most of us—gave rise to recalcitrance as well as a sort of numb fatalism among us grunts. We had a joke, almost a fable, that revolved around an emblematic confrontation between an officer and an infantryman. The grunt refuses an inane order. The officer huffs and puffs and threatens him with severe consequences. "Oh, really," says the grunt. "What are you going to do, *send me to Vietnam*?" They had already done the worst they could do to us.

When the substitute band director told us not to take our weapons up onto the bandstand, we were dumbfounded. A few of the newer guys, intimidated by his rank and not knowing any better, did as he said. But more than half the band—all of the brothers and some of our more belligerent Chicano and white bandmates—simply defied the order. "Fuck you, man," a couple of them even muttered as they hopped up onto the platform with their guns and instruments. We put our rifles down right beside us and set the charts on our music stands.

The conductor was miffed. We stared him down. There was nothing to do but start playing. He gave a downbeat and we launched into a tune. We didn't get more than four bars in when all hell broke loose. A small contingent of Vietcong ambushed us right as we started playing! Easy pickings, they must have figured. We immediately dropped to the ground and returned fire, while we watched the conductor scramble to find cover as the bullets whizzed around him. He was scared to death. I remember looking at his silly ass, thinking, "Yeah, where's your gun now?"

At the end of January 1968, the 4th Infantry base camp was assaulted in what later came to be known as the Tet Offensive, an audacious operation in which the Vietcong and North Vietnamese forces launched simultaneous surprise attacks on Saigon and more than one hundred strategic sites across South Vietnam. The war was unpredictable, but up until then we thought we were in a relatively secure position outside Pleiku, in a sprawling, heavily fortified camp where the general was stationed. But we were wrong.

I was sleeping in a tent near the perimeter when it broke out: we were startled awake by a barrage of rockets that came screaming into the camp, seemingly from all directions. There probably weren't that many enemy soldiers, and they weren't huge bombs, but it was enough to create panic. The frightening thing was that the rockets were flying in low, at about eye level, close enough that we could see the flame coming out of their tails. They left a distinct stench of sulfur in the air: the smell of death. Until you're in the middle of an attack, you don't really think about things like the way it smells. But things like that are the things you remember if you're lucky enough to get through it. And the heat: aside from the explosions, the firefight itself sets the air ablaze.

The sudden onslaught of noise was disorienting, especially in the dark: the quick fizzing of the rocket and mortar fire followed by the distant thunder of detonations, the guttural percussion of large-caliber weapons, and the sporadic bursts of chatter from M-16s and AK-47s. Guys were screaming to get out of the tent. If a rocket hit one of the support posts, the whole thing would come down.

But when I ran out, it was the heat that stunned me. It slapped me straight in the face. I stopped dead in my tracks right outside the entrance. People don't realize that when adrenaline hits, it can go one of two ways. It either can serve as an accelerant—it can give you the strength to lift up a jeep or the legs to jump over the moon—or it can paralyze you. And mine went negative.

Guys were running past me, shoving me as they fled the tent. They ran in a torrent around me. Wide-eyed and mute, I stood there in the midst of the tumult like a stone sitting in the middle of a storm-swollen river.

My friend Belton Narcisse saw me there. He was a fantastic drummer and a sweet guy, out of New Orleans. When it all broke out, Narcisse was on the other side of the tent, and he came running toward the exit like everyone else. "Move, Henry!" he yelled when he saw me stop outside the door. "Get out!"

Narcisse realized I was frozen with fear. He came right at me from behind and hit me between my shoulder blades as hard as he could, knocking me to the ground. The tackle released the adrenaline and I gasped. I felt like I'd been holding my breath for an hour. He looked at me and pulled me up. "Let's go," he hissed.

I still couldn't really move under my own power. I teetered next to him, and he saw the look on my face.

Narcisse had played football at Grambling. A halfback. "Come on, man," he told me. "Put your arm through here." I put my arm through the crook of his elbow and he clenched me tight.

"Come on now, Henry, I got you. Put your head down." I put my head down and let him guide me by my arm. "Don't look," he instructed. "I got you."

And Narcisse went for the run of his life. It was as if those rockets were opposing linebackers trying to take him down. But Narcisse would not be denied. He darted through the fiery maze, cutting to one side and then back the other way to find an opening, dragging me with him the whole way. I kept my head down and followed his lead. We darted and lurched for a hundred yards in an awkward pas de deux and finally made it to the foxhole where everyone had taken cover. He threw me down on top of the sandbags and collapsed next to me.

It was quite a way to spend my first major battle. He ribbed me about it afterwards but, in the moment, it was no joke.

I was injured during the Tet Offensive. I was just finishing a night shift on guard duty on the perimeter with Coleman, my partner, and the sergeant came by in a jeep to pick us up. The lights in the entire camp were out because of the fighting and it was pitch dark: we couldn't even make out the road. We got in the jeep and just as we were backing up to turn around, there was an explosion. The jeep was tossed into a ravine. It flipped over backwards and we were thrown out and trapped under it. We were fortunate: it would have crushed us but the ravine was narrow, so the jeep hit the other bank and stopped just above our heads. Still, I messed up my back when I hit the bed of stones at the bottom of the gully. I wasn't laid up too long at that point, but I did herniate a couple of discs. My messed-up spine has given me trouble ever since. My party favor from the war, and a lingering reminder: on cold winter days, the pain still takes me back to Pleiku.

The Tet Offensive wasn't the only time Narcisse saved my life. There were lots of things that could get you in Vietnam. Beyond the war itself, it was almost laughable sometimes how many threats the environment could throw at you. There were poisonous snakes and foot-long centipedes and vicious wild monkeys and nefarious booby traps in the jungle. Coleman and I would sometimes get assigned to guard duty at what we called "Titty Mountain," a bulbous hill formation near Pleiku where there was a radio unit. Up there you'd often find yourself waist deep in water all night, fighting off endless phalanxes of mosquitoes. You'd hear rats trying to gnaw their way into the bunker. It was miserable. Compared to that shit, the guys would joke, trading a few bullets with Charlie would be a relief.

Stuck in situations like that for hours with nothing to do, I had plenty of time to reflect. Being in Vietnam threw some of my near-death experiences back in Chicago into perspective. Once I was sitting there, staring out at nothing, and I remembered a concert I'd done in Indiana with some singers from the Church of God. I drove down from Chicago with Jo Jo Morris and a few other women to do a show at Anderson College. We came back that same afternoon. People sometimes forget that starting back in the 1920s, Indiana was one of the main hotbeds of the resurgent Ku Klux Klan. In the early 1960s the state map was still pockmarked with "sundown towns," where Blacks were given to know—sometimes with explicit warning signs at the city limits—that although they might pass through, they weren't welcome after nightfall.

We were on a dusty rural highway on the way back from Anderson when we noticed we were being followed by another car. It was hugging our tail close enough that we could see the faces of the four white men inside. They were all carrying rifles. No words were exchanged, but there was no need to say anything. Their stony faces and the aggressive way they were driving communicated the threat clearly enough. I was at the wheel and I remember the anxiety mounting as they rode up on me and forced me to go faster and faster. Finally I made a screeching turn into a side road that ran through a cornfield, and the sedan didn't follow us. The white men gave us a pointed look as they sped by.

I was trying to play it cool, but Jo Jo and the other church-women were beside themselves. I pulled over and waited for the dust to settle before we took off again. But we didn't linger in Madison County.

Unsettling as that episode had been, in some ways American racism was easier to deal with than the unfamiliar menace of Vietnam. Back in the States racism was omnipresent, so it became a fixture in our lives. Just one of the things we took for granted in the atmosphere. Although threats could loom up unexpectedly once in a while, we generally learned how to avoid certain kinds of risk. Black people developed an entire arsenal of subtle strategies that almost became second nature.

But in Vietnam it seemed like there were all sorts of unimagined dangers ready to leap out of the jungle and get you. There were even plants that could choke you to death. We called them "wait-a-minute" vines. The tendrils were thin and they didn't look like much but they were prickly in a way that if they brushed against your uniform or your skin, they would grab you. They were nicknamed "wait-a-minute" because that was what they did: when they got hold of you, you came to a halt. As though the jungle itself were giving you a silent command: Hold up, son. They were known to pull soldiers right out of a jeep or off a tank, leaving them suspended helpless in midair.

Once when the 4th Infantry base camp came under fire, the general ordered a team of us out to pursue the North Vietnamese forces that had attacked us. They had struck quickly and then retreated back into the bush. We rushed out after them. At one point we had to make our way down a hill so steep that the only way to manage it was to slide straight down on our asses, using the butt of our M-16s like a sort of paddle or cane or, more precisely, like a ski pole on an icy downhill. We were coming down in single file, one soldier sliding right behind another.

I was flying down the hill and got caught by some wait-a-minute vines. There was a sudden, sharp sound as though the vegetation itself were exhaling—*chuuhhh*—and the plant stopped me short. I had a grenade clipped to my belt in back, right above my buttocks, and the vines somehow also halfway pulled out the pin as they caught me. I came down on top of the trigger of the grenade, which meant that it was cocked under me. If the pin came all the way out, that was all she wrote for Threadgill.

The vines had me in a stranglehold. I lay there tangled up in an awkward position, watching the other guys slide by me one by one. I was calling for help, but they were skidding so fast they couldn't stop their momentum.

I can't go out like this, I thought. Not like this.

Narcisse was one of the guys coming down after me. He had a machete; when we were going through the thick underbrush, he was one of the soldiers who helped to slash a path open.

"I'm coming, Henry!" he yelled from up the hill. "Hold on. I'm behind you." He launched himself down and was able to grab onto something to stop himself near me. He came over and started to cut me out of the vines.

"Wait, Narcisse, slow up," I warned him. "My grenade is loaded."

"What are you talking about?" Narcisse bent down and looked under me and saw what had happened.

"Oh, my goodness!" he exclaimed. The other cats were still speeding by, watching us as they passed. Narcisse got down on his knees and reached under me. He fiddled with the grenade for a second and was able to push the pin back in.

My brush with the wait-a-minute made me the clown of the week. If it didn't kill you, that shit was hilarious. The guys were especially tickled by this one because it amounted to a devious play on words. Because it wasn't a figure of speech to say that Narcisse saved my ass. No, this time he had *literally* saved my behind.

At times the hypocrisies of the war were so blatant that there was nothing to say. Major General Peers, the commander of the 4th Infantry, would periodically give moralistic lectures about the dangers of sex to those of us under his command. There was a proliferation of lurid rumors that seemed clearly designed to scare us: stories about prostitutes luring randy American soldiers into traps, or mutilating unsuspecting GIs with razor blades hidden in their vaginas. Abstinence was the only option, Peers declared. And yet at the same time, the military had constructed a "Sin City" full of prostitutes outside the Pleiku base camp. So prostitution was condoned—even encouraged, as an ersatz means of decompression for hordes of freaked-out, hopped-up young men hardly past the throes of puberty—in controlled circumstances.

We didn't know what the hell to believe. The basic every-day experience of the war was so preposterous, so continually discombobulating, that it made almost anything seem possible. And, moreover, some of the rumors we saw confirmed with our own eyes—or thought we did. Another thing people used to whisper was that in Vietnam there was an incurable venereal disease known only as Brand X. It was like AIDS before AIDS. If you got it, you were dead. The military was determined to hide its existence, they said, and sure as hell didn't want it to get back to the US. So soldiers who caught it would simply disappear. We heard that they were sent to "the Rock," a top-secret island in some classified location, to waste away in oblivion. It was easy enough to declare them missing in action and let them vanish into the fog of war.

These rumors were persistent and they always seemed to circulate third- or fourth-hand—somebody knew somebody who had heard of somebody—so I was skeptical. I found it hard to believe until I witnessed it myself, when my partner Coleman came down with a mysterious debilitating illness. During the first few months I was in Pleiku, Coleman and I were regularly paired for guard duty. He was a tuba player. A hefty brother, built like an offensive lineman. But Coleman used to go to Sin City, and he also used to frequent the opium houses in town. Those places were bad news: you might go in one of them, get your high on, and wake up in bed with somebody you'd never seen before.

Coleman must have done something reckless. With him it happened fast: he started noticing he was feeling weak and fatigued, and within a few days he couldn't even pick himself out of bed. He started losing weight at an alarming rate. For a little while, he dragged himself around on crutches, and then one day they took him away to the hospital in Pleiku. The next weekend I caught the bus to go into town to try to find him. But when I asked for him at the hospital, I was told that his condition had worsened and he had been moved.

"I'll be goddamned!" one of our bandmates remarked that night when I recounted the story to some of the guys in the rehearsal hall as we smoked and tried to make some sense of it. "They shipped him off to the Rock." Sometimes people would scoff at all the rumors and conspiracy theories that sprouted in the fetid atmosphere of the war. But this time there was no way to refute the fact of what had happened. We sat there in silence.

———

I used to tell my superior officers that I practiced all religions. I told them that my faith ran so deep that in addition to attending Methodist or Baptist services on Sunday, I needed to go to the Seventh-day Adventist church on Saturday. "I can't find what I need here," I complained. "You've got to understand: I am a Hebrew of the Lion of the Tribe of Judah. There's nothing close to that here. So I'm going to be forced to embrace multiple denominations in order to satisfy my religious proclivities."

They must have thought I'd completely lost my mind. (Fortunately they didn't ask me what "the Tribe of Judah" meant.) I went to great lengths to cultivate my spiritual allure: I had prayer rugs on the floor by my bunk, and I went around with a long beard, wearing caps and bead necklaces and amulets and bracelets. Some of the guys razzed me about it. But the majority of soldiers in the division seemed to have their own personal superstitions and lucky charms and talismans—futile as it might have been at the end of the day, there was an odd comfort in the very idea that something could protect you in the midst of all the insanity—so even the most freakish idiosyncrasies and perversions were generally accepted. As long as it didn't interfere with my duties, I was allowed to take the bus into Pleiku to attend services. And I asked to go as often as I got a chance.

I stayed away from Sin City. It wasn't worth the risk. I did have one memorable near-encounter with a prostitute in Pleiku. I had gone into town on a day off and one thing had led to another. I thought we were heading for an assignation in some secluded spot. But this woman led me out of Pleiku on foot and she just kept on walking, to the point that I started to get a little anxious. There were little hotels and whorehouses in Pleiku. Where in the world is she leading me? I thought.

We walked a long way out of town and she took me to an isolated little hut. An old woman opened the door and we went in. I was still wondering why she had brought me all the way out to this place. The prostitute raised a wooden trap door in the floor, and I saw there was a ladder leading down into some sort of cellar. We went down the ladder—when I reflected on the episode later, I had to admit that I must have been rabidly horny that afternoon to have followed her down—into a tunnel that had been dug into the earth under the hut. As my eyes adjusted, I saw that we had entered a sort of catacomb, an underground network of tunnels. And we weren't alone. There were a couple of candles, and I could see that we had come down into a tunnel filled with North Vietnamese soldiers. It wasn't the Vietcong; it was North Vietnamese regulars. But in the idiocy of lust, I had stumbled right into the enemy's den.

The soldiers hardly seemed to register my presence. They were sitting there on the ground cleaning their rifles. A couple of them glanced up at me, but nobody reacted, nobody attacked. It was as though it were a normal occurrence for them to see an American soldier climb down into their hideout.

I thought, Oh, Lord, what have I done? The prostitute walked me through the soldiers to a minuscule room with a single bed and a curtain that served as a door. She pulled the curtain closed behind us and told me matter-of-factly, "You get undressed now."

"Oh, no, no, baby. No, I can't. I don't want to do anything," I murmured. We were right on top of each other; her breath was sweet. I would have backed away, but there was nowhere to go except out into the tunnel.

"What do you mean? You try to say I'm sick?" She started to get offended.

"No, of course not, babysan. No, that's not the problem. It's not you. I'm the one who's sick. I'll just go."

"You lied to me!" she accused. And she stormed out.

Left alone in the little room, I started berating myself. Look at the situation you've allowed yourself to get dragged into, Threadgill. What in the world were you thinking? Did you really need some tail that badly? How far were you prepared to walk? How many tunnels were you ready to jump into?

She came back in, still furious. I was sure she was going to tell the soldiers I'd cheated her. I pulled out all the money I had. "Please, babysan, just take this money. We don't have to do anything. Just let me go."

I realize it's a cliché, but the situation prompted me to rediscover my religious commitment. I thought, God, if you allow me to get myself out of this, there'll be no more problems in my life. Period. Just this one time, God.

I don't know how many times I pulled out that line during the war. At least four or five times. Every time I swore it was the last time that I would ask for one more chance.

She took the money in silence and let me pass. I stepped gingerly through the gauntlet of North Vietnamese soldiers in the tunnel, not wanting to rush and draw attention to myself, but not wanting to delay my departure any further.

And they let me go by. The soldiers certainly saw me. But they didn't intervene. They let me in their camp, and they let me out. It may have been divine intervention, but as I walked to the ladder and looked at them looking at me, I saw something else, something possibly even more miraculous: something that almost came across as a brand of respect. I interpreted it as their response to me as a Black American soldier. It was the converse of my own sentiment: I never had anything against any of these people. As Muhammad Ali famously put it, "I ain't got no quarrel with them Vietcong." I felt that way the whole time I was there. I might have been in the infantry and I might have been given a gun, but I wasn't killing nobody. There would be no preemptive strike for Threadgill. The only way I was going to kill anybody was if they tried to kill me.

This is your enemy, they told us. But I don't have an enemy I don't know. I don't have an enemy I can't see. The men cleaning guns in the tunnel saw me and I saw them. And they let me go. They ain't my enemy.

The sparse population in the Central Highlands included the indigenous Austroasiatic and Austronesian peoples that the French colonizers called Montagnards. The French word ("mountain people") was a translation of the words these people used to refer to themselves: *Degar* or *Ana Chu* ("sons of the mountains"). It reminded me of the situation of Native Americans in the US. Most Vietnamese were barely aware of the Montagnards, because they were concentrated in this hilly interior region. They faced a lot of prejudice: some Vietnamese referred to them pejoratively as *moi*, which means "savages." Hoping for autonomy, some Montagnards aligned themselves with the US and its allies during the war, and many of their villages were decimated during the conflict.

I ended up spending a lot of time with them while I was in the 4th Infantry camp near Pleiku because I was regularly assigned to recruit them as scouts. The Montagnards lived in small settlements in jungle clearings in these elevated longhouses where extended families would share the same living quarters. We would hike out to their villages, which weren't too far from the camp, and hire them to help us with various things. They were legendary trackers and scouts. Some Montagnards could look at prints or droppings or a deserted campsite and tell you exactly who or what had passed by, even if it was hours or days ago. Others were capable of sitting completely still in the crook of a tree for two or three days and reporting on what troop action they spied in the area.

I was often sent to work with the Montagnards because I developed a sort of rapport with them. They liked me for some reason, I'm not sure why. They're mostly darker-complexioned people—maybe it had something to do with that. Whatever the reason, their sense of allegiance was extraordinary. If they liked you, there were no conditions.

After I got to know them well, a couple of the Montagnards from a village nearby got into the habit of sneaking into the 4th Infantry camp before daybreak—they could move like wraiths, slipping right past all our perimeter defenses—to bring me fresh pineapples and other little gifts. It was quite a way to get woken up: a couple of Montagnard girls, still wet from the river, giggling softly over me in my bunk holding out a piece of fruit. I would smell them before I heard them. They had a particular smell. Not a bad smell—just a scent. Especially when they'd just come out of the water. They didn't use shampoos and synthetic stuff. I'd be sleeping and I'd smell that distinctive smell and it would stir me awake a little bit. And all of a sudden one of them would be right next to my bed, leaning over my face, water dripping off. Sometimes I smiled even before I opened my eyes, knowing by the smell that they were there. And they'd see me smile and start laughing. Then I'd sit up and give them a mock scolding. "Shh! Shh! What are you doing here!" I'd stage-whisper, still smiling. "Get out, get out!" They wouldn't say anything. They'd just hand me the fruit and leave, still laughing in the half-light as they snuck out of the tent.

Once my partner Coleman and I were out on a mission with some Montagnards. We'd lost track of where we were, so we were relying on them to lead us. We were both exhausted from walking through the dense brush with all our gear, and we were starving. Coleman and I followed them into a sort of valley and came across what looked like a pocket of tall grass—basically a thicket of weeds. And a couple of the Montagnard girls picked some of the grass and brought it to us. They stripped it and there was a surprisingly sweet sort of pulp inside that was delicious: it tasted almost like coconut and peppermint. It refreshed us. Later that afternoon we noticed a tree loaded with luscious fruit; Coleman started to reach for one but the Montagnards grabbed his arm and signaled to him not to eat it. They made us understand that the fruit from the lower branches was poisonous. You could only eat it if it fell from the top. We formed a circle around the base of a tree and they instructed us to keep our eyes on a particular piece of fruit. Then one of the men shook the tree, and we were careful to pick up only the ones that had fallen from the upper branches.

—Enumerate your full sensory input, in descending order of perceptual primacy.

—Sound: First you hear. Bird calls sometimes, monkey chatter. Unidentifiable things moving through the underbrush. A plane or a helicopter in the distance. Gunfire, far off, still startling you into heightened alertness when it comes. The illusion that you can hear in detail: you start to believe you can hear the vines growing, and the heartbeat of a bat, and the crinkling when a snake's skin starts to molt, and the patient tumescence of a tree as it grows. Your breath coursing through your nostrils. And the silence: it comes abruptly, and you hear it when it comes, as though the jungle comes to an accord to hush.

Smell: Mud. Mildew. Moist canvas. The faint scent of the oil drums where they burn our shit wafting all the way out from the latrine in camp. That ever-present jungle pungency.

Touch: My aching ass on the wooden stool. Feet on the hard earth. The fingers of one hand on the cold metal of the machine gun. The fingers of the other hand bracing myself against the sandbag lip of the loophole as I lean out.

Sight: The sandbags around me, once my eyes adjust. The slight glint of gunmetal in the moonlight. The brown C-ration box and my canteen on the table next to me. Through the loophole, nothing—then, starting about twenty feet away, the dark, indistinct masses of green and blue and black that I know are the beginnings of the ravine. The sky flecked with stars.

Taste: The roof of my mouth. The lingering paste of the last thing I ate: a little chocolate bar.

What blew my mind most of all about the Montagnards was their sense of ethics. Getting to know them destroyed the last vestiges of my devotion to the Church of God folk. Everything

A Montagnard musician with a gong,
January 1968

those evangelical Christians were saying collapsed from a philosophical point of view. All their righteousness—their pronouncements about people being sinners and needing to come to God—started to look pompous and judgmental. Without the slightest flash or pretense, without passing judgment on anybody, in the seclusion of their "uncivilized" lives in the middle of the jungle, the Montagnards were living at what seemed clearly to me to be a higher level of ethical achievement, a state that the church people hadn't come close to attaining even with the help of their Bible and all their praying and repenting and exalting. The Montagnards didn't need a book. It wasn't about professing and striving and backsliding. They just lived it.

The Montagnards didn't lie. They didn't steal. It wasn't that these sorts of behavior were temptations they resisted—they *couldn't* steal! It didn't even occur to them as a possibility. Those of us in the Army who worked with the Montagnards used to marvel at it. You could go to one of their villages and park a jeep with everything you had in it—money, weapons, alcohol, whatever—and they would act like it wasn't even there. That jeep would rot!

I remember being struck by the fact that the Montagnards didn't have locks. The mutual trust within the community was so profound that they had no conception of *needing* to lock anything. Most of their longhouses didn't even have doors.

The other thing I loved about the Montagnards was their music. They had gong bands and these enormous xylophones made out of bamboo. It was my first experience up close with Eastern music. Even with everything on the radio in Chicago, I encountered sounds in Vietnam that I would have never been able to hear without spending time there. The Vietnamese and Polynesian traditions are reminiscent of Taiwanese singing, in terms of aspects like timbre and intonation. And there's also the French colonial influence in some of it. I was especially taken with the resonance of those gongs—hearing that music may have been part of what compelled me to invent the hubkaphone a couple of years later. I remember I even wanted to buy some gongs and bring them home with me. They moved me that much.

>—*Did you communicate with your partner during the night?*
>
>—*We couldn't just chat, because he was up in the tower above me. We had these phones to allow us to talk. Sometimes we wouldn't talk at all for hours. Sometimes we'd talk, whispering to one another about all sorts of shit.*
>
>—*What sorts of shit?*
>
>—*The eternal night; the availability and quality of prostitution; the frustration with colleagues and superiors; the means for the acquisition of certain stimulants; the leaden gulf of boredom; the irrigation system in the Montagnard village; the banality of military comestibles; homesickness; ecclesiastical celibacy; the availability and quality of prostitution (yes, a recurrent topic); the relative merits of the Paul Butterfield Blues Band and Cream; movie-theater popcorn; the soporific effects of staring out into a void.*
>
>—*Did your conversations with your previous partner, Coleman, touch upon any other sorts of shit?*
>
>—*Yes. In addition to the above: The relative merits of Varèse and Stockhausen; the relative merits of Lola Falana and Raquel Welch; the relative merits of Oscar Pettiford and Paul Chambers; the concert we played in Lac Giao; etc., etc. (There were many long nights with Coleman.)*

There were all sorts of drugs floating around in Vietnam. You could obtain pretty much anything you wanted. Guys would carry their own supplies of morphine: if you got wounded, you might not be able to wait around for a medic to show up. But there were all sorts of illicit drugs as well, including amphetamines, opium, LSD, and the most mind-blowingly powerful marijuana most of us had ever had the chance to sample. As with prostitution, with drugs there was a certain amount of moralistic rhetoric from the commanding officers, but in practice they almost always looked the other way. It would have been too difficult to try to rein it in—and they seemed fully aware that in the face of such a brutal conflict, some of us could only get through it by taking a trip once in a while.

One of the most memorable characters at the 4th Infantry camp was known to be a drug supplier. Pretty Freddy was from LA, and he had a particularly West Coast sort of slick style, as though even in his fatigues he'd just strutted in off Central Avenue. Freddy was in the decontamination unit, not in the band, but we used to hang out often during my time in Pleiku.

When the CID contrived to have my papers disappear, I was on the verge of losing my mind. I thought I was trapped in a permanent limbo and I'd never go home. I was mired in a state that alternated between nervous anxiety and utter exhaustion. Most of the time, I was so depressed that I could drink a fifth of cognac at seven a.m. and not even feel it. I'd just mope through the day. I couldn't get over it, because I couldn't see any way out.

One day Pretty Freddy and I were on a bus heading into Pleiku. I was sitting there brooding as usual. He sized me up and said, "Henry, you look really depressed, man. You've got to cheer up."

I raised my head and started to say something cynical. "Cheer up? Please, man. What the fuck do you know—"

All of a sudden Freddy threw a pill into my mouth while I was speaking. As I gagged, startled, he hit me once hard on the breastbone, which made me swallow as I tried to catch my breath. I coughed, but it was too late; whatever it was had gone down.

"What the hell was that?"

Pretty Freddy didn't answer. He just sat there with a smug Cheshire-cat smile as though to say "Just wait and see."

We were sitting there next to each other in a seat toward the back of the bus. After a few minutes, I started to feel a little woozy. I was looking out the window and everything outside turned yellow: the sky was yellow, the ground was yellow, the trees were yellow, the grass was yellow. Then I looked around the bus and everybody was yellow. I looked at Pretty Freddy and he was yellow, too.

He always wore mirrored sunglasses. Every single day. I don't even remember what his eyes were like. So whenever you looked at Freddy you only saw yourself. And now I was looking at myself in his glasses, and I was yellow, too, like everything else.

Freddy seemed pleased as he watched whatever he'd given me take effect.

"What did you just give me?" I asked again.

"Isn't it wonderful?" Pretty Freddy said, sweeping his hand at our surroundings with a flourish. "Everything and everybody is yellow. It's all the same.

"Yes, everything in the world is the same," he repeated. Then he turned back to me and paused before he delivered the kicker with great relish: "Now *that's* what I call democracy."

4

Frame Thy Fearful

—What foreign chemical substances were present in your bloodstream at the time of the purported sighting?

—Well, ethanol for starters, that's for sure, dextropropoxyphene, acetylsalicylic acid, some acetaminophen, a healthy dose of delta-9-tetrahydrocannabinol, possibly a dash of psilocybin, trace quantities of formaldehyde and hexamine and benzene and naphthalene and methanol, nicotine (of course), maybe a little methamphetamine, diazepam, lorazepam, zolpidem, possibly a soupçon of eszopiclone, enough tar to pave a road—oh, I'm just shitting you. What a stupid question. Do you really think we were sitting out there getting high while we were on guard duty? No way. We couldn't afford to nod off. We didn't even dare to smoke, because we were afraid they might be able to see our cigarettes. "Purported sighting"? Fuck you.

Pretty Freddy was a mind trip—literally. At one point he found himself in hot water with the authorities at the base camp. They accused him not just of pushing drugs but also of some sort of pimping, and Freddy went on the run—without leaving the camp. He was sneaking around and sleeping in other people's bunks, trying to avoid discovery. He managed to evade capture for a little while, too. One day I was walking across the camp and he called to me from where he was hiding in the alley between two tents.

"Psst! Henry!" he whispered theatrically, beckoning me over.

"Hey, Freddy—" I started to answer, but he cut me off.

"Don't call me that, man. I can't use that name anymore." He glanced around anxiously and then continued in a conspiratorial whisper. "From now on, call me *Fair Satin*."

I have no idea where he came up with that name. He must have been truly high if he thought a name change was going to throw the MPs off his trail.

"You're out of your mind, man." I stared at him in disbelief. "You can call yourself any fucking thing you want, but it's not going to help you when they catch you." Still, I did have to laugh. He said it with such conviction—he seemed sure that they wouldn't be able to find him if he started calling himself something else. But to select "Fair Satin," of all things, as your code name? Even for a pusherman gone undercover, it was outlandish.

I used to have a photograph of me with General William C. Westmoreland in Dak To at the end of November 1967. As the commander of the US forces in Vietnam, he had come to make a showy declaration of victory—that month, he told the American press that the battles around Dak To represented "the beginning of a great defeat for the enemy"—at the location of what was in fact one of the US and its allies' most humiliating defeats. Hunkered down in heavily fortified bunkers high up on the ridges that dotted the region, the Vietcong and North Vietnamese lured American units into ill-advised uphill attacks through an almost impenetrable jungle. The casualty numbers were appalling: 376 US troops killed and another fourteen hundred wounded.

Back home, it was a public-relations disaster. In early December, there was a haunting two-page spread in *Life* magazine of the memorial service for the ninety-eight soldiers from the 173rd

Airborne Brigade who died on Hill 875 in one of the most notorious battles of Dak To—with their empty jump boots arranged in formation in the red dust. I knew the bugle player who had to play taps for those empty boots. He never got over that.

My unit had been dispatched from Pleiku in the aftermath of the fighting to help with the evacuation process. The photo of me and the general wasn't a buddy shot, of course: Westmoreland had just arrived by helicopter in the base camp near Dak To, and a friend of mine took a picture when I just happened to be standing behind him carrying my alto saxophone with my M-16 slung over my shoulder. The general had no clue I was there. It's more like a grunt photo bomb—the great man in the foreground, intent on delivering his fake news, totally oblivious to the anonymous private behind him.

I wish I still had it, because it seemed so emblematic: the invisible man at the center of the action. But somehow it's only appropriate that even the proof of my one brush with the high command got lost. Vanished evidence that I can now only describe in words: probably the right kind of evidence for a war that was a grand exercise in self-delusion. That sham victory announcement never even happened, in the end. The Army abruptly canceled the press conference and spirited the general out of there. I heard later that—despite the circus atmosphere and the high security around Westmoreland—the Vietcong had somehow snuck into the camp and booby-trapped his oven.

Around the end of the spring of 1968, the central command put out a call for musicians. There were bands like ours that were attached to a given division. But the war also gave rise to its own entertainment industry, the most visible manifestation of which was the USO tours headlined by the comedian Bob Hope. The USO shows would make stops at American bases around Southeast Asia, and large audiences of troops were treated to extravaganzas with Hope and guest stars such as Raquel Welch, Barbara McNair, Joey Heatherton, Lola Falana, and Ann-Margret. The

The only photo I have from Dak To:
me with some Vietnamese musicians . . .

backing band for the USO shows was famous, too: it was Les Brown's Band of Renown. Sometimes other acts came through as well, and that June we were excited to hear that James Brown was going to be touring Vietnam with a pared-down version of the his band that included Clyde Stubblefield, Marva Whitney, and Maceo Parker.

Apparently musicians in both of the bands had fallen ill. And the central command put out a call to Army musicians across the country to audition to find replacements to play with the groups. This was a top priority call from General Westmoreland himself: it superseded any other directive.

The captain in the 4th Infantry was incensed when I announced that I was going to audition. But he couldn't stop me. I tried to convince Narcisse to go down with me, but he said he didn't want to go. He didn't like the idea of being based in a big city. So I went to Saigon by myself and made the audition. They had me play in a band for some TV show.

I didn't end up joining the Band of Renown or James Brown. By the time I got down there, they had already found however many saxophonists they were looking for. But they liked a bunch of the musicians who tried out so much that they set us up as another independent band. It wasn't the flash and dazzle of the USO tours, but we provided entertainment for the troops on a smaller scale. We were three white guys and two Black guys: a singer backed up by keyboards, sax, bass, and drums. We would mainly do covers of pop tunes, the hits of the moment: the Beatles, the Stones, Aretha Franklin's "Dr. Feelgood" and "Respect," and Motown chart-toppers like Junior Walker's "Shotgun," the Four Tops' "Reach Out," and the Miracles' "Tears of a Clown." We would just listen to the records and transcribe them; harmonically most of them were pretty straightforward.

The band toured all around Vietnam, and everything was first-class. We received extra pay in addition to our regular wages. We were based in Saigon in a military hotel where the kitchen was open twenty-four hours. There was no supervision: when we weren't performing, we could just come and go as we pleased. When we were touring, we had papers that allowed us transportation on anything that was moving. We got top priority: if we needed to fly somewhere, nobody could bump us or make us wait for another ride.

Even in the middle of the war, Saigon was throbbing with energy. It was cosmopolitan and sophisticated, with people from all over the world. The South Vietnamese capital reminded me of Chicago, with all the pleasures and perils of a major metropolis: nightlife, food, sex, gambling, corruption. Everything.

I was in my element. Compared to Pleiku, Saigon was paradise. Now *this* is what I'm talking about, I thought to myself. This is my style right here.

That the band had papers allowing us to hitch a ride whenever we needed one didn't mean that transportation was always smooth and easy. One time we were coming back from a gig on a flatboat, making our way down the Mekong River. It was a sheet of metal with no protection from the sun, and after a couple of hours in what was basically an open-air barbecue, the band passed out from the heat. I was the only one still standing. The boat pulled to the shore and they called a chopper to ferry the guys to the hospital. The pilot told me there was a designated landing zone nearby. I was supposed to go there and catch a ride back to Saigon.

I made my way to the LZ and got on the first helicopter that came by. I was the only passenger. The pilot flew back over to the Mekong and started following the path of the river down toward the delta. I don't know why he took that route; maybe it was supposed to be safer than flying inland.

I never did like helicopters. They're almost too mobile, flying every which way with the cargo doors open. They make me uncomfortable.

We were whizzing down the river when we were ambushed by a bunch of Vietcong hiding in the reeds below. They popped up and started shooting at us.

The pilot panicked. He shouted back to me: "Get those motherfuckers off my ass! Get on the gun back there!"

The chopper was a Huey with an M-60 machine gun mounted on a turret by the side door. Not that I had any idea how to operate a 7.62-millimeter machine gun sticking out of a helicopter. I peered at it, trying to discern how it worked. The ammunition magazine was right there on the floor—the split-link belt just fed right into the chamber. As I was trying to figure it out, the pilot was taking evasive action. The helicopter lurched and I almost lost my grip on the back seat as he changed altitude and then made a sharp left turn away from the reeds. He flipped the bird ninety degrees as we banked, which left me looking out the open side door straight down at the river. I almost flew right out into the water.

"What are you waiting for?" the pilot yelled over the thudding of the rotors. "You know how to work it?"

I hesitated. "I know how to work a regular machine gun," I answered. "But I can't make this thing—"

The guy pulled out his .45 on me. He was still swerving to avoid the bullets. But he found time to draw his gun and point it back at my head. "You get those motherfuckers off my back or I'm gonna blow your fucking head off!"

Shooting a big gun for the first time is like trying to dance with a woman you've just met. It's a physical embrace. And guns have a rhythm. You have to intuit the way the gun wants to move in order to gain control over it. You get it wrong, you're going to be stepping on each other's toes all night.

As the helicopter flipped and dove, I struggled to get settled behind the gun. I squeezed the trigger and the kick was much more powerful than I expected. It threw me to the side, and the gun kept shooting as it pivoted toward the chopper's doorframe. Somehow I shot out a couple of our own windows—I may have even shot off the tip of a rotor blade!

"What the fuck are you doing?!" the pilot screamed at me, ducking down in his seat. "Are you crazy?"

"Look, man, I told you, I don't know how to work this damn thing!"

He gave me a vicious look. "I oughta blow your fucking head off."

I was now sitting behind the gun as it rotated on its turret, still as much of a threat to our own helicopter as it was to the Vietcong in the reeds. I glared back at him. "I wouldn't do that, motherfucker!"

The pilot suddenly noticed that I was sitting behind a machine gun.

His expression changed and he put his .45 back down as he sped down the river away from the threat. "What you oughta do is turn your head around and get us down on the ground somewhere," I said.

He was nasty. When we got to the landing zone, the asshole wouldn't set me all the way down. He hovered about shoulder height off the ground, turned around and spat: "Jump out." Fortunately I didn't have much, just a small rucksack and my saxophone case. He even buzzed me as he pulled off, dipping down so the blades came close to my head. He gave me a look right as he did it, as though to say: "Now *that's* for fucking with me, you clueless bastard!" I stood my ground as the blades whipped toward my neck and stared him down. "Well, fuck *you,* too. Good riddance!"

I ran into this little Italian-American kid one day in the market in Saigon. He was with the Green Berets. He provided support for teams out in the field.

We got to talking. "I'm looking for a band," he told me.

"I've got a band."

I looked at him. He was cocky but seemed a little shifty, too. He kept glancing at the crowd around us as though he was worried we were under surveillance.

"Could you guys do a gig for my team?" He offered me five hundred dollars a man.

"Sure, no problem," I said. That was a lot of money—which should have made me hesitate. But I jumped at it.

The next day they picked us up in the market in a flatbed truck. I thought he meant the gig would be right outside Saigon. But we started driving and just kept going farther and farther out into the jungle. My bandmates were giving me puzzled looks.

"How far is this place?" I finally asked the driver.

"We're almost there," he said. But we kept going at least another hour.

We ended up in a hellhole. It was a tiny camp in the middle of the bush, and there were only a handful of Green Berets. There were three guys there when we arrived. The other two team members were out on patrol.

They operated that way: nimble teams out on their own in advance positions. The Green Berets considered themselves supersoldiers. Two or three of them were supposed to be able to take on entire battalions of thirty or forty men. That was their shtick.

We started to get apprehensive when we saw the state of affairs in the camp. Two of the Green Berets were wounded. One had his head wrapped in a bandage, and another had been shot in the stomach. And on top of that, a couple of nights earlier one of them had also been bitten by rats. It was gruesome. Along with an impressive cache of weapons, the camp was littered with whiskey bottles and drug paraphernalia. When we got there we could tell by their bloodshot eyes that they were completely hopped up.

We were supposed to play that evening. But the show ended before it began. Just as we were setting up our equipment, the power went out. When shots rang out, we realized that a unit of Vietcong had snuck up and cut the electrical wires from the generators.

Thrown into darkness, we found ourselves taking cover behind a paltry barrier of sandbags as the Vietcong started firing into the camp. They couldn't really see us, but clearly they figured they had us pinned down and blind. So they were planning to take their time approaching our position and then wipe us all out.

Even in their condition, the Green Berets seemed to welcome the confrontation. They were chomping at the bit for a fight. One dude stood up with guns in both hands, ammunition bandoliers slung over his bandaged chest. "Let's get it on!" he hollered. "Come on in, you motherfuckers. You think you're so bad? Just come on in. Let's get this shit on!"

I always had my pistol and my knife on me. I didn't go to bed without them. But they weren't going to do much good in this situation. One or two of us had rifles, but the band wasn't in the habit of carrying a lot of weapons. Our job was to provide entertainment, not to get ourselves into shootouts.

What finally saved us was that the other two Green Berets on patrol came back just in time. In the little camp there was a sort of pole with a rickety ladder attached to it, a makeshift lookout perch that allowed you to see the surrounding territory from an elevated vantage point. The wounded Green Berets told me to climb up the pole to see if I could see what was going on—how many Vietcong there were and which direction they were firing from. I was scared to go up. It was dark, but there was a little bit of moonlight, and I thought they'd be able to see me up there unprotected. But up I went.

As I climbed, the Green Berets shot off a flare. They told me to look for the patrol. It should be on the way back by now, they said. And I did see the other two soldiers making their way back, coming down through the jungle. In another direction, I could also make out the Vietcong fighters in their infamous uniforms that looked like baggy black pajamas.

The flare gave everyone a glimpse of the situation. And the Vietcong must have realized that there was another team of American soldiers on its way to provide reinforcement. Unsure how many we were and not wanting to get caught between two enemy units, the Vietcong withdrew. And we found ourselves in silence.

The band stayed until the following morning, although we didn't sleep at all. We were terrified that the Vietcong would attack the camp again. But finally it was dawn and the truck came to pick us up.

When we made it back to Saigon, the other guys in the band berated me.

"Why the hell did you get us into that shit, Henry?"

"Hey, don't blame me," I replied. "You all agreed to the gig just like I did. You put your hand out for that money, too."

We all chuckled. But the singer said, "Henry, from here on out you don't get to book the band anymore."

I got sick while I was with the band in Saigon. That shit almost killed me.

The other brother in the band was the drummer. He was from Washington DC, but he was a real country boy, as country as they come. I don't think he'd ever been out of his own backyard before he came to Vietnam. He could play the drums, though. He could have held his own next to Clyde Stubblefield or Pretty Purdie or Zigaboo Modeliste. He was a little simple, sure—but just put him behind a drum kit and get out of the way.

It happened one night when I was running around with him in town. When it came to the many temptations of the big city, I was always cautious. But this drummer didn't have any class. He would hang out in these cheap whorehouses and stuff. He was small-minded. He thought he was being economical. From my point of view, all that meant was that he was taking chances.

We were out this evening, and I stupidly let him convince me to go with him into this area where there were a bunch of low-rate prostitution dens. I was about to turn around and get back to the hotel when the area came under attack. The Vietcong started lobbing mortar fire into the neighborhood. Things were blowing up nearby and we were running down this seedy street looking for shelter. He took me to this place he knew and knocked on the door.

"You no come in unless you spend money," said a voice from behind the door.

"Oh, goddamn, man!" I said to him. "What the fuck are you getting me into?"

"Come on, Henry," he said. "We've got to get off the street."

So they made us pay before they would let us in the door. While the assault continued outside, we sat there to wait it out, and of course we got to drinking and stuff. I remember I got sleepy and I went to lie down for a little while, and the next thing I knew this woman was in the bed with me. I was hardly conscious. I don't even remember what happened. But that must have been where I got it.

Over the next few days I started to feel this itching and burning in my penis. It was not pleasant. But I told myself I could handle it. I started trying to self-medicate, giving myself various painkillers and antibiotics. I was cooking up all sorts of concoctions. It was easy enough to get drugs in Saigon. But I didn't have the slightest clue what I was doing.

One morning in the shower what had been a small sore suddenly split open—it was like someone took a razor blade and sliced me. I almost fell over right then and there. I knew I had to get to the hospital immediately. I tried to bandage it as best I could and got dressed and went out into the street. The pain was going down my leg, and I could feel the blood and pus oozing down. I must have looked like a zombie stumbling down the street.

Somehow I made it to the hospital. But only that far. It was right around high noon. I collapsed on the steps at the entrance. They told me later I fell flat on my face.

—What course of action did you take when you thought you perceived two eyes looking at you?

—Nothing at first. I wasn't sure. I saw them, and then I

couldn't see them. And then I saw them again. That might
have been a coincidence. My mind playing tricks on me.
But when I saw them a third time, I became convinced
there was something there. I stared at it.
  —And what transpired next?
  —I stared and stared, trying not to lose them. Trying to
figure out what it was: a human being? an animal? Was
there more than one? I kept looking. And then I realized
something: the eyes were coming closer. They were stay-
ing in the same lane, if that's the right way to put it, but
very slowly moving toward me—low to the ground, as
though there were a creature of significant size painstak-
ingly crawling inch by inch toward my position. That was
when I started to freak out.

I woke up in a hospital bed. I didn't know how long I'd been out.
There was a doctor there at my bedside.

"Well, well! Welcome back, Dr. Frankenstein!" he pro-
nounced. "It seems someone's been experimenting on himself."
He looked me in the eye, making sure I heard him before he continued. "Let me tell you, you'd have been dead if you'd kept that
up a day or two more."

They shot so many different types of antibiotics in my
butt that I couldn't even sit down. They said what I had was
extremely serious. It wasn't Brand X, but it was a particularly
virulent strain of venereal disease. It was like some sort of triple-
strength gonorrhea. They decided to transfer me to a rehabilita-
tion center run by the Royal Australian Medical Corps down at
the very southern tip of the country in Vung Tau. They had to
have me stand up in the jeep to the airport. There was an attendant on either side of me holding me up in the back. And when
they flew me down to the 1st Australian Field Hospital, they also
had to strap me standing up in a harness in the plane.

I have only vague memories of those first days at the Australian hospital. I was in and out of consciousness. I may have been

in an induced coma at one point. I don't know how long I was out.

One thing I do remember is that when I woke up, I scared the shit out of my nurse. I'd been lying there in this room in the dark with the blinds pulled shut. She was used to coming in and seeing me lying there still. And one day she entered the room and I was sitting up on the side of the bed in my nightgown. She gave a little scream and ran over and grabbed my arm to steady me. And then I stood up. The Return of the Mummy!

She rushed out and got the doctor. Eventually they brought me outside and started having me walk around the grounds to regain my strength. At first I could barely move my legs.

It turned out that the Australians had been rooting for me. They were pulling for me to come through, they told me. The field hospital was in this gorgeous spot on the edge of the South China Sea, and there was a pool on the grounds. When they brought me outside for the first time, the Australian doctors and nurses all lined up on either side of the poolside deck and toasted me with great big mugs of beer. The nurse propped me up and I gingerly made my way through the crowd, blinking in the dazzling sunlight and smiling bashfully as they cheered, "Hip hip hooray! Hip hip hooray! Cheerio, old man!" Gradually I started to regain my strength, and eventually I got to the point where I could eat on my own in the dining room. They gave me this English dessert called trifle that was a revelation—I said to myself, Forget strawberry shortcake!

When I started to regain my strength in the 1st Australian Field Hospital, I was allowed to take walks in the area. The doctors gave me one instruction. "Don't even look at a woman!" one of them warned me. "Even if you put four prophylactics on—even wearing a Coca-Cola bottle! Don't even think about it. You're out of action for now."

"I'm not going to be doing nothing," I promised.

One of the first times I went out in town, I got lost on the way back and found myself in the jungle. I was trying to regain my sense of orientation when I heard music from off in the distance. It was very faint, and it seemed to be coming from farther out in the bush. But it was jazz. And something familiar, too. Curious, I followed the sound.

After a while I came to a clearing at the edge of a little town. There were lanterns swinging from lines strung in the trees. The music was Coltrane, being piped through some speakers. There was a Black American soldier standing on top of a jeep with a machine gun strapped to his back. He had a little bamboo flute in his hands, and he was miming playing along with the music, leaning back and gesticulating like he was taking Coltrane's sax solo.

I stood there for a minute, astonished. What in the world was this? It seemed like some sort of weird surrealistic vision.

The spell was broken when the guy noticed me. He spun around and pointed his gun at me. "What the fuck are you doing here?" he demanded. "Who are you?"

"Whoa, whoa!" I held up my hands. "I'm a brother."

"What are you doing, coming up on me like that? Where did you come from?"

"Man, I don't know. It was the music. I heard Trane. I was just following the music."

He gave me a look. "What you know about that?" He kept his gun on me and carefully got down from the jeep. When he almost tripped over himself, I realized he was high as a kite.

"Come on," he ordered. "You're going to see the boss."

I didn't know what he was talking about but I was in no position to object. He walked me into the little town. It was clearly not a military installation, but it was hard to tell what to make of it. It was like some cartoonish stage set from a Hollywood western. There were people gambling in the street and drinking and screaming at each other. Most of the men appeared to be African American, which seemed odd. Two Vietnamese women were going at each other viciously, rolling in the dirt and slapping at each other, while a group of men looked on, laughing.

The would-be Coltrane took me up to one of the men, who seemed to be the one in charge, prepared to hand over his prisoner. But before the guard could say anything, the head man noticed me.

"Henry?" he said, surprised.

"Dan?" I exclaimed. "What are you doing here?"

"What the fuck are *you* doing here?" He waved off the guard. "Put your gun away. This is my partner. We grew up together!" Dan clapped me on the shoulder.

I asked him again what was going on and he signaled me to walk with him. "In due time, Henry. In due time." He gave me a smile.

It was a bizarre coincidence. Dan's family lived at 61st and Peoria, just a few blocks from my mother's house. He was one of four or five brothers. We weren't close friends, but I used to see him all the time around Englewood. Everyone called him Dirty Dan, because he was a little bit of a hustler and used to get into trouble—small-time stuff.

It quickly became apparent that Dirty Dan was the leader of the band of outlaws. Black outlaws on the lam in the jungle in Vietnam! Who would believe it? But we had heard stories of renegades roaming around AWOL during the war. I'd even met another one earlier, a cat they called Six-Gun. He was a short little dude, but he was a legendary shot with any weapon. He could jump on a howitzer and shoot off a mosquito's wing from a thousand yards. He never missed. My friend Hall, a piano player from Dallas who replaced Pete Martin Malijewski in the 4th Infantry Band, had told us about him—they'd been in an artillery unit together.

Once, the band had been playing in some village somewhere and we were all standing there smoking a pipe after the concert. Suddenly this cat walked up on us in the dark and startled us. He was standing right there among us, and in the dark we hadn't even seen him come up. He just appeared. He said something softly to Hall and the pianist recognized him. They spoke for a few minutes. And then the stealthy visitor vanished back into the jungle. Once he left, Hall explained: "That was Six-Gun."

Dirty Dan and his outlaws had figured out a way to scrape together a wild existence on the margins of a wild war. They would loot and steal and commandeer equipment and supplies wherever they could, staying one or two steps ahead of the various organized armies around them.

"Come on, we've got to move," Dan told me. "We're going back to headquarters." The group convened in a small motorcade of vehicles and drove down to a hotel on the South China Sea. Damn, I thought. The complex was huge—the main building must have been twenty stories high—and it must have been luxurious when it was functioning. Now it was in complete disrepair. The place was trashed, with champagne bottles and opium pipes and discarded clothes strewn around.

"You want one of these girls?" he asked me, waving his arm at the various women who were with the group.

"No thanks, man," I replied. "I'm not interested in none of that right now."

Dirty Dan smiled. "Well, if you change your mind, just let me know."

"Come on, let's catch up," he declared. He took me up to the room he was using as his personal flat. It was the middle of the night by the time we got to the hotel, and we stayed up all the rest of the night smoking, sharing war stories, and reminiscing about home.

Around dawn, one of the guys came up and announced, "Boss, we gotta get out of here. We got spotted on our way back."

Dan snapped into action. "Henry, we're going to have to get going." He started to pack some things in a bag.

"What about me?" I wondered.

"You'll be all right, baby. We'll take care of you."

The outlaw convoy rushed out of the hotel. On their way to another hideout, they dropped me off. "Check you later," Dan said, giving me a faux salute, and they roared off.

The problem was, they let me out on the side of the highway on a stretch where the road ran right along the coastline. It was gorgeous but utterly desolate. It was just me and the seagulls caw-cawing at the sunrise as they glided over the sand.

I started walking but I had no idea where I was. I just picked a direction and headed off. After a while, a single vehicle appeared on the horizon, coming my way. It was a cycle rickshaw. Once he got over his astonishment at encountering an African American infantryman out in the middle of nowhere, the driver gave me a ride back to Vung Tau. Fortunately I didn't have to report to anyone at the hospital. They didn't even notice I'd been out all night.

Once when I ventured into Vung Tau from the Australian rehab facility, I met this fabulous woman. I didn't think I'd ever seen anyone so beautiful in my life. The beach isn't really my thing, but I happened to go to the seashore that day. And these two women came up to me. I think they were both Cambodian, or of some mixed heritage. They were both wearing bikinis, and everyone on the beach was openly staring at them. They were that fine. One of them in particular was like a walking sculpture. She looked like she had been molded out of copper—she had this absolutely unbelievable skin tone. And these stunning curves. She was working that bikini. Her eyes were a color that seemed to change depending on the angle—they were greenish-gray and almost iridescent—and the overall effect was mesmerizing.

The woman and her friend came right up and planted themselves next to me on the sand. It was clear they were intending to start a conversation. I felt myself start to perspire. It was like the women were radiating some sort of heat. Oh, man, I thought, this is not good for me. The doctors told me not to start anything.

Down the beach there were some white American soldiers who had also noticed the women. And when they saw them approach me, the rednecks started making aggressive noises and egging each other on. I could tell right away that they were offended that these fine women had chosen to sit next to a Black guy. They weren't going to let that pass. I knew that one way or another, if I hung around too long I was going to end up getting hurt. I've got to get out of here, I told myself.

So I got up and walked away before the women could say anything. I tried not to look at them. They were just too fine and there was nothing to discuss. I sheepishly beat my retreat.

I walked around for a little while to cool down before I went back to the hospital. I was coming down a street and crossing an alley when a rickshaw pulled up in front of me, blocking my path. I looked up and there she was: the copper woman, sitting in the rickshaw, queen of the fucking world. And the only thing she said was "Get in." What was I to do?

Ironically enough, the war solved the age-old American race problem—at least temporarily, in the isolation of its hothouse atmosphere. Vietnam forced us to deal with it. The stark realities of the situation made serving in the military feel like living in a cowboy town. Anything goes. As a result, some guys had no hesitation in responding with aggression if they felt somebody insulted them or cheated them. You call me out of my name? Then you and I got a problem. And I don't play no games. Fuck decorum. Fuck rank. I don't care if you're a lieutenant or a major or whatever. Just try it. Let's see who's got the quickest draw, right now.

A lot of the brothers got politicized during the war—*because* of the war. We were reading about what was going on at home. We listened to the news on the radio, too, and we were intently following the conflagrations of 1968 from a distance. I was corresponding with a few friends at home. My homeboy M'Chaka Uba used to send me books: Dick Gregory, *The Autobiography of Malcolm X*, Stokely Carmichael. Even in the midst of everything, we were hungry for information about what was going on. So we didn't miss the Black Power movement: we lived it from Pleiku and adapted its lessons to our situation.

In the war, racial prejudice started to look even more stupid than it did at home. We're facing a common threat. Somebody's trying to kill all of us. You think we're going to waste time squabbling over your ignorant prejudices? No, my friend. Listen, if you insist on traveling with your racist baggage, you should understand that *you* might become the problem. We can tell you right now: we are not going to die because of your hangups. We might have to eliminate you.

The shift in mindset was mostly tacit. But now and then guys would say it straight out. Vietnam was such a free-for-all that some of these sentiments were voiced, and even acted upon.

In the Army we found a camaraderie across racial lines that felt new to many of us. Many years later, Pete Martin Malijewski told me that he'd been thinking about our time together in the war.

"We'll never have what we had, Henry," he said. "You know what I'm talking about."

And I did know. In Vietnam, we were joined at the hip for the first time. It brought us together, and the solidarity we shared was deep and pure: I wouldn't have hesitated to take a bullet for Pete or for Napoli, the little drummer from First Avenue. It's like that line in the Billy Joel song about the Marines: "We would all go down together . . ." In the war, death was the common denominator. We were all facing the same ultimate jeopardy. And that brought us together. There was no time for foolishness.

At the same time, death was also the universal indicator, like in chemistry. Dip anyone in that solution and his true colors come out. I don't mean that anybody got cured of racism in Vietnam. There were still plenty of rednecks in the Army. But it was right out in the open for everybody to see. So it wasn't hard to deal with. In fact, even when there was lingering hostility, it was much more civilized, because the circumstances removed the pretense. With the unreconstructed bigots, there was an agreement that was blunt even though it remained unspoken: I don't like you and you don't like me. You stay over there and I'll stay over here. But let's be clear: you even think the word "nigger" and I'll blow your fucking head off.

But when we returned to the US, we realized that the polarity was different. That's what Pete meant. We'd never have that same camaraderie again, because things hadn't changed back home. There were the same old familiar undercurrents of hate. I remember being struck by it as soon as I got back to Missouri that fall. The resentment was palpable. There weren't a lot of infantrymen in my situation, guys who had served substantial time in Vietnam and then came back to spend their last few months on a base in the US. At Fort Leonard Wood I had to put on a dress uniform for some special event. I had campaign ribbons and insignia and stuff. The white career-military guys in the company were seething: it was as though they couldn't stand the visible proof that I had gotten through it. The war was another excuse to divide us rather than a shared experience that brought us together. And the matter-of-fact cross-racial solidarity of the war vanished—I realized I'd left it on the other side of the world.

The copper-hued goddess had a fantastic bungalow apartment. It turned out that she was a high-class call girl. Clearly her needs were being taken care of.

I wasn't sure why she had approached me. Part of me wanted to pretend that I was all that, but I was just pipe-dreaming. Deep down I knew she was way out of my league. I wasn't in any shape to do anything anyway.

It turned out she had another agenda. She had a kid. She told me that she had had an affair with a Black soldier. They were in love, she explained, and she got pregnant. But some officers wanted her to themselves and got jealous. And they got rid of the brother. She couldn't find out what had happened to him.

Their son was placed in a boarding school or orphanage in town that was run by Catholic nuns. She wasn't even allowed to visit her boy. And so she asked me to visit him in her place. She gave me money and I would bribe the nuns to let me spend time with the kid.

He was just a toddler. "Your mother sent me to come see you," I told him. "She misses you so much. She can't come right now, but she asked me to come by to see how you were doing."

It was a pitiful situation. I ended up becoming friends with her. I felt awful, and I wished there were something I could do aside from delivering these futile messages to her child. But there didn't seem to be any solution.

From our base in Saigon, the band traveled all over playing music, from the South China Sea at the bottom tip of South Vietnam all the way up north to the so-called Yankee Stadium, where the 5th Fleet was anchored in the Gulf of Tonkin. We were living the sweet life. And then we got busted. It was the piano player in the band. He was a blond guy from Southern California. Real friendly—although involved in some serious business action on the side. My man turned out to be a major drug runner. Unbeknownst to us, he was carrying around an entire duffel bag full of opium, and he was making deals everywhere we went. I don't understand how he was moving so much product. He must have had suppliers somewhere. And I don't know how he was getting paid. In the military you bought everything with scrip; it was strictly forbidden to possess currency, whether local or dollars.

The only thing we noticed was that he always had his duffel bag with him. And he never seemed to change his clothes. It seemed a little peculiar, but it didn't bother us—he didn't smell. Well, we eventually got the explanation: he never changed clothes because there were no clothes in that bag! It was all just opium.

The Criminal Investigation Division had been tracking him. The CID was like the FBI of the US Army; they investigated felony crimes and violations of military law inside the service. We were up north, scheduled to play a show for sailors in the 5th Fleet. We were staying in these houses on the beach the night before we went out to the ships to play the concert. The CID raided us in the middle of the night and arrested all of us. We didn't find out until later, but the piano player had already been caught. They'd arrested him earlier that afternoon making a drug deal.

We never saw him again. They dealt with him quickly and shipped him off to jail somewhere. I remember he had a beautiful, pearl-handled Colt pistol, and after he got busted I tried to get it—I was hoping to send it to his mother back home. But the authorities wouldn't give us any of his belongings or even tell me his family's address so I could write them.

The CID tried to intimidate the rest of the band into confessing that we were involved. But we didn't have anything to confess; we had had no idea what he was up to. Eventually they let us go and told us to head back to our original assignments.

We said our farewells right there on the steps of the courthouse in downtown Saigon. A couple of the guys broke down crying. "I can't believe this shit," the singer groaned. "I've got to go back to artillery?" The other brother, the drummer from DC, had it even worse: he was a foot soldier. And so that was the end of my big city idyll. I got my stuff together and headed back out to Pleiku.

—What was your next course of action?

—I called the cat up in the tower and I told him, "I don't know what's going on, man. Something's coming toward me."

"What do you mean?" he asked. "What is it? I don't see anything."

"I don't know what it is. But you've got to put the light on it. Turn the spotlight on right now or I'm going to start shooting."

"Wait a second, Henry. You know you can't just start

shooting. And I can't turn on the light unless we're sure. I need to call the command post."

The protocol was that unless there was an immediate emergency—an attack coming in—we weren't supposed to draw attention to our position. We were required to call in a report and wait for them to tell us what to do.

Well, I wasn't about to sit around and wait for whatever this thing was to rush me. I didn't have time for that. So we had a stalemate.

I left Saigon and returned to the 4th Infantry base camp outside Pleiku in August 1968. I was scheduled to be there for another month or two before I was sent back to the States. My final weeks in Vietnam soon turned into another improbable chapter in my war experience. For a while I wasn't sure they were even going to let me get out.

There was a captain on the base who for some reason developed a grudge against me. Some of the officers in Pleiku were still pissed off that I had auditioned for the band in Saigon. This captain launched an investigation to try to find out whether I had broken any rules and regulations while I was stationed in Saigon. I knew some people in the communications unit in camp, and they informed me that he had been sending messages to people in Saigon, asking about my whereabouts. It was a fishing expedition and there wasn't anything to catch. But in their frustration not to be able to pin something on me, they passed the case over to the CID.

I don't know if it had to do with the piano player getting busted while I was in the band, but the CID got extreme. Since they couldn't prove that I'd done anything untoward, they simply made all my papers disappear. Effectively I didn't exist. And if there was no record of my existence, then of course I couldn't be discharged. I couldn't clear. Which meant I wasn't going anywhere. I couldn't leave the country; I couldn't do anything.

I suspect that what saved me in the end was the eruption

of civil unrest back in the US. After the assassinations of Martin Luther King Jr. and Robert F. Kennedy earlier that year and
the convulsion of urban riots over the summer, reports started
to emerge in the American news media about racial tension in
the armed forces in Vietnam. That summer we heard that both
a congressional committee and a delegation from the United
Council of Churches were scheduled to come to Vietnam specifically to look into allegations of racial prejudice in the military.
In preparation, an emissary visited the 4th Infantry camp and
interviewed soldiers. And all of a sudden—that very same day—
all my papers turned up. I existed again. The documents were all
stamped and in order, and my discharge was approved. I was on
a plane out of there a few days later. They sent me back to the US
to spend my final few months in Missouri.

When I left Vietnam, I had to pass through a processing center
in the south of the country. Arrivals and departures were regi-
mented during the war. I had arrived at Cam Ranh Bay, which
at the time was a sort of indoctrination and training center as
well as a hospital where you got climatized to the conditions
and trained in the specific perils of jungle warfare and chemical warfare. But when I left, I was sent to this processing center
that was right next to a notorious place called Long Binh Jail.
We jokingly nicknamed it LBJ. It was a penitentiary for the sick-
est dudes on the planet. Most of the guys that ended up there
were completely nuts, and they had committed awful crimes.
LBJ was where they sent the renegades who had gone AWOL,
like Dirty Dan's merry pranksters, but it was also where they
sent the hard-core offenders, men who had committed rape and
murder and serious war crimes.

  LBJ was famously unruly. In fact, there had been a violent
uprising by the prisoners there in August 1968, a little more than
a month before I arrived, in which they burned down the mess
hall and a good portion of the facility. By the time I got to the

processing center, LBJ was hardly functioning as a detention facility at all. There were guys who had escaped from the prison milling around the processing center, hoping to steal someone's papers.

The environment was completely chaotic. The authorities had basically relinquished control; they communicated with us by announcements over a loudspeaker. The MPs seemed scared to come in. So those of us on our way out were left waiting to get processed in this big compound that had been infiltrated by deranged escapees from the dysfunctional prison next door.

When I arrived, I noticed these vicious-looking guys hanging around the Quonset hut that was the main office of the processing center as well as around the surrounding yard and barracks. The tension was palpable: they were like packs of wild dogs waiting for a chance to strike. I walked into the building and I could feel them sizing me up, trying to figure out whether I could be taken. They weren't stupid, and they knew how dangerous it was to underestimate an adversary in Vietnam: one mistake and everybody could go up in flames.

I had heard how dangerous the situation was, and so I came prepared. I had my left arm completely bandaged up. I also taped my cassette recorder to my upper arm, so I was walking around wearing it like some sort of cyborg. I could see that those hyena desperadoes weren't sure what to make of that. What they didn't know was that before I left Pleiku I had emptied the bowels of the cassette recorder and concealed my 9mm pistol in there. I also had a big hunting knife down my pants as an extra measure. You weren't supposed to bring weapons to the processing center. But I had heard about LBJ, and I wasn't going to go down without a fight.

I went to my assigned spot in the dormitory and I chained my duffel bag to my cot. Some of the criminals were still watching me from a distance. After a little while they sent over an emissary. A dude sauntered up and started trying to engage me in conversation. "Look, man . . .": bullshit about needing help with something, wanting to make a little trade. I didn't say anything. I just stared at him. I wanted him to understand that I was not to be messed with. After a few minutes he slinked away.

This tense predatory game played out over the next couple of days. They would announce departures over the loudspeaker: "Specialist Prettyman and Corporal Tinsley will be departing at 1800 hours this evening on the flight to Honolulu." At this information, the crooks' ears always perked up. They intently scrutinized the soldiers who were departing, trying to discern who were the lucky bastards that day. "Where the fuck is that motherfucker? Maybe we can snatch his dog tags and papers."

While I was waiting to be called, I tried not to take any chances. I just ate and stayed by my bunk. After a few days, I was filthy. The shower at the processing center was right in the middle of an open yard: it was just a big elevated tank with a cord that you pulled to release water over you. I finally decided to wash up. I left my clothes by my cot and strode out to the shower. Everybody was looking at me: this skinny naked dude with a big bandage on my arm and a tape recorder strapped to it. I took my knife, too—I just walked out in the buff with a huge blade in my hand and my towel over my shoulder.

I came back from my shower and walked into the dormitory. When I came in the door I pulled up in surprise. All my clothes and the duffel bag were gone! They'd taken everything—even the cot.

I maintained my composure and went directly to the master sergeant that handled requisitions. He looked up at me standing there in nothing but a towel and asked me what was wrong. I didn't tell him what had happened. I just said I needed a new set of fatigues, boots, underwear, and a jungle hat.

"Oh, and one more thing," I added. "Give me a couple of ponchos, too."

"Two ponchos?" the master sergeant said, befuddled by the request. It hadn't rained there in days.

I nodded and he got the stuff and handed me a pile. I went back out and put on my clothes. The criminals were still lurking. But this time I wanted to make sure they saw me. I carefully unwrapped the bandage on my arm, and then I opened up the cassette player and took out the gun. That put them on notice. I took the gun and my knife and went out of the dormitory and set myself up under a tree in the middle of the yard. That's why I asked for the ponchos. I slept on one and kept the other to cover myself with at night if it got cold. I sat down with my bag against the tree, pulled my jungle hat down low over my eyes, and cradled my 9mm under my arm. If anybody tried to sneak up on me, I was prepared to defend myself.

They still didn't give up. Another emissary made his way over. He started trying to talk to me, and I lifted up the brim of my hat and looked him in the eye.

"Come here," I said. He hesitated and then advanced a step closer, leaning down.

I pulled out my gun and pointed it at him. "Start breathing, motherfucker."

He pulled back and instinctively raised his hands from his sides. "Wait, man, be cool, I just wanted to talk to you—"

"Breathe, so I can pull the trigger," I interrupted him. "Just breathe." Finally I shouted it again: "Breathe!"

He turned around and scurried off. And after that they didn't mess with me anymore. They knew I was packing and they saw I was on edge—they figured I might just be unhinged enough to take somebody out. They had seen my gun and knife, but they didn't know what else I might have, what other craziness I might be capable of. So they let it go.

When I eventually left the tree, I met a skinny white kid who had been a clerk in the secretariat in Saigon. He was carrying his release papers with him, just waving them out in the open. Completely innocent—he had no idea of the danger he was putting himself in. I went up to him and said, "Goddamn, man, what you got your papers out like that for? You can get hurt around here like that." He thanked me and folded them up and put them in his pocket. We chatted for few minutes. This kid had never been around any of this sort of stuff. He had spent the war in an office, so he was sheltered from the storm.

Well, they killed that boy. They killed him and took his papers.

> —*For what reason were you skeptical about the efficacy of calling the sighting into the command post?*
> —*I didn't have time to wait around to see what some half-asleep officer might say! And I knew they wouldn't believe me anyway. Back in May, I was in the exact same position with Coleman and I spotted movement out in the ravine. I thought I saw guys darting from one position to another, appearing and then vanishing into the brush again. I told them but they wouldn't listen to me. It was only when the camp was attacked by the North Vietnamese Army that they realized I'd been telling the truth. After we repelled the attack, we found that the NVA had built tunnels all around the base camp. They must have been working for months. They were right at our doorstep.*

I rode the plane back with a criminal who had stolen somebody's papers. He wasn't the one who had killed the white kid. But he was an accused murderer who had slipped out of LBJ and swiped some credentials to get on the plane heading out. Although I knew he had boarded under false pretenses, there was nothing I could do: the situation was too volatile, and I was determined to make it out myself.

The flight went straight to Washington State. From there I would take another flight home to Chicago. I had a brief stopover at home before I had to report to Missouri, where I'd been assigned to spend my last few months in the service. While we were en route across the Pacific, I had a brief exchange with the fugitive from LBJ. He knew that I knew what he'd done. He told me, "Listen, man, I don't care." He told me that his mother was terminally ill—with what, I didn't catch. "I don't care what they do to me. I'm going home to see my mama," he declared.

By the time the plane landed that night in Washington, they had somehow figured out that the fugitive from LBJ was on board. The FBI was waiting for us. They put searchlights on the plane as soon as we touched down—we didn't even taxi over to the terminal. The authorities came out onto the tarmac and brought a mobile staircase to the door. They made us deplane slowly, one by one. The fugitive was behind me. I stepped through the door and started to make my way down the stairs. As soon as he came out, he leaped over the side of the staircase down to the ground and ran toward the woods next to the air-field. The feds starting yelling: "Stop! Get that man!"

They made quite a fuss, although I noticed that none of them actually took off in pursuit. They were yelling the order as though somebody else were going to go after the convict. I paused at the bottom of the staircase—only after my feet were safely on the ground—and watched the charade for a few seconds. I certainly didn't want to draw any attention to myself. But I was bemused. I was thinking: You all don't know what you're getting yourself into. You're really going to run into the woods after a crazy motherfucker from the Army who had been desperate enough to steal somebody's papers to get home? This cat had nothing to lose. And they didn't have any idea what he might have been carrying.

When I finally got called to board the flight back to the States, I'd had to walk over a little bridge and past a set of big oil drums next to the runway. It's finally going to happen, I'd told myself. I was hyped up and ready to get the hell out of Vietnam.

The authorities checking our papers had instructed us to turn in any illegal weapons or controlled substances we might have before we got on the plane. They had a whole list of things we couldn't have, and some of it was macabre. (I remember that one of the prohibited items on the list was "foreign body parts.") They knew they'd created monsters.

"Just throw it all into the drums," they'd said. "Once you

cross this line and board the plane, you will have technically entered United States territory, and you will be prosecuted for the possession of any illicit items."

I'd tossed in my 9mm and my big knife, too. It felt like a purification ritual. I never wanted to see another weapon again in my life. But of course it was just a gesture. It wasn't just about the things we carried or hid in an empty cassette player. The war had reshaped my insides. And some of the changes there was no way to discard.

I found out later that all my medical records from my service in Vietnam had been washed. I tried to get them and they informed me that they had no documentation of my treatment. After I hurt my back during the Tet Offensive, they had prescribed me a powerful narcotic that was illegal back in the States. They never told me precisely what it was—I think it was some sort of super-strength laudanum or some similar sort of opiate cocktail. There were all kinds of drugs being tried out on the sly over there, in the chaos of the battlefield, that hadn't been approved for use back home. I suspect they wiped my records to get rid of any documentary evidence of what they'd done to me.

When I arrived at Fort Leonard Wood in Missouri, I still had a few of the pills they'd prescribed me in Pleiku. When those ran out, I went to the infirmary and asked for the prescription to be refilled. But when I showed him the bottle, the doctor said it was against the law to give me the same thing I'd been taking.

I was taken aback. "What are you talking about, against the law?" I asked him. "It was Army doctors who gave it to me in the first place."

But he told me the rules in Pleiku—or the lack thereof, apparently—didn't apply in the USA. Instead he gave me a prescription for Darvon, a much less powerful painkiller. After a couple of days, I went back to the doctor and complained. "What is this weak stuff you gave me? It doesn't help at all." But he told me that was the best he could do.

I had been taking the painkillers regularly ever since the Tet Offensive in early 1968. I was still on them all through my period in the band in Saigon. I realized that whatever it was they had given me, I had gotten hooked. It took me a good while to kick that habit. Without the stronger drug, the pain was so bad that I had to wear a back brace for a while. During my first month back in Missouri, I was in and out of the hospital at Fort Leonard Wood, trying to shake that addiction. It was brutal.

Fort Leonard Wood is in central Missouri, about two hours southwest of St. Louis, and throughout the fall and winter of 1968 I got in the habit of heading up to the city when I had time off on weekends to play with some of the musicians in the Black Artists' Group. When I had my stopover in Chicago before I reported to Fort Leonard Wood, I reconnected with my friends in the Association for the Advancement of Creative Musicians. The guys were all happy to see me—and especially relieved to see that I'd gotten over my devout period. They welcomed me right back into the fold.

By the time I got back, the trumpeter Lester Bowie was collaborating closely with Roscoe Mitchell, Joseph Jarman, and Malachi Favors; they were already recording together, and what started out as a group under Roscoe's leadership soon started calling itself the Art Ensemble. Lester had grown up partly in St. Louis, and as the AACM began to hum with creative activity he brought some of his associates from Missouri up to play in Chicago. So when I returned, I met people like the alto saxophonists Oliver Lake and Julius Hemphill and the baritone saxophonist Hamiet Bluiett.

In St. Louis, Lake, Hemphill, and Bluiett had founded an arts organization with a number of artists working in different disciplines (including the painters Emilio Cruz and Oliver Lee Jackson; the actors Malinke Elliott, Vincent Terrell, and Portia Hunt; and the poets K. Curtis Lyle and Shirley LeFlore). Whenever I could, I would go down to St. Louis for the weekend and stay at Oliver's house. I started hanging out in Gaslight Square and at the spacious headquarters building that the Black Artists'

Group had leased on Washington Avenue. Until I was discharged from the Army and moved back to Chicago permanently in April 1969, I spent most of my time between Fort Leonard Wood and St. Louis, and the BAG scene was the main milieu where I continued my explorations as a composer.

One day I was walking across Fort Leonard Wood and I noticed a bus coming in with a load of soldiers. But these weren't just regular soldiers returning from the war: as the men started to file off the bus, I saw that they were all in chains. These guys were prisoners—some of the military criminals from Vietnam that had been locked up in places like LBJ.

Back home in chains, they weren't as rowdy as those jackals lurking around the processing center. Seeing them brought back the memories of what I'd gone through a month or two earlier. But then a guy shuffled off and I recognized his face. I was startled: it was Dirty Dan!

So they had finally caught him. Dan didn't look injured, so I presumed he must have surrendered without a fight. Still, it seemed strange to me that they had brought him back to the US so quickly. The normal procedure was that you would serve the time at LBJ for whatever you had done over there, and then you owed the military whatever time you spent in jail. In other words, in addition to finishing your term of enlistment you'd also have to go back out into the jungle for however long you'd been incarcerated. You had to pay it back. I figured Dirty Dan must have talked some miraculous bullshit to get himself sent back home so soon. Dan always did have a fast mouth, though.

He didn't see me and there wasn't any way to approach him. The next time I saw him was a few years later. Air was playing its first concert at Grant Park, downtown in the Loop near the Art Institute of Chicago and the Buckingham Fountain. I came up from the South Side on the regional railroad. In the station there was this shoeshine stand, one of those old-fashioned ones where the clients are seated up on a platform while they get their shoes shined. I was walking by and there was a guy sitting up there reading the newspaper. His face was hidden but I noticed his shoes: the guy was wearing these loud two-tone patent-leather Stacy Adams wing-tip Oxfords with white stitching along the seams. They were ostentatious, and I was thinking, Who the hell still wears garish shoes like that?

The man suddenly lowered the newspaper and addressed me. It was Dirty Dan. He just intoned one word: "Thread." He was suave and unruffled, as though it were perfectly normal to run into me in the station years after he'd dropped me off on a highway by the South China Sea.

Dan was sharp as a tack. He had on a bespoke dark-azure-blue three-piece suit. He pulled out a wad of bills in a silver money clip and paid for the shine.

"What are you doing here, Dan?" I asked. "How'd you do it?" I didn't voice the real question in my head: Why aren't you still in jail?

He didn't say much. Apparently he had gotten a dishonorable discharge, but at least he wasn't locked up. And it looked like he was doing pretty well for himself back in Chicago. I saw him once or twice after that. He never came to my shows himself, but he would send these associates of his. I don't know what they were involved in—an endeavor of dubious legality, I assume. But Dan knew how to take care of himself. He was a natural leader: he had a way of congregating disciples around him. And he had a brilliant mind for scheming up rackets of one sort or another. Dirty Dan was not exactly the most upstanding member of the community, but still I found it hard not to marvel at him. He was something special: a complete original—and even an artist, in his own unrepentantly unclean way.

Especially when I switched my main base of operations to New York in the mid-1970s, it dawned on me how many of the musicians on the scene were veterans. In one respect this isn't surprising at all: service in Vietnam was a defining experience for my entire generation. It was simply the period when we happened to come up. But so many of us saw action that you have to wonder what effect it had on the development of the music.

We were mostly scattered around in different postings, but I almost certainly crossed paths with some of the musicians I met later in downtown Manhattan. Talking with my friend the trumpeter Ted Daniel years later, I realized that it was likely he had seen one of my concerts with the Saigon band, possibly in Bambi Tuit. I met the tenor player Frank Lowe in New York and we quickly figured out that he probably saw me with that band in Chu Lai. When I became close to the cornetist and conductor Butch Morris, we realized that he was posted right there in Pleiku during the same time I was at the 4th Infantry Division camp. Butch was a medic, and the bus into town would let you off right in front of the clinic. I was there every weekend. We must have seen each other, even if we didn't know each other yet.

Just before I shipped out, I met my replacement in the band. He was a saxophonist from Detroit named Allan Barnes. I remember him showing up just before I left: a truck rolled in with a group of new arrivals, and I noticed this wide-eyed beanpole wearing his brand-new digs and carrying a shiny new saxophone case. That's got to be the new kid, I said to myself. I could tell he was totally green. I left the next day and so I didn't get to talk to him then, but I caught him once years later when he was playing with Donald Byrd's crossover group, the Blackbyrds. (Barnes is the one who played the laid-back flute solo on their biggest hit, "Walking in Rhythm.")

I went backstage to introduce myself after their set. I reminded him that I was the guy he'd replaced in the 4th Infantry Band.

"It was you?" Barnes said. By then he'd heard some of my music, probably one of the early Air records. But he hadn't realized I was the same person.

All of a sudden Barnes got a serious look in his eye and said, "You know, Henry, I really should kick your ass."

"What for?" I responded, nonplussed.

Barnes broke out laughing. "I got you for a second there, didn't I?" I was relieved to know he was kidding. But I still didn't get it.

"Henry, I didn't know who you were or what you had done, but the officers fucked with me the whole time I was there. They wouldn't let up! The other guys in the band told me they'd been pissed at the guy I replaced. Shit, man, whatever it was, I was the one who caught the backlash."

I started to apologize but it felt far too late to say I was sorry—and beside the point, too. (Does a boat apologize for the waves it leaves in its wake?) And it seemed silly to apologize for something I hadn't even done. Those resentful officers had been so frustrated not to be able to get me that they took it out on the next guy that came in.

I only spoke to Barnes that one time, but something subtle shifted between us as we laughed about him getting caught up in the turbulence of my legacy. We'd both been put through the same shit. Hell, once I was gone they gave him my bunk, so in more than one way he slept in the bed I'd made. It was funny and it was fucked up, too. We looked at each other and that familiar feeling of solidarity came back. Neither of us said anything, because the connection came through on some lower frequency and I don't think we could have put it into words. But in that moment we both understood that even if we hadn't quite served together, we shared something indelible.

—How did you resolve the stalemate with your partner?

—The eyes moved closer and closer until they were no more than fifteen feet away, right at the edge of the ravine. There was definitely a mass there, a body, and I was more and more sure it wasn't human.

I called my partner again and said, "Look, I can't take it anymore. It's right there."

"Okay, okay, hold on! I'm going to call them up."

"I don't give a fuck whether you call them or not. As soon as this thing gets close enough that I can really see it, I'm going to start shooting. I don't care what it is. I'm going to shoot it as soon as it comes into view. If you don't want me to do that, you better throw some light on it so we can see what it is."

He finally suggested that he could try to flip the klieg light on real quick so we could see what it was. A flash of light would be better than the cacophony of a machine gun. Even if it was enemy soldiers, they wouldn't be able to pinpoint our position from an unexpected flash.

"Go on and do it, then," I said.

When he threw the light on it, that's when it came up. It had been crouching on the ground, dragging itself gradually on its belly. Now it stood all the way up. It was right in front of me. And I could see what it was: a huge tiger.

In a single motion, the cat stretched out the full length of its body into a majestic leap. In the sudden glare of the light it extended into the air and we could see just how large it was. Extended, it was easily more than a dozen feet long.

It didn't jump at me—it leapt to the side. It seemed to hang there suspended in the air: a fearful vision framed in the light.

The tiger sprang to the side back into the shadows. My partner tried to swing the klieg light to follow it, but as soon as it hit the bushes it was gone.

As it jumped to the side, the tiger turned and looked over its shoulder right at me in the bunker. Even in the speed of its retreat—from launch to landing it couldn't have taken more than two or three seconds—it took the time to take a long, deliberate look at me. And its eyes delivered the universal message of the predator to the prey after a miraculous escape: "Catch you next time . . ."

———

One of the main ways that war transforms you has to do with your sense of hearing. It's partly an expansion of your aural palette, all the new stuff you become attuned to in the new environment: the sounds of helicopters and distant howitzer fire, sure, but also the ribald banter among the guys you serve with, or the voices of the Montagnards, or the unfamiliar patter of rain on a triple-canopy jungle, or the melodious cries of street-food vendors in Saigon hawking their goods.

But it's not simply a matter of hearing more—it makes you hear *differently,* too. You acquire a heightened sensitivity to sound. Your body learns quickly that listening can be a matter of life or death. Your ears start to pick up things you wouldn't even have noticed back at home, because in the war missing the slightest signal at the wrong moment could get you killed. Your body learns to hear things with great precision even while you're asleep, and to jolt you awake at any hint of a threat. For any artist, such a profound transformation of your understanding and perception can't help finding its way into what you're doing.

It's like I grew a set of antennae over there. When I returned, my reception equipment was different. And even if the war messed up my head in a million other ways at the same time—and even if I didn't ask for any of it—I'd have to admit that that heightened sensitivity became one of the main things that shaped me into the composer I've become.

5

Apprenticeship of a Tail Dragger

I didn't shed my war experiences when I got off that plane from Vietnam, or when I was discharged from Fort Leonard Wood and came back to civilian life. Vietnam stayed with me, and it took me to some dark and twisted places even once I returned to Chicago. The simple fact of it was, I was really fucked up. Everybody that came out of the service and out of that war was fucked up. We were in flagrant denial about that fact. We acted like everything was all right just because we were walking around with all our body parts, just because we weren't alcoholics or sleeping on the street or acting like raving psychopaths. But we were all fucked up.

The entire country was in denial. The US Army didn't provide us with any counseling to help us confront our demons. The service just regurgitated us as though nothing had happened: spat us back into the communities we had come from. And our communities ignored it, too. If anything, returning veterans were met with hostility, since we were the symbols of an unjust war. We were careful not to bring it up, because we didn't want to provoke that resentment; we didn't want to be associated with what was quickly becoming a national travesty.

I came back to Chicago and nobody asked me anything—not my family, not my friends. They acted like I hadn't even been away. No comment, no concern, no acknowledgment, no questions, nothing, not even a measly "How you doing?" It left us psychologically isolated. There was no one to talk to, no one with whom we could share the confused thoughts that were roiling our heads. The horror, the absurdity, the drudgery—all of it lingered with us and transformed us inside. I still carry all of it. And the story of my experience felt all the more indelible because there was no one to tell it to. Even the most terrifying or fantastic episodes came to feel precious, proof of what I'd been through, even if I had to keep it locked away.

To put it another way, nobody ever asked me about the tiger. That dialogue happened only in my head, only in hindsight, as I recounted what happened to myself in the form of a mathematical catechism. I had to imagine my own debriefing.

When I came back to my mother's house, I couldn't even sleep. It took me months before I was able to get a decent night of rest. It wasn't that I was frightened. The problem was that I'd gotten so acclimated to the sounds of the war. I couldn't sleep because even in the city, it was too quiet: there was no gunfire going off in the distance. No helicopters passing overhead. The silence was driving me crazy.

I used to walk the streets all night. I'd slip out of my mother's house and wander around Englewood in a sort of somnambulist daze. I was walking around late one night and, without really planning to, I ended up at 63rd and Morgan at the home of a kid named Edgar Caver, who had been my best friend in grammar school. Edgar was a talented singer; he could sing the hell out of the blues when we were kids. He had a great collection of Howlin' Wolf records and we used to listen to them together.

I found myself standing there in front of Edgar's front door. It was probably five or six o'clock in the morning. His mother must have heard me, because she came to the door. Fortunately she wasn't too startled to see someone standing there. She peered out and recognized me.

"Henry, is that you?" she asked. "I haven't seen you in years!"

"Yeah, it's me," I confirmed in a monotone. It was ludicrous but I asked for my old friend. "Is Edgar around?"

"No, Edgar's married and moved on." She told me that Edgar's sister, Didi, had left the house, too. "Now it's just me."

She looked at me with concern. "You don't look too good, Henry. Come on in. Let me get you something to eat." She didn't ask me what I was doing out there wandering around at the crack of dawn. Instead she fixed me some eggs and toast. I suddenly noticed that I was famished.

She stood there by the stove and watched me while I sat at her kitchen table and ate. Then she suggested, "Why don't you go lay down in the back?"

The house sat right behind the El train. The tracks ran past the window. I went in that back room and lay down on the guest bed, and I don't know when I woke up. I slept all day long. The train would rumble by at regular intervals, and there was something comforting in that racket. It was loud enough that I could finally pass out.

We never spoke about what was going on with me. But somehow Edgar's mother understood, or at least she sensed that I needed to be there. I got in the habit of going by her house and taking these long naps. For a while it was the only place I could sleep.

Today, the experience of the aftermath—the trauma of coming home, on top of the trauma of the war—is far enough behind me that I can almost joke about it with a few friends who also served. "Damn, we were screwed up!" we say to each other now, ruefully. At this late date we can finally acknowledge the damage. We certainly weren't in any shape to be in a committed relationship or to be having children. There's a reason all of us got married more than once.

When I came back from the military, the plan was to resume my studies at the American Conservatory. But I needed to save some money for tuition, so I didn't start back immediately. I heard that veterans could qualify to get Illinois funding to attend one of the state schools, and so in the meantime I used that grant support to study at Governors State University, which was south on Route 57 in Park Forest. I enrolled there as a composition and woodwinds major.

At Governors State my main instructor was the bassoonist Cedric Gay. He was the only Black bassoonist I knew of who had achieved some prominence in the classical world. But he had done all sorts of other things, too. He was always trying to write a hit musical—that was his dream.

Mr. Gay told me incredible stories about his experiences in classical music. In the late 1950s he had performed with the Lyric Opera of Chicago. There was no question about his ability. He was at that level. But the music world was still infused with so much racism that it was unimaginable that an African American musician, no matter how talented, could ever be seen sitting on stage or in the orchestra pit among white colleagues. Mr. Gay told me that when they couldn't find a white player, organizations would call him in. But in some circumstances, they went so far as to make him sit behind a screen while he played so he wouldn't be visible to the audience.

I was dumbfounded. I couldn't imagine anyone coming up with something so blatantly stupid. To separate a musician physically from a group he's in the midst of performing with is just a way of advertising the irrationality of racism. It's just a way of spotlighting the contradiction on stage.

I remembered I even declared to Mr. Gay, "What? I could never do that." He just looked at me. I didn't really think about it more carefully until later. When I did, I felt bad about mouthing off. This had happened to him in 1955 or 1956. What was he supposed to do? He was the best bassoonist in Chicago. He knew it and they knew it. What was he supposed to do?

There has never been a serious conversation about the experiences of that generation of Black American classical musicians and composers in relation to the history of the music more broadly. I knew people who had nervous breakdowns trying to get into that world. Imagine being a young musician then, on the cusp of the changes that the civil rights movement would bring over the course of the next couple of decades. What had seemed inconceivable even a few years earlier suddenly started to seem like something one might be able to aspire to. But the door wasn't open yet. And as opportunities arose, they didn't arise equally for everyone. Things changed in one orchestra, but others remained staunchly segregated. There started to be room for a few Black singers in opera—but mainly women, very seldom Black men. The powers that be never want to confront the perverse fits and starts of desegregation.

If you think about it from the perspective of the Black artist, then you have to ask about the toll of these sorts of situations on a performer or composer. Think of the investment—financial, psychological—that Black families put into supporting young musicians who had the dream of breaking into the classical music world. Think of how hard it is to make it even without these barriers. What kind of artist does that produce? Who can withstand the vicious fire of that sort of forging and come out on the other side?

Lester Bowie took over the presidency of the AACM from Muhal in September 1968, just before I landed back in the US at Fort Leonard Wood. Lester started a mimeographed newsletter called *The New Regime* and asked us all to contribute articles. I wrote an essay that appeared in the first issue in December next to pieces by Kalaparusha Maurice McIntyre and Braxton.

WHERE ARE OUR CRITICS?
by Henry Threadgill. . . . . .

"*. . . take over our own destinies . . .*"
—*Richard Muhal Abrams*

Inasmuch that Jazz has not been able to be defined whereby the greater number of its advocates and creators have accepted any such definition, especially in this day. What could be said concerning the past history of Jazz up to some recent contemporary date, with no clear mark timewise, is that the essence or spirit of Black Rhythm and Blues was involved aesthetically if not emphatically.

The question has been tossed about many times in recent years primarily by Black artists, that the term JAZZ had taken on too many false and bad connotations, stigmas, etc., and in what is basically a commercial-materialistic-capitalistically oriented country, taken on a too limited conception in terms of art. Thereby setting the stage for a foreseeable dead end in terms of progressive creativity— [un]less the fruits to be born were to be derived from within what has become a preconceived Music-concept-thought-mode, better JAZZ.

Why so much rejection, negative criticism of the newer music, Jazz nomenclature of lesser importance—in a word, ignorance. Our information medias being subject and geared to and by the same aforementioned system in the prior paragraph has not kept abreast of the movement progression of development.

Who or what then would this entail: disc-jockeys, promoters, agents, publishers, newsforms, profiteers, and at the top of the list critics or so called critics.

It is a very strange fact that only one significant book has been written to date, of my knowledge, about the contemporary music scene of which we speak. *Black Music* by LeRoi Jones [Amiri Baraka], stands alone in recording history in this instance as it happened and is happening. Well aware that his book was not attempting to be comprehensive, it did make known facts about the music and artist[s] that would be familiar and understandable in that exposure had found it and them in greater and lesser degrees. The point being that much significant and invaluable information has been compiled by one such writer not

il

WHERE ARE OUR CRITICS?
by; Henry Threadgill......

"...take over our own destinies..."
-Richard Muhal Abrams

Inasmuch that Jazz has not been able to be defined whereby the greater number of its advocates and creators have accepted any such definition, especially in this day. What could be said concerning the past history of Jazzup to some recent contemporary date, with no clear mark timewise, it that the essence or spirit of Black Rhythm and Blues was involved aesthetically if not emphatically.

The question has been tossed about many times in recent years primarily by Black artists, that the term JAZZ had taken on too many false and bad connotations, stigmas, etc., and in what is basically a commercial -materialistic-capitalistically oriented country taken on a too limited conception in terms of art. Thereby setting the stage for a foreseeable dead and in terms of progressive creativity-less the fruits to be norn were to be derived from within what has become a preconceived Music-concept-thought-mode, better JAZZ.

only about the music but culture also of broad awareness and concern, today.

When we look at western Music History, some of the best critics and writers were themselves first musicians and composers. Why? Because they knew where the music was "at" at the time they were talking about. Not leaving the task of writing and reviewing to the "out-of-time-of-tune reviewers of society."

It would appear possibly, that we, as musicians and composers, don't really care about this particular aspect of the music. This could not possibly be true with all the talk and platitudes on spirituality, expansion of intellect, and wholesome aesthetics being an integral part of the ideology. With such an ideology for what other purpose could such high ideals and ideas be for if not man.

It is with this point, however, that I would caution the reader not to infer or otherwise be led to believe that the music came forth as a result of obligation or necessity to or for man initially. The music created as such that it is, because the spirit of creation has moved to this point as it moves independent.

Lest the responsibility of writing about the music fall heavily upon us, we cannot expect much good from the critics and writers other than creating a serious gap for a large number of people.

Who else in this Aquarian Age would be better suited to speak about this product than the instrument through which it appears? Surely, if such highly creative music can come from such minds, the same minds can give some insight about it and themselves in relationship—that is, not just by being its creators and performers.

When I wrote this, I was a twenty-four-year-old private first class in the US Army, hardly just back from Vietnam. I had had my fair share of experience as a musician. But I hadn't made a record yet, or finished my degree at the conservatory. Reading it again so many years later, what I find striking is how self-conscious I was about my own professionalization. And how clear I was about what was needed: not promotion, not commercial exploitation, not sensationalism, but instead honest and accurate information about who we were and what we were trying to do as serious artists. In the AACM we shared a conviction that, aside from a few exceptions like Baraka, that information wasn't going to come from journalists and critics. And we were undaunted at the prospect of having to take on the task ourselves of fostering what Lester (in his own article in the same issue) called "lines of communication" with our audiences. Green as most of us were, we weren't intimidated at the idea of having to become the historians and explicators of our own creativity.

Back in Chicago in 1969, I couldn't help feeling that I had some catching up to do. The pace of advancement among my peers in the AACM was unbelievable. For example, I was blown out of the water when I heard *Sound*, the album Roscoe Mitchell made while I was away. Out of the blue he opened up an entirely new route in terms of tempo and space and silence. It was a giant leap ahead. The first time I listened to it, I thought, Man, what the hell happened here? Then there were the records Jarman had done, *Song For* and *As If It Were the Seasons*. Braxton, Leroy Jenkins, Kalaparusha, Lester Bowie: they had all started to throw down the gauntlet.

Like all of them, Wadada Leo Smith had developed a strong musical identity by the time I returned to Chicago. When I first met him that summer, he was living up on the North Side of the city, in an area where an experimental theater scene was starting to bloom. I went by his place and he had Webern scores laid out on a table. He was listening to the recordings and carefully analyzing what Webern was doing in his music. I tried to act cool but I thought, Damn, man, you're just going through Webern on your own? Wadada, Braxton, Amina, Roscoe—even by then, all these AACM composers were painstakingly working out their own individual musical vocabularies and even their own notational systems. It's a vast legacy when you think about it, a contribution that still hasn't really been acknowledged. There was a competitive aspect to it, of course, but it was also always supportive.

The first paying jobs I was able to get when I returned to Chicago were in blues bands. I had loved the blues since my childhood, but I had to learn how to play it. And it required as much practice and discipline as anything else. The blues is fundamental, but that doesn't mean it's primal or simple—some sort of raw outpouring. In fact, the blues is a highly intricate music, both on an emotional level and on a technical level. You can't coast or meander in the blues. The execution of every note is a highly sophisticated event. It's less a matter of harmonic complexity or melodic elaboration than of the sheer *sound*. That's what blues musicians focus on first and foremost, and it's incredible what some of them can do on their instruments.

People often think of the blues as having a strict formal structure: a twelve-bar harmonic pattern that repeats like clockwork. But the real blues isn't fixed. The blues is an internal thing. That's what makes it so difficult. If you really pay attention, you can hear that each tune has its own organic development and its own structure. It has nothing to do with set patterns. Just like the gospel music I was playing with Horace Sheppard, the blues can take any direction and any form at any time. It has a starting point, but you never know what's going to happen with the music until you're in it. The blues is a spirit music: the direction emerges through the spirit. So that's what you have to attune yourself to.

I played in a number of places around the South Side, but my regular gig was in the house band at the Blue Flame, on 39th Street right off Cottage Grove. All kinds of big names came through there: Buddy Guy, Mighty Joe Young, Hound Dog Taylor, Memphis Slim.

In the jazz world, jam sessions would happen on Monday
night. But in the blues world, they start on Sunday afternoon.
So I would go in on Sunday toward the end of the afternoon and
we'd play until about three or four o'clock in the morning with
everybody who came up on the bandstand.

The headliner of those jam sessions was the guitarist and
singer Frank Craig. Frank was a jovial, muscular dude originally from Mississippi who specialized in a gritty version of vin-
tage Chicago blues. Everybody called him "Left Hand Frank,"
because he was left-handed and played his guitar upside down,
with the treble strings at the top.

Frank's core house band was a small unit: lead guitar, rhythm
guitar, me on alto and maybe another horn player, bass, and
drums. There weren't set arrangements where I was reading a
part. This was more about blowing. I knew Frank's repertoire,
and I might put in a riff or double the melody line. When he
wanted me to solo, I'd take a solo. It was pretty free—as long as
you could play the feeling of the blues with conviction, you could
let the spirit of a tune take you wherever it took you. You could
pretty much play what you wanted to play, however you wanted
to play it. I could certainly go "outside"—there was no squabble
about that.

Eventually the range of music I was playing started to catch
up to me. Some days I would play clarinet for a parade one afternoon and then switch to alto for another gig in the evening, or
to flute or tenor the next day. Playing the blues was physically
demanding, especially given the long hours. Then a session with
the AACM big band would require a different set of challenges
with extended techniques. My embouchure was really suffering
from all the hard playing on different instruments in different
contexts. After a night of blowing, I'd show up the next morning
for a flute lesson at the conservatory and sound terrible. I was
so inconsistent that my instructors would ask, "What's going
on with you, Henry? One week you sound great, and the next
week you sound like you can't even play." "It's my chops," I'd
explain. "My lip is out of it. I was out playing all night!" None

of the other students were doing anything like what I was doing. It took me a while to figure it out. I eventually had to rebuild my embouchure so that I could switch between instruments without a hitch.

I played on some rhythm and blues recording sessions, but it was uncredited work. From time to time I would be asked to step in and play in a horn section—friends like Sonny Seals would call and I'd run over to the studio. To my mind the first recording that really counted was Muhal's *Young at Heart/Wise in Time*. The second track on the date was a quintet with me on alto, Lester Lashley on bass, Wadada Leo Smith on trumpet, and Thurman Barker on drums joining Muhal's piano. It was important to me because this wasn't just a job. This was creative music. We recorded it only a couple of months after I returned to Chicago, in August 1969. To my mind, it served to announce my arrival— even if my arrival was actually a return—bringing me publicly into the AACM fold after I'd been away the previous two years. And it meant a lot to me that Muhal trusted me to help him lay down a permanent record of his music.

Young at Heart/Wise in Time was recorded for Delmark, the Chicago blues label that came to play a key role in documenting the AACM in those years. A little later, Muhal, Wadada, and I considered founding a record label of our own. The idea emerged out of our discussions about the issues I brought up in my article for *The New Regime*. Just as we were dissatisfied with the coverage of our music from mainstream critics to the point that we were prepared to take the initiative of writing about it ourselves, we were also dissatisfied by our interactions with the record industry. This was a longstanding concern among Black musicians, of course. Like Max Roach and Charles Mingus before us, we wanted control over our art: we wanted to decide how it would be documented, how it would be packaged, how it would be marketed and promoted, how it would be distributed. It wasn't easy, but we were looking for ways to move these other partics out of the picture in order to have the final say on our output.

Even while I was still stationed at Fort Leonard Wood and finishing up my military service, I was getting reconnected with my colleagues in the AACM, coming up to Chicago whenever I could. In addition to the time I was spending in St. Louis with Oliver Lake and the Black Artists' Group, I would also drive up to Chicago to play with the AACM big band and other ensembles. So there wasn't really a transition period when I finally got my discharge and moved back in April 1969. I slipped right back into the swing of things.

It was a strange time to return, though. On April 15, one of the members of Jarman's band, the bassist Charles Clark, collapsed from a cerebral hemorrhage in the Illinois Central train station on Randolph Street. It wasn't the first tragedy to strike the AACM, either: a year earlier, while I was in Vietnam, the pianist Christopher Gaddy had passed away suddenly of kidney disease. Both of them were twenty-four years old when they died—just about the same age I was. Even before these losses, a sort of dispersal had started, with AACM musicians leaving Chicago. In 1967, the drummer Steve McCall moved to Amsterdam with his family, settling there for a time before making his way to France. My old running buddy Abshalom Ben Shlomo went to Israel. The bassist Leonard Jones went to Germany. At the end of May 1969, after a farewell concert at the Blue Gargoyle next to the University of Chicago campus where they called themselves the Art Ensemble for the first time, Jarman, Bowie, Mitchell, and Favors departed for Paris, later to be followed by Braxton, Leroy Jenkins, and Wadada Leo Smith.

Things didn't disintegrate, but the center of gravity shifted in Chicago. Muhal was still there, and a somewhat different group of us took the lead in continuing to present concerts and to teach at the AACM School: Amina Claudine Myers, Thurman Barker, Kalaparusha Maurice McIntyre, Ajaramu, Lester

In the AACM big band, I was still playing alto exclusively.

Lashley, Wallace McMillan, John Stubblefield, M'Chaka Uba, John Shenoy Jackson. In the AACM big band, I was still playing alto exclusively. I hadn't gone back to the tenor since that incident in church. Even if I had been so inclined, in that band the tenor section was chock-full of monstrous voices. I looked across at Kalaparusha and Stubblefield and thought, Damn, I'd better stay in my lane!

In the summer of 1969 I also made a reconnaissance trip to New York. I wanted to get the lay of the land. I thought I'd check it out before deciding whether it made sense to move there.

I was in town for a month or two, staying in Spanish Harlem with some friends of Jo Jo Morris, the singer from the Church of God. I remember that I met the Panamanian saxophonist and flutist Carlos Ward at the airport. We happened to arrive at the same time and struck up a conversation when we noticed each other's instrument cases.

I had met the bassist David Izenzon in Chicago at some point and I knew that he was playing that week at the Village Gate with the Argentinian tenor saxophone player Gato Barbieri. Carlos and I went by and asked if we could sit in. But Gato Barbieri wouldn't even acknowledge us. So we walked around downtown looking for somewhere else we might be able to play. We ended up at Slugs' Saloon on Third Street between Avenues B and C in the East Village. Leon Thomas and Pharoah Sanders were playing that night, and they let us join them. In the middle of the set, Kalaparusha Maurice McIntyre came in, too—it turned out that he was visiting from Chicago. Not bad for a first night in the city.

Carlos ended up staying in New York, and pretty quickly he was getting jobs with people around town; he made his first recording with the vibes player Karl Berger in August 1969, when I went back to Chicago for the session with Muhal. I knew I would make the move myself someday. But I also knew that I wasn't coming to New York to be a sideman. I wanted to write music. If I came to the big city, it was going to be to play my own music with my own group. I wasn't about to jump into the fray. There were too many talented musicians lurking on the sidelines, ravenous for work. I wasn't interested in that type of competition, trying to play solos to please this or that bandleader. Either you have the aspiration to be Billy the Kid or you don't. And I knew I wasn't a gunslinger.

Along with teaching at the AACM School, in the fall of 1969 I got a gig as an adjunct instructor at Columbia College teaching a course in Black music history. And there I found myself pulled into an entirely different performing-arts universe, not so much in the music department as in the theater-arts program, which took an educational approach of involving students in hands-on productions in the city. I started seeing a gorgeous theater student named Catherine Slade, who was a friend of Charles Clark's widow, Marabia. Through Cathy I met a number of the people in the theater and dance programs at Columbia College. I started getting gigs as an accompanist, composer, and music director for productions in the avant-garde theater scene that was emerging on the North Side, east of Lincoln Park on Lincoln Avenue around Fullerton and Sheffield, near the neighborhood where Wadada Leo Smith lived.

The energy up there was amazing. Little experimental theater companies were popping up like mushrooms: the Body Politic Theater, the Organic Theater (where André De Shields was performing before he moved to New York and got the title role in *The Wiz*), the Free Street Theater, the Kingston Mines Theatre Company, and over the next few years others, including the Victory Gardens, the St. Nicholas, Wisdom Bridge, and Steppenwolf. By the mid-1970s these troupes would come to be renowned for nourishing the careers of playwrights like David Mamet and Sam Shepard. I worked the most at the Kingston Mines, which was founded in 1969 by the director June Pyskacek in an old trolley barn on Lincoln Avenue and later became known as the theater where the musical *Grease* premiered in February 1971. But the shows I worked on there were farther out.

When I was still in high school, I met an older musician on the El train coming from the Loop down to the South Side. This guy was sitting across from me with an instrument case next to him. I could tell by the size that it was a trumpet or a cornet. I was coming back from my saxophone lesson with Jack Gell, so I had my tenor with me in the case with "SONNY ROLLINS" stenciled on the edge. He started talking to me. His name was Phil Cohran, he said, and he asked me if I wanted to come play with him and his band.

If he had hit on me a few years later, I might have been tempted to check it out. But at that stage, I knew I was a long way from being ready to play with any serious adult musicians. For some reason, just from looking at him, I could tell that Cohran was advanced. And I was well aware that I needed to work on my craft. It was too soon. So I simply thanked him and took his information, without any intention to call him or track him down.

Years later I realized that the cat had been one of the founders of the AACM. Early on there had been a break between factions about the direction the association should take in terms of privileging original compositions versus the traditional musics of the African diaspora. And Cohran decided to go his own way. Toward the end of 1967 he acquired a former movie theater on 39th and Drexel in the South Side that he named the Affro-Arts Theater, and it became an important cultural hub in the emerging Black nationalist scene in Bronzeville, centered around the music of Cohran's Artistic Heritage Ensemble. A number of important artists became associated with the theater, including the choreographer Darlene Blackburn and poets such as Haki Madhubuti.

During that period, I was traveling with Horace Sheppard and then away in the war, so I didn't see any of this firsthand.

Playing alto saxophone in Phil Cohran's Artistic Heritage Ensemble
with Pete Cosey (bass), John Stubblefield (tenor saxophone),
and Steve McCall (drums)

But when I came back I met Cohran again, and I started playing with him, too. I heard that there had been some sort of falling out, but there wasn't any bad blood. It wasn't a problem to play in both the AACM big band and with Cohran.

The Affro-Arts Theater closed in 1970, and by the time I got involved with Cohran we were mainly performing in other venues. But it was a great band and another important learning experience for me, because Cohran was a major bandleader, composer, theoretician, and musicologist. John Stubblefield was in the band, too, along with the tenor saxophonist Eugene Easton and the guitarist Pete Cosey.

I even got involved for a minute with the Pharaohs, the Afro-funk band that emerged out of the Artistic Heritage Ensemble and included Don Myrick, my friend from high school, as well as the percussionist Derf Reklaw, the bassist and trombonist Louis Satterfield, the trumpeter Rahmlee Michael Davis, the tuba player Aaron Dodd, the alto saxophonist Black Herman Waterford, and the trombonist Willie Woods. They put me on percussion—that was all they would let me play. They assigned me to play frying pan! It was like a probation period. You didn't just stroll into that band. They were serious. Some of them had been session musicians at Chess. And a few years later Satterfield, Myrick, and Davis formed the nucleus of the Phenix Horns, the horn section of Earth, Wind & Fire. It was briefly amusing. But I quickly got tired of waiting for them to say, "Okay, we're going to let you get your alto now."

I played under Phil Cohran's leadership for only a short period. But it taught me an important lesson. One difference from the AACM big band was that Phil put you in a uniform. There was a certain discipline in that band in terms of how you were expected to present yourself and how you were expected to play.

There was serious discipline in the AACM, too, of course,

and it was something unprecedented due to the concentration of performing composers. I don't just mean musicians who write tunes now and then. I mean artists who consider themselves composers in the most expansive sense of the term. Our ambitions on that score were no less than those of, say, Elliott Carter or Philip Glass or Charles Wuorinen or Meredith Monk or John Adams. The challenge of the AACM was that it was set up as a collective of performing composers on a fully democratic basis. You had to be able to play everybody's music and give one hundred and fifty percent of your energy and focus to the aesthetic they wanted to explore, whatever it was.

In the AACM, it didn't matter what you thought about your colleagues' music. It didn't matter whether you liked it or not. It didn't matter whether you shared the vision. You were expected to give your all to everyone else's compositions. No half-stepping, no compromise. A lot of guys couldn't do that. Braxton would stand up and tell people, "I want you to play this chart with no feeling. I want it cold as ice." And people couldn't handle it. There was intolerance; there were places some folks just couldn't make themselves go. That radical democratic orientation shrunk the ranks to those of us who had that openness and commitment to one another's work.

With Phil Cohran and the Artistic Heritage Ensemble, it was a different brand of discipline. There was a togetherness and warmth to the group, but it wasn't collectivism. It was Phil's group and his music. So the discipline was a matter of following his lead with absolute conviction. You had to get in line. And I had trouble with that. I was young and cocky. I said to myself, This is some old-fashioned authoritarian shit. I've already been in the military—I don't need this.

Phil Cohran actually ended up firing me. And Stubblefield, too. We wouldn't do what he was asking us to do. He wanted us to improvise using only a limited set of notes, and we thought that was out of date or immature or overly constricting. There were people in the saxophone section who could adhere to the rules and still come up with inventive solos. Gene Easton was one—

whew! Gene made all our whining sound silly. But Stubblefield and I thought it was too much of a pain. We were convinced that it would cramp our creativity. So we insisted on trying to play all these other things on top of the music. At a certain point, Phil had had enough, and he told us he had to let us go. He said that we were talented musicians, but we just didn't get it.

I only realized much later that it was all part of my growth. I needed to be slapped in the face right then and there. Eventually I came to understand that what Cohran was asking us to do was actually extremely advanced. It was *too* advanced for us to grasp at the time. To find creativity within constriction, to invent within conditions of restraint, isn't elementary—it takes nuance and great self-control.

This is a major blind spot in the way so-called jazz education has been institutionalized in the past few decades. No one took the time to think about the way we'd been doing it all along. The thing is, we'd been doing it successfully from the beginning. That's why the music is so powerful and so deep. We'd figured out our own ways to pass it down. And something like my experience with Phil Cohran is a good example.

Up through my generation, we all followed the same path. Despite all the incidental differences of individual experience, we all took the same route to becoming musicians in the Black tradition. You start playing an instrument. You start having musical experiences—not just sitting in a classroom playing scales or practicing in student ensembles, but instead out in the world: in little bands you put together with your friends, in churches and funerals and parades, at parties, at school dances, wherever. This is laying the groundwork. And it needs to go on for a significant period of time in your life. It might seem haphazard or juvenile, but it's extremely important in terms of your development as a musician. It might seem insignificant, but in the accumulation of these little forays into the music you're starting to develop a sensibility—an awareness of aesthetics, of history, of society situations—even before you're really conscious of it.

I once heard that for his first gig Coleman Hawkins was

assigned to play one note. That's it. One note. He had to get that one note right. The point wasn't to curb him with a beginner's exercise. He wasn't being held back. Along with learning the technique—taking the time to hone a voluptuousness of sound, rather than the velocity of reading a chart—he was being socialized into the music. Learning how to behave, picking up the subtle codes, the things people don't explain overtly. None of this is taught in an MFA program—and I'm not convinced it can be taught in school.

Where is the love affair? If you haven't had a love affair with the music, I don't know what you're doing in it. You have to give yourself over to it wholeheartedly and humbly without the thought of any kind of reward. The reward comes when you eventually can hold your own. A few years ago I read an interesting interview with Roy Hargrove in which he was criticizing the lack of curiosity among young musicians and saying that music schools should have them listen to more music. I agree with the critique. But at the same time, that's not the school's role. Young musicians should already be listening to music on their own, before they get to school. That thirst for the tradition, it has to come from inside.

You have to come to the tradition on its own terms. It's not a fixed curriculum that can be handed to you premade. You have to find the music by yourself and with your friends, learning standards on your own, hanging out together in the basement. You have to go through that laborious process together: you have to dive into the music and deal with the fact that you've got a passion for it. To skip over that process creates an imbalance, and an unjustified sense of entitlement.

Young musicians have to find their way on their own, in the company of their peers. It's the only way to develop those modes of behavior, those ways of playing together, that are deep in the music. If they don't come at it that way, they don't develop a sense of allegiance among themselves. And they don't develop an understanding of the real lessons at the foundation of the music.

Or to put it simply: they haven't been fired enough.

———

At Columbia College I ended up working as music director for
a number of shows, including a production of *The Threepenny
Opera*. Ronnie Davis, the founder of the San Francisco Mime
Troupe, who espoused a confrontational, politicized version of
commedia dell'arte he called "guerrilla theater," directed the
theater arts program at Columbia College for a couple of years
in the 1970s, and I composed the music for his production of
Fanshen, based on William Hinton's 1966 book chronicling the
impact of the land-reform program of the Chinese Communist
Party on a small village.

But my most sustained collaboration was with the choreographer Shirley Mordine, who started the Dance Center of
Columbia College in 1969 and directed it for the next thirty
years. Her dance troupe performed in a renovated movie house
at 4730 North Sheridan Road, and I ended up playing accompaniment for technique classes as well as performing music for a
number of shows. I also regularly went with them on tour in cities around the Midwest. At one point the company performed a
piece choreographed by Merce Cunningham and I did the music
for it, which was an interesting experience because his dances
were not set to any particular score. When he worked with John
Cage or David Tudor, they would famously develop the dance
and music separately, and only bring it together for the performance. Cunningham came through Chicago to teach them the
choreography and I got to play music for his classes.

I met the dancer Kim On Wong either through one of Shirley's dancers or through Jarman (who had done the music for
Wong's December 1968 production of *The Tibetan Book of the
Dead*). Kim On Wong was a charismatic performer who had
studied multiple Asian dance forms: born in southwest China
near the Tibetan border, he was taken to India as a child to
train, before spending time doing Kabuki in Japan and then
studying under the legendary Balinese dancer I Ketut Mario. In
the 1960s he did shows at the University of Chicago and the Field

Museum and offered workshops in Asian dance on the South Side.

I worked with Kim on a show called *Earth, Air, Fire.* I used four or five musicians, including the violinist Jason Kao Hwang. The catch with Kim On Wong was that if you wanted to play with him, you were required to take his Balinese dance classes. Three times a week—it was rough! When you see Balinese dance on stage, it looks refined and hyper-stylized: all these minute hand gestures and tilted heads. But it was a serious physical challenge, staying bent down in plié and trilling your two middle fingers. You had to hold your head still and flit just your eyes back and forth in rhythm. We weren't in any sort of shape for that. I'd get out of the studio with aches in weird places from my calves to my eyeballs. At least one of my musicians ended up quitting. "I can play the music, Henry," he told me, "but I can't take any more of these dance classes!"

The advantage of getting a foothold in the North Side theater and dance scene was that I didn't have to worry about trying to get straight-ahead jazz jobs, which was the main thing available in the conventional nightclub world. Most of those guys didn't want to hire me anyway, because they knew I wasn't going to play the same old bebop licks. In the end, being forced to cobble together a living on my own was an advantage, because it expanded my horizons. I couldn't just sit there and stagnate in the same old cloistered world playing the same old standards.

Being rejected is the best thing that can happen to you—as long as you know how to think laterally. When people shut one door in your face it can help you see that there are plenty of other doors. I ended up getting a much broader and deeper musical education. Admittedly it took longer than it might have otherwise, if I'd slipped right onto the straight-ahead career path. I got shut out and forced into a bigger world that it took much more time to explore.

I got all kinds of pickup work and I learned something from

all of it, from every little corner of the performing-arts world I got the chance to see. The AACM tenor player Vandy Harris hired me to transcribe hit R&B records on the Brunswick label to make lead sheets. Vandy had served in the war, too, and for a while when he came back he was afflicted with a bad case of jungle rot on his hands that made it impossible for him to play. While he was recovering, I replaced him a few times in the band of Brother Jack McDuff, the great organist.

Around 1969 I also got a regular job in the backup band of the Dells, the vocal quintet that was one of the biggest pop groups of the era. Lester Bowie's brother Byron was in Chicago at the time, working as a music director for a number of R&B and soul acts around the city, and he got me into the band. Jimmy Ellis was the other alto player. We played package dates with the Dells with groups like the Main Ingredient, the Isley Brothers, the Chi-Lites, and the Stylistics at the largest clubs around town, places like the High Chaparral and the Peppermint Lounge. We also toured around most of the major cities in the Midwest, from Missouri to Michigan.

Then there were the one-off gigs. I played with Latin bands and polka bands up on the Northwest Side of Chicago. Dances, parties, small neighborhoods bars and clubs. The different kinds of work forced me to keep up my chops on my other instruments. With polka, I exclusively played clarinet. But the Latin bands wanted me on tenor and sometimes baritone. Never alto. I hadn't gone back to tenor in the AACM context yet, but the Latin gigs forced me to pick up that horn for the first time since I laid it aside in the Church of God. Those bands were brassy trombone-heavy outfits designed to get people moving.

The funny thing was, they didn't hire me to play the charts. The Latin bands only used me as a featured guest soloist. I used to beg them to let me do more, because some of the arrangements were intricate. "Oh, no, Henry, you don't need to worry about that. We've got enough guys in the horn section. We just want you to blow."

———

Along with Latin and polka bands, the other sporadic gigs I used
to support myself with were parades. In fact, I played parades
longer than anything else, all the way up to the point when I left
Chicago. I started getting my first paid parade jobs with veteran
organizations that had bands back around my junior year in
high school. The first time, my old friend Milton Chapman and I
went down to audition together. We were just looking for opportunities to play, but it was nice to get paid. They were groups
like the VFW (the Veterans of Foreign Wars), the Elks, and the
Shriners. Some of the marching bands were similar in style to the
sort of marching band you might hear in New Orleans, playing
classics like "St. James Infirmary," "Tiger Rag," and "Didn't He
Ramble." Others were closer to military bands, doing things like
Sousa marches. And there were a few others that had their own
books of arrangements. There were quite a few of them on the
South Side.

Cedric Gay, my teacher at Governors State, also worked as
a contractor for parade bands, and he regularly hired me and
other friends: Milton, Don Myrick, Louis Satterfield, Sonny
Seals. I mostly played clarinet for these marching-band parades,
but occasionally Mr. Gay would hire me to play tenor. You could
make good money playing parades, as much as sixty-five to sev-
enty dollars a gig. I could play a couple of them and have enough
to cover my rent and expenses for the month. They ran all spring
and summer, culminating in the second Saturday in August with
the annual Bud Billiken Parade and Picnic, the oldest African
American parade in the country. I enjoyed it, too. A lot of the
arrangements were challenging, and there was sometimes space
for improvisation: we had the scores they gave us, but we had
to come up with riffs and other things. Another challenge was
that you had to learn how to walk while you were playing. You'd
have the score on a lyre attached to your horn, and you'd have to
be able to read the music without clipping the heels of the guy in
front of you.

There were some fantastic musicians in these groups. When Milton and I first started, most of the guys were much older than we were, of course. We must have made a motley crew, two teenagers marching next to seventy-year-old veterans, all of us in matching uniforms and wearing a Shriners fez.

For some of the senior guys, stamina was an issue in more than one sense on those long marches in the hot summer sun. Some of them used rubber bladders so they could pee if they needed to. They'd attach the bladders to their johnsons like a condom, except that the bladder was hooked up to a tube that ran down the inside of their pant leg and under their spats. "Get over here, boy," one of them would bark at me or Milton as we were all dressing before the parade, and we'd tape the end of the tube under the guy's shoe. It was an efficient system: they could relieve themselves as they walked without missing a step. The urine would trickle out from their shoes, and the only ones who would notice would be the guys marching right behind them in the formation.

I learned a lot just from being in these different environments, seeing how the musicians handled themselves, seeing their interaction with the crowds. The whole aesthetic. How something is delivered. How the human voice is viewed in a given type of music: is the voice just a pretty-sounding thing, or is its role to convey a message, or does it contribute to the musical texture just as much as the horns or the piano or the drums? In some kinds of music, the trombone or the clarinet might have more to say than the singer—the instrument might have much more content to communicate than the voice. Does the vocal melody serve to convey some sense of uplift, or is it secondary to some other effect? In the blues, for example, melody isn't there to take you higher, to give you that sense of weightlessness. On the contrary: when Howlin' Wolf sings "I'm a tail dragger / I wipe out my track," he's not striving for melodic transport.

We don't always appreciate the depth of knowledge possessed by some so-called popular performers. Otis Redding was one of my great heroes. People just think of him as a singer, but he was an incredible arranger, too. He really knew how to put a horn section together. I was watching a fundraiser on public television and they showed some footage of Marvin Gaye sitting at the piano playing something by Duke Ellington from memory. This wasn't a concert: this was informal backstage footage or maybe a sound check. Even in this off-the-cuff moment, you could see that Marvin had imbibed the tradition: he had the touch, he knew the voicings. A lot of these so-called pop stars have a lot more information than we generally give them credit for. And that information is what I picked up on when I played in these other kinds of groups.

None of this is digested whole. But it all goes in. Some people might have a tendency to forget the full variety of their experience—to dismiss all the stuff that was supposedly irrelevant, the gigs you do to pay the bills. I hold on to all of it. I don't ever reproduce any particular influence in a straightforward manner. What would be the point of that? Still, I keep going back to the traces, and they get woven into my music. I wouldn't even describe it as a deliberate process: it's something subtler, something beyond or behind my control.

It's like those distant memories of my great-grandfather. It was a long time ago, and I was just a child. But it feels like I have his name branded into my mind somewhere so I won't ever forget what I learned from him—so the love I got from him won't fade. No tune I've ever written is "about" him. And yet he's there in it. It's not an overt thing; the music won't tell you he's there or conjure his image. But sometimes I'm working on a composition and I sense his presence.

Around the spring of 1970 things between me and Catherine Slade started to become serious. I moved into her place at 48th and Drexel, and later that year we decided to get married. Cathy and I also started working together. By early 1970 some of the

AACM expatriates had started to return from Europe. Leroy Jenkins, Wadada Leo Smith, and Braxton were the first to return, with the Art Ensemble following that summer. Wadada and I started collaborating with another AACM member, the trombonist, bassist, and cellist Lester Lashley, who had played on seminal early sessions like Roscoe Mitchell's *Sound* and Jarman's *As If It Were the Seasons*. Lester also had an MFA in visual art from the School of the Art Institute of Chicago and was a talented painter and printmaker. We called the group Integral, and it also included Cathy and Lester's soon-to-be wife, Marilyn.

Cathy was an actress and Marilyn was a dancer, so they brought those disciplines into the mix. But our idea was to do something thoroughly multimedia. So Wadada, Lester, and I would play, but we also sometimes recited poetry or got entangled in theatrical skits. Sometimes I would bring cassette tapes of things I'd recorded off the radio, and we would loop them and play them in our shows. I remember one show where I had John Stubblefield up on stage as a ghost on a throne in church, wearing this white sheet, sitting there in enigmatic silence as a chorus intoned a litany around him. We'd read about the "happenings" that were going on in New York, and we thought of some of our performances as similar sorts of semiscripted events and political interventions. If we were getting so involved in providing the music for those troupes on the North Side, Wadada and I decided, we might as well do a little experimental theater of our own.

One day that autumn, I drove into an epiphany on the Dan Ryan Expressway. The elevated highway passes by the Maxwell Street Market, where I used to go as a child with my grandfather. I glanced over as I went by, and there was a brilliant glare coming off something metallic in one of the stalls along the sidewalk. The sun was hitting the metal at just the right angle and the reflection was lighting up a whole patch of the expressway. It was blinding—I had to turn my eyes back to the road. I could see that it was coming from across the street from Leavitt's Delicatessen near the corner of Maxwell and South Halsted, but I couldn't tell what was giving off that light.

I pulled my big blue Chevy off the expressway at the next exit to check it out. After parking the car, I waded into the throng on Maxwell. When I got close to Halsted I could see what was reflecting the sunlight, across the street from the deli: a large display of hubcaps, laid out in rows and layers on top of cardboard boxes on a bunch of tables in the market.

For some of us it takes a road-to-Damascus moment to appreciate the aesthetic qualities of the everyday industrial objects that surround us. I liked cars, but I'd never really thought much about hubcaps until that light hit me. I found myself standing there mesmerized by the beauty of fourteen-inch discs of stamped steel coated with chrome. And suddenly, with dozens of them gleaming there in front of me, I noticed the variety: the Chevy Impala cap with the characteristic checkered racing flag emblem and the eight perforations around the rim; the angled fan blades around the flat central circle of a Ford Thunderbird; a Mercury with its concentric rims gravitating out from the trademark crest; the luminescent greenish-golden spokes fanning out from the shields at the middle of a Buick LeSabre; or the stately pyramid-like steppes of a Cadillac Coupe DeVille. Some of them were almost floral, others domed and austere, and others with bulbous nipples protruding from their cores.

Reaching across the table for one, I inadvertently knocked a couple off the table and they clattered on the asphalt. I was struck by the sound. Hubcaps have a beautiful indistinct pitch. And they all sound a little different. I was so taken with the noise the first couple made that I deliberately pushed another off the table, just to hear it. I realized that the tone and timbre varied depending on the hubcap's size and shape.

The guy selling them gave me a quizzical look. But when he saw me start to gather a pile, he chose to overlook my clumsiness.

The ones I liked the best seemed to come from classic cars from the 1950s and 1960s: the heyday of American industrial

workmanship. You could hear the quality: back then, facto-
ries in this country made everything in tune. Picking through
the boxes, pinging hubcaps to test the pitches, I started to get
excited: I'd found a readymade gong set, right off the Detroit
assembly line!

Ever since I'd been in Pleiku, I had been searching for some
approximation of the Montagnard gongs. It wasn't going to be
an exact match, because in Asia—whether in Vietnam, or with
the kulintang ensembles in the Philippines, or the Indonesian
gamelans—the gongs were hand-cast out of bronze and carefully tuned as a unit. I couldn't replicate that craft. But I was
looking for something like that sound. I tried some other stuff;
I remember I fooled around with license plates at one point, but
they didn't have enough resonance, and there wasn't enough dif-
ferentiation among the pitches. As soon as I stumbled across the
hubcaps, though, I was confident I could make them work.

My hubcap mongering may seem idiosyncratic, but in the
context of the AACM at the end of the 1960s it didn't really
stand out at all. Almost all of us were fascinated with unusual
timbres and with the sonic potential of what we started to call
"little instruments," which could include almost anything, from
a variety of instruments from around the world (finger cymbals, zurna, conch, conga drum, kelp horn, balafon, zither,
angklung), to sound-making devices not usually privileged for
their aesthetic potential (whistles, sirens, bicycle horns, Swiss
cowbells, door chimes), to various invented instruments. Soon
after they formed the Art Ensemble of Chicago, Joseph Jarman,
Roscoe Mitchell, Lester Bowie, Malachi Favors, and Don Moye
started incorporating an entire forest of instrumental options
in their concert performances. Wadada Leo Smith, Anthony
Braxton, Leroy Jenkins, Douglas Ewart—we were all the same
way, always on the lookout for timbral potential. The epitome of
this compulsion might have come in 1978 with Roscoe's record

The Maze, which featured an octet of us playing his carefully arranged "sound collages" on dozens of little percussion instruments. On that session, across the room from my hubkaphone and Jarman's rack of small cymbals and temple gongs, Braxton set up a contrivance he called a "garbage can machine."

Even as we all strove to reach a level of virtuosity on the instruments we had studied, we were also determined to expand or even to destroy the narrow conservatory conception of technical mastery. Something new and unexpected could happen when you had to figure out a way to get sound out of an instrument you weren't familiar with—or out of an object that wasn't even an "instrument" in the conventional sense. The point wasn't that technique was taken out of the equation: on the contrary, you *could* become a virtuoso on cowbells or door chimes—or hubcaps—if you took the time to figure out what they could do. But technique wasn't something codified, something you could get at the conservatory. You might have to come up with an entirely different way to practice. Beyond that, we thought of ourselves as composers as much as players, and as composers we wanted the broadest potential palette we could find.

It took me some trial and error to invent the hubkaphone out of that epiphany at the Maxwell Street Market. I realized right away that the hubcaps couldn't just be laid out on a table or held like a tambourine: they needed to be hung or suspended somehow, like the ride cymbal in a drum kit, so they could resonate. I went to the hardware store and ordered pipes cut to build a rack. If you bought the materials from them, they'd custom cut the pipes to your specifications.

"I need two three-foot lengths of one-inch pipe that I can stand up vertically with a one-foot horizontal piece attached with a tee joint at the top and another one foot down," I told them. I got to the point where I could sling around the lingo like a plumber. "The top horizontal bar should stick out one way,

Playing the hubkaphone for a
performance at Roberta Garrison's dance
studio on Crosby Street in New York in the
late 1970s. Photo © Jacki Ochs

and the lower horizontal in the opposite direction. Put caps on all the open ends. And then I want to attach the two verticals with a crossbar halfway up."

I wasn't sure how to make legs or feet for the armature. One day I was in my grandmother's basement putting clothes into the washing machine, and I noticed that there was a small sewer plate in the floor. She would let the water out and it would go down the drain. I knelt down and poked at the plate. It was flat and heavy. It occurred to me that it might be able to serve as a base. I went back to the hardware store and asked them to screw the vertical pipes into sewer plates. It worked: it was stable, but I knew I didn't want it to be too snug—there needed to be a little give so that the hubcaps could really vibrate when I hit them.

I strung two nylon cords between the two top horizontal pipe lengths, and two more between the lower pipe lengths. Then I attached the hubcaps lying flat in rows along the cords, four across the top and four across the bottom. I realized that if I had the horizontal pipes stick out in opposite directions from the vertical stand, it created distance between the two levels, almost like the graduated terraces of organ manuals. It set the lower row of hubcaps closer to me and the upper row farther away from me, making it easier to play across the two levels.

I spent hours testing out various hubcaps, noting down their pitches and designing modes. Many of the caps had more than one pitch, just like a drumhead or a cymbal: you'd get one pitch if you struck the edge and others if you struck a ridge, or the knob in the middle. I didn't worry about trying to follow scales or classical modes. The whole point of inventing a metallophone wasn't to replicate the Lydian mode. Instead I made up my own combinations of pitches. Of course, I could change the array if I wanted to—switch out one hubcap for another in order to get a different sequence. I hung a few small gongs on strings from each side of the hubkaphone, and I had a huge set of sounds to work with. My own microtonal arsenal.

————

I had missed the boat on the AACM exodus to Paris in the late 1960s. It seemed as if everybody was leaving just as I got back to Chicago from the war. I wasn't ready to head off to Europe right when I returned from Asia. But in the back of my mind I was thinking that I'd like to travel at some point. An exploratory urge was a key part of the AACM mindset, too: there was an expectation in the air that it was important to cultivate a curiosity about other cultures, other musical traditions. Around the end of 1970, after Wadada and I been working together in Integral for a while, we started to talk about taking our act to Europe. Paris is over, we said to ourselves. We should try something different.

One of the North Side theater troupes I'd been working with asked me to do the music for a show they were doing in London in early 1971. It seemed like the perfect opportunity. Once I had finished the gig in London, Wadada and I decided, we would meet up in Amsterdam to test the waters there.

While I was in London, I took some time to try to get a sense of the scene there. One day I was wandering around and I happened upon the office of some African newspaper or magazine. I went in, hoping to get some information about what was going on culturally. On the office wall there was a stunning painting: a large impressionistic canvas with vibrant colors swirling through it. I asked one of the guys working there who had painted it. "That's by Jan Telting," he said, "the famous Dutch painter. He's Black; he grew up in Suriname." I told him that I was on my way to Amsterdam and he suggested that I look up Telting while I was there. He gave me the painter's phone number.

I already had a contact in the Netherlands. Wadada had the number for some Dutch musician who had said we could stay with him. But when I left London and made my way over to Amsterdam, the guy changed his mind. I think he was fearful that we were going to storm in and take over the scene there. He wouldn't even let me stay over for one night. It was unbelievable: he met me at Amsterdam Centraal Station just to tell me I couldn't come to his place. He ditched me right there.

Well, if this isn't an auspicious start to my Dutch sojourn, I thought. I didn't want to go to a hotel if I could avoid it. I was right there on the Singel in the middle of the city. But I had no idea what to do.

I remembered that I had the painter's number and decided that I might as well give it a shot. I called Jan Telting and when he answered, I heard a Charlie Parker tune playing in the background. I took that to be a good omen. I explained who I was and what had happened. We hit it off immediately. In perfect English, Telting told me he'd spent time in New York and knew a lot of jazz musicians. He had worked in a record shop downtown— for a while he'd even worked at Slugs'! "Come over to my place," he told me. "We'll figure something out."

I had no sense of the city, so he told me to get a taxi and give the driver his address. "It'll be a schoolhouse," he added.

When I arrived at his building, I found his name on the list at the entrance and he buzzed me in. It was a former school that had been converted into artists' studios. I didn't know where to go, so I just went into the building to see if I could find his place. It was a big building and there were a lot of people working there; in every room there seemed to be someone sculpting, welding, painting—the whole place was buzzing with activity. It was loud, but I as I entered the stairwell I heard Charlie Parker again and I figured that I had to be going in the right direction. I followed the sound of Bird up to Telting's studio.

He opened the door and greeted me as though I were a friend from the neighborhood he was used to seeing every day. He welcomed me in and told me to put my instruments down and made me some tea. I told him that Wadada was coming and that we needed to find a place to stay. "It'll be fine," he reassured me. "Look, my apartment is too small for guests, but you all can stay here in the studio." There were a couple of beds, a hot plate, basic supplies. The toilet was down the hall, and we had to heat up water to bathe. But it was fine—better than fine: right in the middle of an art scene teeming with energy.

Quintus Jan Telting was about fifteen years older than I was.

He left Suriname at the age of sixteen as a stowaway and ended up serving in the merchant marine for a decade. After taking up the trumpet and studying painting in the Netherlands, in the late 1950s he moved to New York and became close to musicians including Sonny Rollins, Kenny Dorham, Art Blakey, Milford Graves, and John Tchicai. Apparently it was Telting who came up with the name of the New York Art Quartet, the pivotal avant-garde group formed by Graves, Tchicai, Roswell Rudd, and Lewis Worrell. (Tchicai wrote a tune called "Quintus T.")

Amsterdam was a lively scene. All kinds of artists and intellectuals would stop by Telting's studio: painters, sculptors, writers, musicians, philosophers, dancers. Almost every day, Telting would meet a group of friends in a terrace café in Leidseplein square, on the south side of the central ring of the city. He went there for lunch.

When he left me in his studio that first day, he told me to meet him in a particular café in Leidseplein the next morning. "But I don't know how to get there," I said.

"Don't worry, you'll find it." He led me over to the window and pointed. "You see that canal?" I nodded doubtfully. "Just follow that canal. It'll take you right to the square."

Oh, man, I thought. I just got here, I don't speak Dutch, and this guy is sending me out on my own. On the other hand, he clearly trusted me enough to give me the key to his studio with all his artwork in it a few minutes after he'd met me. I had to trust him. And he was right. The next day it turned out to be a straight shot to the Leidseplein and I found him easily.

There was a group that would congregate there and hang out for hours in the afternoon. Telting introduced me to the others: a talented Vietnamese painter, a sculptor named De Fries, a bunch of modern dancers. I also met the poet Dobru (Robin Raveles), also from Suriname, an imposing brother with a booming bass-baritone voice like Paul Robeson's. The group would have intense philosophical debates about art. Sometimes the whole entourage would head back to Jan's studio and continue the discussion there. It was frustrating not being able to

Practicing the clarinet in Amsterdam.
Photo © Leonard Jones

understand very much Dutch, but I'd catch a few snippets of the conversation, and occasionally they'd switch into English. Sometimes Telting would translate something from Dutch for me so I'd know what was going on. I strained to follow as much of it as I could. I got completely immersed in their intense arguments about aesthetics: what was permissible, what was valuable in art—how art could make a difference in the world. It was the first time I'd been around a group that was primarily visual artists talking about aesthetics. Telting even ended up painting a portrait of me.

Often they would meet at one of the oldest bars in Amsterdam, a place that dated back to the late sixteenth or early seventeenth century where the wooden tables were stained with tobacco from generations of sailors. Everybody seemed to be smoking enormous quantities of hashish. They would pull out these bricks of hash, almost the size of cinder blocks. The guys from Suriname were especially ostentatious about it, blowing prodigious puffs of smoke. Oddly, there seemed to be some unspoken rule that the Black guys could smoke wherever they wanted to. When the police strolled by, it was the white guys who would scurry inside, because according to the law you weren't supposed to smoke in public. But the authorities never hassled the Black guys. It was amusing to observe. I'm not in Kansas anymore, I thought.

When Wadada arrived, we moved out of Telting's studio because there wasn't enough room. Jan knew somebody who owned a houseboat on the canal around the corner. So we stayed there. It was moored in front of a fabulous bathhouse, too. It struck me as a brilliant system: you paid the equivalent of about fifty cents and got full access to the locker room, the showers, the sauna. Coming from Chicago, it seemed like an almost unfathomable luxury.

The year before, the AACM bassist Leonard Jones had moved to Hamburg. We got in touch with him and asked him to come over and join us in Amsterdam. Wadada and I went to meet Leonard in Hamburg and hung out with him there for a

My photo of Leonard Jones on bass in the foreground and Wadada Leo Smith in another room in the background as we practiced in the houseboat in Amsterdam

few days before making our way back to Holland. In Amsterdam, Leonard moved into the houseboat with me and Wadada.
We hooked up with a couple of dancers we met through Telting,
too, and that way we reconvened Integral in a new form and did
a number of performances around the city. Our first concert was
at the Paradiso. After a few weeks we bought a cheap used Ford
van and cobbled together some gigs elsewhere in Amsterdam,
eventually venturing to Munich for a little while as well.

Integral never got the chance to record, but getting back into
creating music and the multimedia happenings was crucial for
me. During my brief but focused period with Wadada in Europe,
I really started to figure out what I wanted to accomplish as a
composer and player.

Practicing on the houseboat was an unexpected challenge.
There weren't really waves on the canal, but the boat would rock
back and forth a little bit and that made it hard to play. If the
three of us stood on one side, it would tilt that way. Eventually
we figured out that the best solution was to distribute ourselves
evenly across the cabins so that our body weight would keep
things more or less steady. The houseboat didn't have a single,
open cabin: instead it was a warren of interconnected chambers.
To balance the boat we had to play in separate rooms. We put a
mirror on the wall at one end so we could all see each other as
we played. As we rehearsed, we would time our downbeats to
the rocking of the boat.

I brought my hubkaphone with me to Amsterdam, along with
all my horns and flute. At that point I had designed the instrument but I hadn't figured out a way to play it. It was in the Netherlands that I developed my technique.

Telting had a platform on wheels in his studio. It was sort of
like a moving dolly: a wide, flat wooden platform on four swivel
casters. On the platform was a vertical board, and he could
attach a canvas on either side. So he could be working on one
painting on one side and another on the other side.

The windows in the old schoolhouse were huge, and the light in Holland is very unusual light. There must have been six or eight big windows in the studio and throughout the day Jan would move the platform with the light. Having the movable platform allowed him to change the natural lighting as he worked.

The way he painted was amazing to watch. Jan would start by putting the platform in one spot. He'd stand there next to it with a handful of brushes, looking at his work. All of a sudden he would start to move: he pushed the dolly into motion across the room. He would jog along with it and then leap onto the platform himself and ride it as it moved. And as he glided across the studio he would paint. It was like he was dancing on a moving stage.

While I was staying with Jan before we moved to the houseboat, I would watch him from the bed where I was sleeping on one side of the studio. The thing that mesmerized me was the sound of the brushes. Jan used all these different techniques, swirling and flicking the brushes with these flourishes of his wrist. The first time it happened, I heard him before I saw him, and I thought, What is that sound? It was the wheels running on the floor and then the swish of his brushes as he went at the canvas.

His initial jump onto the platform would set it in motion. And then he would change the angles as it moved: push it back in the other direction, grab the frame to slow it down or stop it. He would jump off and reposition the platform to get the light he wanted. And then he'd strike the surface again with another kind of stroke.

It was the sound of his brushes and his constant movement, his way of shifting the angles, that inspired me in terms of approaching the hubkaphone. Up to that point I had been thinking about it like somebody playing a marimba or the vibraphone: the posture is basically static, and the player's hands move the mallets across the tone bars that are laid out in the arrangement of the chromatic scale of a piano keyboard. See-

The hubkaphone in Jan Telting's studio in Amsterdam

ing Telting, I started practicing steps. I could move from left to right, from right to left. I could accelerate and dip and hop. I also started designing combinations of strokes: not only charting the unusual combinations of pitches I could get on various hubcaps, but also planning out different ways to hit them—dab, slap, swipe, scrape, jab, whisk, tap, smear. Taking full advantage of the instrument, I realized, wasn't just a matter of scoring its unique modes. I also had to choreograph the way I would move as I played.

Cathy was pregnant when I went to London for the show and then to Amsterdam with Wadada. I ended up staying in Holland longer than I'd originally planned. In fact, I didn't get back to Chicago until shortly before Cathy was scheduled to give birth. I was having so much fun that I lost track of time, or at least that's what I told myself in the moment—looking back now, I'm sure that my trepidation about becoming a father had something to do with my tail-dragging. Parenthood was a real leap into the unknown, and I wasn't sure I was ready for the responsibility.

Our son Melin was born in April 1971. A couple of weeks before the arrival—in that interregnum of nervous anticipation and the odd sort of fatalism experienced by every expectant parent—Cathy and I went out for a midday walk in the neighborhood. We set off down toward Hyde Park and the University of Chicago campus, which was about ten blocks south from where we lived in Kenwood.

I was feeling good that day—I don't remember why. Those are the best days, when you feel good and you don't even have a reason. Anticipation, maybe. Or pride, despite my anxiety about fatherhood. The weather was gorgeous and I was strolling around the neighborhood with my beautiful and very pregnant wife. I had felt an impulse to dress up a little, as though we were some Victorian couple out for a promenade, and I felt sharp as I escorted her down the block.

These teenagers came up behind us and started harassing

us. Talking smart. It was just low-grade adolescent belliger-
ence. Maybe we stood out because we looked so happy. Maybe
that pissed them off. The ingenuous glow of our contentedness
exposed their sorry, monochrome existence. In other words, their
hostility was a form of self-hate: the mentality of the colonized.

Cathy and I just kept walking and ignored their jeers.

But then one of the kids pulled out a pistol and held it up
to our heads. "Oh, yeah, homeboy, you still think you such hot
stuff now?"

We froze. My wife looked at me as if to say, Henry, don't give
them no problems. They're kids. Let's just get through this and
get back home.

I just stared him down, putting myself between him and
Cathy. The other teenagers knew their friend had taken it too
far. "You oughta cool out, man," one of them said. "Put that
thing away." We were in a standoff for what must have been no
more than a few seconds, but it felt like an eternity.

Finally the kid lowered the pistol, snickering like it had been
an innocent gag. "What, you thought I was gonna shoot them
or something?" The other teenagers seemed impressed by his
audacity. The group sauntered off unceremoniously down the
sidewalk and left us standing there.

"It's over, Henry." Cathy took my arm. "Let's just go home."
When she touched me, I realized how tense I'd been. I was rigid,
coiled. After a few seconds, I relented and we started to make
our way back in silence. The mood was spoiled; there was nothing to say.

I was struggling as we walked home, trying not to let Cathy
see how angry I was. But inside I was seething. I've never felt so
bad in my heart. You pull a gun on my pregnant wife? For kicks?
Are you kidding me?

In my head I went through an exhaustive fantasy of what I
would have done. I would have found them. I would have hunted
them down, and they would not have enjoyed what would have
happened.

I would have taken my time. I would have been thorough. I

would have tracked each and every one of those maggots back to his house. I would have camped out in the sewer and surveilled them for weeks until I knew everything about them. Who they lived with. What time they woke up. What they ate for breakfast. Where the gas lines ran in, what corner of the basement the furnace was in.

I would have been methodical. Just to sneak up and kill them would have been too easy, too quick. I would have taken out all their friends and family first. Blown up their houses. One by one. Not all at once, but sequentially. I would have made their suffering last a long time. It would have been an extended campaign of terror beyond anything they could have imagined in their worst nightmares. I would have prolonged it, so they could see it coming on and feel just as helpless as I had.

When I would have finally shown myself, to make sure that thug with the gun understood who did this and why it happened, he would have been sputtering with fear, begging me to take him out of his misery. No, motherfucker. I'm not done with you yet. You had no right to do that to me. I didn't do a damn thing to you.

No, I wasn't going to lose it.

But if I ever did lose it—if I made the *choice* to lose it—it wouldn't be quick and simple. I wouldn't just scream and flail around and lash out. It would be systematic. The truth is, the terror is the only thing that's going to change people. It's unfortunate, but it's the only thing that works. If I were going to lose it, I would go all the way. If I were going out, I would set the whole thing on fire.

We brought this back from the war, too. This propensity for violence. We realized we were capable of killing somebody, given the right circumstances. We didn't always know what might trigger it, what might set off our temper all of a sudden. We came back with the knowledge that it could slip out of our control. It was always simmering inside. We repressed it, of course—there was no one to talk to, anyway. But we carried that knowledge and it affected us. It changed our behavior, knowing

that there was something hot under our skin that might erupt at any moment. Even on the days when we almost forgot we'd been in the war, even when things seemed idyllic. Even when we thought we weren't being affected by it, we were.

Toward the end of July 1971, I go to see Duke Ellington with his orchestra. This is at the High Chaparral, the big ballroom where I perform with the Dells, near 77th Street and Stony Island on the South Shore. There are hundreds of people in the crowd, and it's a lavish affair. I know my way around the place, so I slip backstage during the intermission. I'm hoping to be able to say something to him—just to introduce myself and tell him how much I appreciate his music. But I go back there and there are all these people swarming around him, all these men in tuxedos and high-society women in gowns with diamond brooches.

Ellington is holding court as only he can, talking to two or three fans at the same time. "Oh, yes, my dear, it's been so long—when was the last time, in Paris? . . . And how is Horace doing these days? Is he still thriving in Antibes? . . . You enjoyed *The Goutelas Suite*? Yes, Mr. Gonsalves is indeed in fine form this evening. I'm so deeply honored that you appreciated our efforts. . . ."

I stand there for a minute watching him work the crowd. I can't get within ten feet of him. Oh, well, I think. I get it. He's surrounded by money. It's obvious that I'm not supposed to be in the middle of this scrum.

All these refined people in their fancy clothes are brazenly shoving each other as they try to get in a word with the great man. The crowd ebbs and flows and then the current shifts and I find myself propelled a little closer to him.

I don't even realize that he's noticed me. But all of a sudden he reaches out and grabs me and pulls me next to him. He's got his arm tightly around my waist, like he's about to pull me onto the dance floor for a waltz. I think, What the hell is this? But he's got me, and he's still talking to all of these people, he doesn't actually miss a beat in the multiple simultaneous conversations he's having. He doesn't look at me, he just keeps chatting in that debonair way he has. "Ah, yes, the weather in Newport was lovely, we just played there two weeks ago . . ."

Finally he looks over at me, still clutching me close by the waist. I lean back away from him, stunned by his attention and a little petrified at the same time.

"So," he says, "what do *we* do?"

Just like that. I gape at him, astonished by his deployment of the royal "we." I have no idea how to introduce myself. Ellington looks back away and continues a conversation with someone else in the crowd.

The only thing I know immediately is that I'm not going to tell him I'm a composer. I'm certainly not going to say that. So when he turns back to me, I say, "Um, I play woodwinds."

My answer only serves to annoy him. "I know *that*," he says. I think to myself, How could you possibly know that I play saxophone?

He looks me in the eye. "And what else?" And then he looks away again, still talking to people around us, still holding me close.

After a few more exchanges he turns back to me. He's waiting for an answer and I'm in his clutches. So I confess, "Well, I write music sometimes."

"Oh!" Ellington exclaims with mock surprise, hugging me tighter. "We write *music* sometimes, do we?"

I don't know what to say now.

He's got me and he's talking, and he's moving and dragging me with him, and the crowd is pressing in around us. Somehow he maneuvers us toward his dressing-room door. He's still smooth-talking the aristocrats. Then in a single motion he enters the dressing room and pulls me inside with him. The door closes and we're alone.

Duke always has a piano in his dressing room when he's on the road. As we spin in through the door, he's pulling me backward into the room, and before I even realize what's happening he turns me around and sits me down at the piano. Finally he releases his grip on my waist and takes a step back to sit down on a couch behind me. Ellington leisurely pulls out a cigarillo and lights it and looks hard at me.

"So. Let's hear some of our music, shall we?"

I'm sitting there looking over my shoulder at him, wondering how he flipped me down in front of the piano.

I'm so starstruck that I couldn't play a C-major scale to save my life. I'm paralyzed. It does occur to me to play him something I'd been working on recently, a piece called "Melin," after my son. But I can't even lift my hands up to the keyboard.

Duke cracks up. But I can tell he's not making fun of me. He gets it. He can see that I'm nervous because of who he is. He stands up from the couch and puts his hand on my shoulder. "I know," he says, smiling. "I understand. You can stay, right?"

Of course I'm planning to stay for the second half of the show.

"Yeah, I'm staying."

"Let's go back out," he says. "It's time."

He takes me out and gets me a spot where I can watch the band from the wings. And when he gets ready to hit, he looks over to see if I'm still there. I'm standing right to the side of Harry Carney—I place myself there deliberately to try to get a look at what he's doing on the baritone. Ellington looks over at me with a twinkle in his eye and then he counts off the band and they start up.

"We write music sometimes, do we?" I'm standing there, listening to them launch into the *Togo Brava Suite*, and it occurs to me that maybe it isn't such a bad thing that I froze. Maybe it's lucky I was starstruck. Look what happened to Billy Strayhorn: he was a beast, a genius, he was beyond category, and he got swept up into Ellington's world. What if Duke had made me an offer to work with him as an arranger? I have a feeling that if he had heard the music I was working on at that time, he might well have asked me. And I wouldn't have been able to say no.

I'm glad that didn't happen, I tell myself—I'm glad I didn't even have to run that risk. I love him madly, but I can't go work for Duke Ellington. I want to lead my own band and play my own music. I need to work for me.

I had started my studies at the American Conservatory in 1964 and resumed them soon after my return from Vietnam, having first enrolled in Governors State University. In the wake of the war and all the other disruptions along the way, it took me until 1973 that I finished my course of studies there and earned my BA degree in music, mainly focusing on composition.

Stella Roberts was my last teacher. Once I got to her, all my previous composition teachers basically didn't count. She was the only master pedagogue I encountered in my time there. I wouldn't have made it through the program without Gail Quillman, my piano teacher. If you major in composition, you might as well be majoring in piano. You had to play a constant diet of recitals. Quillman was the one who somehow got me to a point where I could give a performance of a Beethoven piano sonata. I know I didn't get through that on natural ability alone. So I'm eternally in her debt. But in terms of learning something new, something that shaped me, it started and ended with Stella Roberts.

By that point I had been engaged for some time in a thorough analysis of the European classical canon. And I was trying to figure out how to use all that information and to merge my own ideas with that. That was where I was. I was obliged to compromise, however, in terms of what I could turn in at the conservatory, because there were assumptions about what counted as "composition." Most of the faculty wouldn't have understood what I was trying to do anyway.

I certainly couldn't bring in anything that had had anything to do with improvisation. If you were paying any attention to contemporary music, it was obvious that such a prejudice was ludicrous. Plenty of composers (from Cage and Earle Brown to Xenakis and Varèse and Stockhausen) had been experimenting with "indeterminacy" in one way or another in their scores: leaving certain elements (duration, meter, pitch) unspecified, or experimenting with graphic scores rather than conventional notation, with the result that the music was unavoidably shaped by the performers' choices in the moment. But conservatories were notoriously behind the times. Of course their attitude also had to do with an idealistic understanding of the musical work of art as being crystallized in the mind of the composer and realized in the supposedly fixed form of the written score. And it was rooted in ideological and sometimes racist bias against other understandings of music, including many of the richest and most venerable traditions in the world.

My closest friend in the composition program was a Greek American composer named Chris Granias. We were like two peas in a pod. In the composition program, we were the black sheep, because we were both willing to push against those expectations a little bit. We'd sometimes do pieces together: duets for piano and flute that made space for certain kinds of improvisation. We were both comfortable improvising, so we composed pieces for each other and played them ourselves. We'd bring them to student recitals and it would provoke the usual half-veiled sneering. But we didn't care.

But for assignments, we had to follow the rules. Even in doing them, I pushed back in other ways. I would be assigned to compose a woodwind quintet. "Okay," I'd say, "but I'm not going to do it in the sonata form." Stella Roberts would support my little acts of rebellion. We discussed it; I explained my reasoning. "It's not relevant," I told her, "in terms of what I want to learn to do. You know I understand sonata form. There's no need for me to be chained to a harmonic system to do this assignment. Let me figure out my own way to do it."

She would usually relent. Stella Roberts didn't need to be convinced that I understood musical analysis and advanced harmony. I had the highest grades in the school. I even used to assist her with her classes for master's and doctoral students. She'd bring me to her graduate classes and then call on me to shame them. We might be looking at a Stravinsky score in class and she'd berate them: "Henry is in the bachelor's program. Why is it that he can analyze this passage and you seem unable to understand what's going on?" She'd point to a particular measure in the score and ask me to explain it. "Henry, please tell them what this is." The grad students would squirm silently as they listened to me break it down.

Stella Roberts never taught me anything. That's what was so fantastic about her. That's what made her great. She never taught me anything that I could recount or quantify.

Instead, she knew how to make you educate yourself. She knew how to give you the additional resources you might need to find answers on your own. But she wouldn't lead you there. She didn't really give me assignments in the sense of making me do perfunctory exercises for the sake of proving I could go through the steps. She just expected me to compose, and I'd bring in whatever piece I was working on.

I'd meet her in her office for the tutorial and hand her my score. She didn't make me try to play it on the piano—the point was the composition, not my facility as an interpreter. She would take the score and sit with it at the piano. But she wouldn't touch the keys. Her hands would float above the keyboard as she read through it. She could hear it in her head.

Sometimes her hands would stop at a spot in the score and she'd pause and look over at me, sitting there in a chair next to the piano bench. She wouldn't say anything. But if she stopped, I knew there was something wrong—something that didn't work. I could tell where she was by following her hands as they moved above the keys. And I'd make a mental note of where the problem spot was.

She never said anything discouraging. She wouldn't pronounce a verdict. She wouldn't say, "That was great up until measure nineteen" or "This isn't as good as what you brought in last week." Instead her comments were always oblique. After a while I understood that she was giving me hints about ways to repair or improve things without talking about it directly.

There were long silences. After sight-reading my score, she would walk over to the window and stand there for a while. I would watch her from behind: her hands clasped behind her back, her short gray hair. Finally she'd say, "Henry, have you read Archibald MacLeish's book *Land of the Free?*"

"I used to read his poetry in the library at the University of Chicago," I'd respond. "But I'm not sure I know that one."

"Look in that cabinet." She had a beautiful wooden cabinet with glass doors. The shelves were full of neatly arranged books. Her office was in the Fine Arts Building on Michigan Avenue across the street from Grant Park and the Art Institute of Chicago. You could see the lake out of her big bay windows. The décor was tasteful and refined; you felt like you'd been invited into an exclusive salon. "The second shelf down from the top. See it? Go ahead, take it out."

She'd lend the book to me and tell me to bring it back when I came for my next lesson. I'd take it home and study it. It never contained a direct answer or a technique I could simply adopt, but often the reading would provoke some insight about form or composition that I could figure out how to apply to what I was doing. I'd notice that the MacLeish book was a juxtaposition of poems and classic American photographs, and the way they were put next to each other suggested something about the way you could use different sorts of materials in tandem to imply a certain rhythm or pattern running through a work. She only gave me books on music a couple of times: once it was Vincent Persichetti's *Twentieth-Century Harmony*, another time a biography of a particular composer. Most of the time the references would be off to the side of what I was supposedly doing—a book about architecture, or something about modernist literature.

She never told me anything. And that's why I learned so much. I learned how to think for myself, how to search for what I needed. It was never about jumping through hoops to garner her approval. I kept working on my compositions, but it wasn't that I was expected to come back the next week having fixed whatever wasn't working. She didn't waste time on that. We just kept on moving.

Stella Roberts had studied in Paris with Nadia Boulanger, the legendary teacher who had been a mentor for dozens of composers, including Virgil Thomson, Elliott Carter, Aaron Copland, Astor Piazzolla, Philip Glass, Lalo Schifrin, and Quincy Jones. At one point she tried to convince me to follow in her footsteps and go to Paris to study with Boulanger. But I declined. I thought I was too old to be trying to learn French. These were highly advanced students working with her one-on-one or in small groups, and I assumed you had to know the language. On top of that, it struck me as redundant. "I'm honored that you think I might have the potential," I told Ms. Roberts. "But why do I need her, when I have you?"

I haven't played the hubkaphone in concert for years. It's not that I no longer appreciate the palette it provides. But it's gotten harder to keep up with the physical demands of playing the instrument, with all the choreography I developed.

The last time I used the hubkaphone for a production was in March 1994 at the Kaaitheater in Brussels, Belgium, for a show directed by Jan Ritsema called *Philoktetes Variations*. Featuring the American actor Ron Vawter (best known for his work with the Wooster Group) and Belgian performers Dirk Roofthooft and Viviane De Munck, it combined three different renditions of the story of Philoktetes, adapted from Sophocles' late play. During the journey to Troy, the Greek general Philoktetes, a renowned archer who was bequeathed the magic bow and arrows of Heracles, is bitten on his foot by a snake. Unable to bear the sound of his moans and the stench of the festering wound, his compatriots abandon him on the uninhabited island of Lemnos. Years later, an oracle informs the Greeks that they will only be victorious against the Trojans with the help of Philoktetes. The play is set on Lemnos, as Odysseus goes with Neoptolemus, the young son of Achilles, to find their former colleague and convince him to come to Troy.

Philoktetes Variations sequenced three versions of the story in three languages. In Heiner Müller's German, Odysseus (played by De Munck) takes center stage, rationalizing his abandonment of his friend with the argument that in times of crisis, the needs of the nation take precedence, even when it requires falsehoods and personal betrayals. In André Gide's French version, Philoktetes' status as an outcast lends him a moral authority; he rejects their pleas and remains in the solitude of his island exile. John Jesurun's English is otherworldly, by turns crude and lyrical, coruscating and meandering, brimming with American slang and yet weirdly out of time. In it, Philoktetes speaks from beyond the grave to his former colleagues: "The cadaver will direct the autopsy, a talking corpse narrating."

We rehearsed for weeks. I had prerecorded tapes as well as the hubkaphone and my alto and flute. Ritsema had me play on an aerial platform about twenty-five feet above the stage. I had to ride a Genie boom lift to get up there. I designed my own costume: I was supposed to be a sort of spirit haunting the action from the clouds, and I wore a white gown made out of gauzelike material. I had heavy makeup around my eyes, so the audience saw what looked like a spectral figure with bright eyes, floating in the air in a thicket of glinting metal. I had to be careful. It was like the houseboat in Amsterdam; the platform would sway as I moved around, and I had to make sure not to fall off.

The performance was given another layer of impact by the fact that Vawter was dying of AIDS. He spent much of the show naked, and the sight of his body covered in purple Kaposi rashes made it impossible to ignore the parallel between the story of Philoktetes and the AIDS crisis. It ended up being Ron's last production: we did the opening night but then it closed almost right away because he was too weak to perform. They tried to bring him back to the US under medical supervision. But Ron passed away in April on a Swissair flight back to New York.

In 2003 I used the hubkaphone on my band Zooid's LP-only

album *Pop Start the Tape, Stop*, which emerged out of a residency at Engine 27, a former firehouse converted into an art gallery on Franklin Street in lower Manhattan. Even for that, I didn't perform it live: I set up the hubkaphone and prerecorded myself playing, and then had the tape broadcast through sixteen loudspeakers spread out across the ground-floor exhibition space as a sound installation while the band and I performed a live concert. I used a sound processor to shift the hubkaphone track an octave up or down at certain points to make space for the music I was writing for Zooid. I also had a foot pedal so I could stop and start the tape and have the hubkaphone coming in and out when I needed it. We designed the installation so that the prerecorded hubkaphone soundtrack traveled at a designated speed from speaker to speaker around the room. It created a shifting sonic atmosphere around the band, the pings and clangs seeming to bob and weave, advance and recede, almost the way my body used to skip, hover, and pounce behind the suspended chrome when I danced with my invention.

6

Mirror over the Water

I once saw footage online of an interview with Sonny Rollins where he was talking about his close relationship with Clifford Brown, and about how hard it was when the trumpeter was tragically killed in a car accident in 1956. He had some problems playing for a while after that, Sonny explained, simply because he'd been with such a giant. Suddenly that sound wasn't there with him anymore. It left him unmoored. He said he found himself calling on Clifford's spirit.

I knew what Sonny was talking about. You call on that presence as you're playing, to help you through.

But then, Sonny added, he realized that he had had to stop doing that. It was becoming a crutch. He had to let Clifford's spirit go wherever it was headed.

When I heard Sonny say that, I had to stop watching the interview. I couldn't even go there. Because I knew exactly what he meant. Even with your closest collaborators—no, especially with your closest collaborators—you can't sit there in the mausoleum of your accomplishments. You have to learn to let them go.

Great bands get constructed the same way great baseball teams or basketball teams do. It's all about the combination of players. The Duke Ellington Orchestra would not have sounded the same with just any musicians in those seats. Count Basie without

Freddie Green, without Lester Young, without Herschel Evans? The Chicago Symphony Orchestra under Frederick Stock: there were key people in that orchestra who made that sound. It's always a team effort. People forget that sometimes and only look at the leader's name on the date. But the musicians are the ones who realize the blueprint. And it's the ability to open up a blueprint that brings a work to life.

When I returned from my little jaunt to Amsterdam, I tried to accommodate myself to the rhythms of domestic life with Cathy and the baby in our apartment in Kenwood at the corner of 48th and Drexel. Even after indulging my wanderlust, I struggled to settle down into normalcy. I wasn't sure what it really meant to be a husband or a father. And I was still carrying around my demons from the war—feelings I hadn't ever spoken about, even with Cathy. I just couldn't shake my discontent, and eventually it cost me my marriage. I ended up getting my own place a few blocks away, first at 52nd and Drexel and then at 56th and Maryland.

It was only in my music that I felt like I had a sure sense of direction and purpose. After my time in Europe, I was even more determined to be something more than a sideman. I wanted to find my own group: a band I could write for. Starting back in 1969, when I first got back from the war, I'd been trying to put a group together, in addition to all the gigs I was juggling around town. I tried out various configurations with players on the scene—Joel Brandon, Wallace McMillan, Corky McClerkin, Frank Walton—but I still hadn't found the right mix.

Kenwood is known for its architectural extravagance. There are some low-rise apartment buildings, but it's a neighborhood full of sprawling thirty-room nineteenth-century mansions with expansive gardens. This is where the royalty lived: Muhammad Ali, Elijah Muhammad. Many of the mansions have adjoining coach houses that have been converted into residential spaces.

While I was still living with Cathy and Melin, I would often hear the sound of a bassist practicing alone from a coach house that was right behind our place. I think he might have heard me practicing, too. One day I saw him coming out of his building and we started talking. His name was Fred Hopkins. He was playing all the time, although he wasn't performing too much. He was working to support himself by stocking shelves and bagging groceries at the A&P across the street on 47th. We decided to start playing together. He had a huge open space upstairs, a sort of loft above what had been the garage for the coaches. We'd rehearse up there. There was plenty of room to set up my hubkaphone.

Fred had gone to DuSable and studied under Captain Dyett. Dyett encouraged him to continue his studies, and in 1969 Fred ended up being the first recipient of the Charles Clark Memorial Scholarship (established in honor of Jarman's late bassist) at the Civic Orchestra of Chicago, where he studied with Joseph Guastafeste, the principal bassist for the Chicago Symphony Orchestra. Fred had gotten involved a little bit in the AACM scene, too: in the fall of 1970, Kalaparusha brought him into his band to record the album *Forces and Feelings*. Around the time I met him, Fred had also started playing with Muhal's Experimental Band.

It so happened that the drummer Steve McCall came back from Europe right around then and moved a couple of blocks away, near 51st Street. Steve was more than a decade older than me and Fred, and he had a lot of experience: he had played with everybody from Braxton and Muhal to Don Byas, Dexter Gordon, Gene Ammons, and Marion Brown. Steve had been one of the cofounders of the AACM in 1965, and so I knew him from those circles. I remember being impressed with his playing when I made the trip up from Kansas in the fall of 1966 to attend the recording session for Jarman's first record, *Song For*. Soon after he came back to town, I ran into him at a concert at the University of Chicago, and when I realized we were neighbors, I asked him if he wanted to try playing in a trio with me and Fred. Sure, he said. So we brought his drum kit over to the coach house, too, and started playing together.

Upon my return from Amsterdam, I fell right back into the experimental theater scene on the North Side. Cathy or June Pyskacek introduced me to another director named Donald Sanders, who preceded Ronnie Davis as the chair of the theater arts program at Columbia College. The department had an initiative called the Chicago Project, which was set up to give students hands-on experience in mounting productions around the city in collaboration with professional performers and designers. Sanders asked me to do the music for a play they were doing at the Columbia College Theater Center on West Barry Avenue just north of Lincoln Park.

The show was initially called *Hotel Diplomat*, after a specific hotel in that neighborhood. Every city seems to have a Hotel Diplomat, and it's never a good place to check in. They always seem to be near the train station or the bus depot. The name tries hard to give off a whiff of prestige—as though foreign dignitaries are constantly passing through—but Hotel Diplomats are almost always transient dumps.

The Chicago Project productions involved a sort of research component in which the students were supposed to study the social and historical backgrounds of the environments they were depicting. According to the Project's program materials, the idea was that drama should function not in isolation but instead as "an active part of a total sociocultural context."

This particular show was developed through an unusually extensive research process. There were about twenty actors in the show, and they infiltrated the community around this hotel. They were trying to obtain a sort of cross-section portrait of the whole area. So one of them got a job in the pharmacy down the block, another in the liquor store, and another at the corner deli, while some others took rooms at the hotel itself. They did this gradually and covertly, each of them working independently; they pretended they didn't know one another. This neighborhood was near the intersection of North Sheffield and West Belmont on the North Side. It was an unstable mix, a hodgepodge of various immigrant and ethnic communities. The actors integrated themselves into the area and gathered material for months.

This Hotel Diplomat was a residency hotel. Over the years it had accumulated a unique colony of eccentric long-term residents. There was an older woman who had been an actress on Broadway; she had copies of all her theater programs and head shots, and at times she seemed to operate under the delusion that she was still living in that world. "I'm on call at six thirty this evening!" she'd declare, as though she had a show to get to. Another guy had been a moderately successful country-western composer, and you'd hear him in his room strumming away on his guitar. Another slightly deranged resident would talk obsessively about his dreams; he'd accost you in the lobby and start telling you about these lurid recurring nightmares he was having. There was one in which he was being tormented by a woman with gigantic breasts. So that got incorporated into the play: in one scene, the character recounts these nightmares as he's squeezing these red tomatoes into pulp in his kitchen—compulsively, one after the other—ranting about the dream as the juice runs down his hands.

It turned out that the hotel and most of the businesses in the area were owned by one mob family. They deliberately kept their affairs nebulous, but many suspected that they were using the legitimate businesses to cover for other, more dubious enterprises, including small-time drug-dealing and gambling. During the period when the actors were collecting material, the patriarch of the family passed away, and they held the wake in the deli. It turned into a tense scene: a power struggle over who was going to run the family—with the guy's body lying right there. That got put into the play, too: the body lying in state surrounded by all the cold cuts and chopped liver as the surviving relatives argued about who was going to take over the operation.

The actors surreptitiously documented the goings-on, taking notes on everyday interactions and incidents, and then Sanders developed it into a script. As a way to work, it was fascinating. But the ethnographic approach got them into trouble, because the play ended up being too close to reality. The theater was just a few blocks away from the hotel, after all. Everybody in the neighborhood knew all these characters. And not surprisingly, the family didn't want the spotlight on their business dealings.

The show was supposed to premiere in March 1972. But on opening night they shut us down. Somebody called the fire department and claimed there were code violations in the theater. And when that didn't work, some goons showed up to intimidate us. It was totally clichéd, like a scene in a bad gangster movie. They informed us that we weren't going to open if we used that title.

Fortunately, the issue did turn out to be the name. Once we made it more generic—calling it just *The Hotel* rather than *Hotel Diplomat*—they didn't give us any more problems. "Spend an evening at *The Hotel*," beckoned the revised program, adding the vague promise that the show would deliver "99 rooms of unwelcome awarenesses." We were finally able to open a couple of days late, and the show ran through mid-June. In the end, Sanders didn't have to revise the content at all: there were still all the eccentric characters, and even the thinly veiled portrait of the family. They just didn't want the connection to be explicit.

Don Sanders had the idea of using ragtime in the show, and when he asked me to write the music he handed me the two-volume *Collected Works of Scott Joplin* that Vera Brodsky Lawrence had edited in 1971, one volume featuring Joplin's works for piano and one volume with his songs. Sanders didn't give me any specific instructions about instrumentation or arrangements. "Use whichever ones you like," he told me, "and we'll weave them into the scenes." He told me I could bring some of my own compositions in addition to the arrangements. I'm not sure how Don came up with the idea of using Joplin. The pianist Joshua Rifkin had released his unexpected hit album *Piano Rags by Scott Joplin* in the fall of 1970, but the so-called ragtime revival didn't really erupt until a few years later, when Marvin Hamlisch's soundtrack for *The Sting* won an Oscar for best score in 1974. I suppose you could say that along with a few other things—including the staging of T. J. Anderson's orchestration of Joplin's opera *Treemonisha* in Atlanta (coincidentally also in the spring of 1972)—we were part of what helped to build that momentum.

I was just beginning to work on the Joplin arrangements when I started playing with Fred and Steve, so naturally I brought the scores over. The first day we started rehearsing in the coach house, that's what we played: the rags that I'd started orchestrating.

It was an interesting challenge, because ragtime was so closely associated with the piano. There were no models of how to proceed. There was nothing to listen to for examples of trios of saxophone, bass, and drums playing rags. I had to figure out how to make them work for our format. And we all had to rethink how we played our instruments. The constraints of the form pushed us in some interesting directions stylistically. Fred already had that fullness—that thick Chicago sound that comes out of the great Wilbur Ware tradition. But playing all these rags forced him to come up with an approach that wasn't what you'd end up with if all you were playing was show tunes and jazz standards. It was great training material. We were already mature as individual players, but as a unit, ragtime shaped us. We stuck close to the form: rags are structured like little suites, we realized, but if you maintained the flavor of each section they allowed room for expansion and improvisation. We warmed up with other stuff, sometimes equally unusual: little arrangements of James P. Johnson, Mozart, marches.

In the program for *The Hotel,* I'm credited for the Joplin arrangements but not for my original compositions. As for the band, it just says:

MUSIC PLAYED BY HENRY THREADGILL
STEVE MCCALL
FRED HOPKINS

After the show concluded, we started playing concerts around town: I remember we did a ragtime concert a few months later at Ida Noyes Hall at the University of Chicago, and we also performed at Alice's Revisited, the North Side fixture on Wrightwood Avenue that now and then hosted AACM bands but mostly featured big-name blues acts like Howlin' Wolf, Otis Rush, Sunnyland Slim, Buddy Guy, Muddy Waters, and Junior Wells. We kept playing together, and I kept writing for trio.

Even as we started to perform around town, we'd identify ourselves just by listing our three names. I was doing almost all the composing so my name was first, but we wanted to make it clear that the band was a collective endeavor rather than a leader and sidemen. It never occurred to us to label ourselves the Henry Threadgill Trio.

By early 1973 we started calling ourselves Reflections. Sometime that year we put together a three-fold brochure with a multiple-exposure photograph of the three of us superimposed over one another, suggesting the way our music was a true interweaving. You couldn't have one of us without the others. Inside the brochure was a short text Steve and I wrote to introduce the band:

Reflections is a co-operative effort on the part of three musicians who have been together since the latter part of 1972, and whose collective backgrounds encompass everything from polka to gospel, show tunes to classical, rhythm

REFLECTIONS

By early 1973 we started calling ourselves Reflections.

and blues to marching bands, spirituals, folk, dance music, traditional jazz, and what has been variously termed as New Music, New Jazz or simply playing free. Such a varied preparation has created a broad musical experience which is historical, and yet contemporary in nature.

The group's idea of collective playing has led us to a revitalization of the original New Orleans concept. The result of this effort was a concert series at Alice's Revisited in 1972, which subsequently generated a revival of Scott Joplin's ragtime music. Another manifestation of the group concern for what we call "foundation music" was evidenced in a concert series presented through NIA and the Chicago Front for Jazz, in which urban blues and gospel traits were strongly prevalent.

In the area of theatre, Reflections has jointly composed and performed the music for Don Sanders' *Hotel,* produced the "Dance Series" in coordination with the University of Chicago and Columbia College, and created the Children's Theatre Music Series, which was first presented at the Jazz Showcase in Chicago.

Reflections is also interested in a variety of educational media. Since we consider ourselves to be a visual experience as well as an auditory one, we have been involved in various recording performances through a creative use of video tapes at the University of Illinois, the Art Institute of Chicago and the Academy of the Arts in California. We are further prepared to present lecture, workshops or seminars on a wide spectrum of subjects from the music of Black Americans to special topics in dance, theatre and multi-media.

An unusual characteristic of the music played by Reflections is a multi-instrumental approach and the constant use of ethnic instruments and new instruments created originally by members of the group.

In addition to the programs described in this brochure,

Reflections is prepared to engage in night club dates, recordings and the creation of music for films, etc.

Rereading our self-description now, it's striking to me how the trio was coming to serve as a vehicle for me to continue many of my explorations over the previous few years. The trio with Wadada and Lester Lashley had been more overtly theatrical—we were acting and reciting as well as playing—but Reflections retained some of that multimedia inclination, even though it was much more about the music. From the beginning, we really did "consider ourselves to be a visual experience as well as an auditory one," and that was reflected in the way we dressed and the way I'd move between my saxes and flutes and the hubkaphone. Our work with video wasn't very well documented, but it was an important part of our concept in the early years: we even did a show with the pioneering video artist Nam June Paik at the Art Institute of Chicago. The Children's Theater Music Series was a weekend matinee series for kids that Joe Segal organized at his famous club the Jazz Showcase: for those shows, we'd often do things that included a theatrical element, sometimes in collaboration with poets such as Ajule (Bruce) Rutlin, whom I'd met hanging out with the Black Artists' Group in St. Louis.

We started to build a reputation, and soon Reflections was touring around the region, making little loops around the Midwest: Milwaukee, Detroit, Rockford, Gary, Iowa City. Occasionally we ventured farther afield. We drove out to Tucson, Arizona, for example, to work with some dancers I knew who were based there. I remember it not only because of the long drive through the changing landscapes going out to the Southwest, but also because I had an opportunity to see some of Harry Partch's homemade instruments, which were on display in a museum next to the dance studio. (Years later, I got a chance to hear some of Partch's dazzling inventions—Cloud-Chamber Bowls, the Chromelodeon, and the massive Marimba Eroica—in action

Air in concert with the hubkawall at the Museum of
Contemporary Art in Chicago, December 1976

when I did an arrangement of "Meditations on Integration" for *Weird Nightmare*, the album of Charles Mingus interpretations produced by Hal Willner in 1992.)

Touring around the region, we quickly built a reputation as an exciting new group. But we hadn't had an opportunity to record yet. In the end it was the press coverage that opened that door. I don't think I've ever seen anything like it: in review after review, journalists covering us were clamoring for us to make an album. It's a travesty that this trio hasn't been recorded yet, they would complain. Eventually all the noise got the record industry to sit up and pay attention.

It was a Japanese company that approached us first. In the summer of 1975, the producers Masahiko Yuh and Kazuo Harada came to the US with the intention to record a wide range of new music coming out of Chicago, Philadelphia, and New York: Walt Dickerson, George Cables, Joe Bonner, Charles Sullivan, Joe Lee Wilson, Chico Freeman, Donald Smith, Ted Curson, Monty Waters, Andrew Cyrille, Muhal. By the time we went into the recording studio in September, we had decided to change the name of the trio from Reflections to Air. Our first record, *Air Song*, was the third release on their label, Whynot.

We had been playing together for a while as Reflections before we decided to change the band's name. Around the spring of 1975, Steve started seeing a woman named Susana Cavallo who was a graduate student at the University of Chicago. I remember she was working on translations of Spanish and Latin American literature by writers such as Gabriel García Márquez, Francisco Ayala, and José Hierro. She would have us over for these wonderful dinners at her house. One night we were sitting around and Susana started asking everybody when their birthdays were. "All of you are air signs!" she observed. It had never occurred to us, but it was true: I'm an Aquarius, and Steve and Fred were both Libras. She knew some astrology, and she figured out that there were other parallels, too, in our ascendants and secondary progressions.

"Air," Susana mused. "You know, that would be a much better name than Reflections. It's economical. Elemental, even. Nobody would expect a jazz band to have a name like that—one of the five basic elements."

I exchanged glances with Steve and Fred. We had never quite been satisfied with Reflections. Something about it seemed vague: reflections of what? And it didn't really suggest our sound as a trio—our particular approach. A group named after a basic natural element wouldn't be completely out of the ordinary, given that Earth, Wind & Fire was one of the most popular bands on the planet. But it was true that a name like that would be unusual in the jazz world. And there was something intriguingly enigmatic about it: just the one element, as though that some-how said it all. It seemed to fit what we were trying to do musi-cally as a collective trio. Air suggested a quality or substance that was fundamental, even ubiquitous, yet hard to see and hard to grasp. The name implied something that was everywhere but elusive—it had that openness we were aiming for.

When we eventually relocated to New York, we found that the name took on other levels of association in that context. Many journalists and listeners later assumed we called our-selves Air in reference to the little placards posted in the lobby of many converted loft buildings in lower Manhattan, which the Fire Department required when artists started moving into those formerly industrial spaces. (In that context, the "A.I.R." sign in the lobby indicated that there was an "Artist in Residence" in the building, so that, in the case of an emergency, the firemen would know there were residents to be evacuated.)

"And besides, it's a three-letter word, and there are three of you!" Susana exclaimed, as though that settled the matter.

I had heard Sonny Rollins playing in a saxophone trio, and I may have heard Sam Rivers by then as well. I've already explained that Sonny was my polestar. As much as I loved him, I knew I wasn't going to be able to approach it his way, with athletic displays of bottomless improvisational brilliance. I decided that I had to approach my writing for me, Steve, and Fred from a compositional point of view: exploring the full range of what we could get out of the trio format in terms of orchestration and texture.

In composing for the three of us, my thinking was influenced most of all by the sound of the Ahmad Jamal Trio. It was a piano trio rather than a saxophone trio. But what I learned had to do with the way the music was arranged—the sense of space. They could lock into a groove, but they also knew how to be elliptical: to play a hint or a dollop in a way that suggested more.

You get the hand you're dealt. And this was my hand. I was thrilled to have it, too: a dedicated group of three musicians, living in the same neighborhood and playing together all the time. What more could I want? But it required a particular approach compositionally speaking. I was working with a minimal palette. How much can you do with seemingly limited means? It meant learning how to write by implication. I didn't have a brass section to work with, or an arsenal of violas to bring out some timbral nuance. As I said to a journalist once, it forced me to learn to write the silhouette of the thing rather than the thing itself.

The proposition that live music is "a visual experience as well as an auditory one" wasn't a new idea, of course. And it didn't necessarily have to be a matter of multimedia art, like an installation that combined music and video. The great masters of the music have always understood the importance of that visual aspect.

A number of years later, we were playing a double bill with Dizzy Gillespie. Even later in his career, he was insatiably curious—and crafty: he would stand in the control booth during our set to try to figure out what we were doing. And he understood, too, because he was brilliant. He watched the way we captivated the audience.

The next night he sent his band up on stage in the dark. He had them turn out all the lights. And he told the lighting guy to put a blue spotlight on the main microphone. People were still allowed to smoke in clubs then, so the smoke was wafting up through that blue light. People in the audience were chatting and sipping their drinks. And then suddenly Diz stepped into that light and hit a note, with a Harmon mute stuck in that iconic angled trumpet bell. Out of fucking nowhere. It was like a postcard.

He just stepped up to the mike and became a visual subject. And the room was his. He knew it was a way to steal the moment. With that simple trick, before he even hit that note, he upstaged everything we'd done.

That time I was the one in the control booth, watching. I had to laugh. Damn, Diz, I thought. You sure got us. You stole the moment with lighting!

I saw him do something similar another time at some jazz festival in the 1980s, playing as a special guest with the V.S.O.P. Quartet when it was comprised of Herbie Hancock, Ron Carter, and Tony Williams (the rhythm section of the great Miles Davis band) along with a young Wynton Marsalis on trumpet. Diz had slowed down by then due to his age, but he still knew how to conquer a room. He came out on stage and started playing an unaccompanied intro. No tune had been called, so the band didn't know what he was doing at first. They sat there patiently waiting for him to launch into an identifiable melody. I was watching in the wings with some other great trumpeters, including Lester Bowie and Jon Faddis, and we were all standing there wondering what Dizzy was doing. At first it seemed like a casual display of virtuosity. But then it started to take shape, gradually, even though you still couldn't guess what the tune was. Finally he reached a culmination with this glorious run up to a high C. It was only when he hit that last note that we all simultaneously realized we were in the Jerome Kern standard, "All the Things You Are." The rhythm section got it, too, and went right into the changes. But somehow Diz set that high note that opened the door to the song up in the air. He placed that note in the room and it stayed in the room. It was incredible: the note seemed to linger there like a shimmering bubble up above the audience.

That one note was the note of the evening. It was the only thing anyone heard.

The truly great ones know this stuff. They know how to use lighting and posture and acoustics to make themselves stand out. Just like opera singers vie to get to certain places on the stage. They know there are hot spots. From certain places the sound is bigger, richer, more direct, and more volatile. Dizzy was a pure showman. And he knew how to command a space. I learned early as a musician that it was crucial to study the masters when I had a chance. Sometimes it was subtle musical things: a way of phrasing a line, or a way of modulating dynamics. But just as often it was these little unspoken tricks of the trade. To the untrained eye, Diz carried himself in a manner that seemed casual, even lackadaisical. But watching him, I knew I was getting a master class in the aerodynamics of stage performance.

From the beginning, people tended to assume that the music of Air was largely improvised, even "free." It's related to broader assumptions about the music. There's a tendency to underestimate the intellectual component in Black music across the board, as though we don't possess a sophisticated understanding of what we're doing. We're just playing. The fact is, the music of Air was largely composed. On the first couple of albums, there are some tunes that involve melodic statements followed by improvisation. But we quickly moved away from that. By the time you get to albums like *Open Air Suit* and *Montreux Suisse Air*, you're listening to music that is almost entirely written. Ninety percent of it is represented on paper in some form, including the sections that might sound like individual solos. There's a subtle line between zero improvisation and total improvisation. In Air we tried to hover right at that point of undecidability.

That said, how it was *executed* was another matter. I was responsible for bringing in material, but then things would get changed in rehearsals. That's where the collaboration lay. I wrote for the personalities in the group and how we all played. I tried to write for people rather than just writing music. Of course, Duke Ellington was a genius at this: writing a part that was tailor-made for Johnny Hodges or Harry Carney and no one else. But with Air, it fed into our collective dynamic. I'd bring in a piece of writing and suggest that we could approach it one way. But then Fred or Steve might do something a little different in rehearsal: revise the intonation of a phrase, or elaborate a melodic figure. And that might become part of the piece. Sometimes I'd written something for one of us, but we'd start playing it and realize that that person needed to lay out. So we might cut a section. This could happen in the rehearsal process, but it could also happen on the bandstand.

In this way the music was constantly unfolding. And it kept changing form—an ongoing recombination of elements. The musical architecture was something less like a skyscraper or a bridge than like an octopus or a spider. The tentacles move independently, but there's a coordination under it all.

This is another way of saying that Air was collaborative in the best sense. Every session, every day, it was a process. Interpreting the written material, we all had to sense each other's needs and change things accordingly. You work it out together as you go along. In terms of the way we ended up sounding, the major difference between Air and other great trios that might come to mind is that radical commitment to the collective statement. It changes the whole frame of reference. We didn't simply want to support one another. We wanted to kill the idea of accompaniment altogether.

Composing for Air, I came to realize that it was possible to stretch the palette by taking advantage of the tonal possibilities of each instrument. Maybe it was composing for hubkaphone that got me to think about percussion that way. But early on, I started having Steve tune the drums, which allowed me to use them as another voice in the tonal fabric. Steve already had that orientation. He had been experimenting with different tunings for some time. And he thought of the drums as a melodic instrument. He could swing, but it was never just about playing time.

Because I was thinking about it compositionally, I also used myself in multiple ways, as you can hear even on our first album, where I play alto, tenor, and baritone sax as well as flute. In this sense it was a little bit more like Sam Rivers, where in his trio he would switch between tenor, soprano, flute, and piano. In the Rivers trios there's a great deal of textural variance, but it's different because a lot of what they were doing was in fact freely improvised. I wanted to approach the trio form as a *composer*, first of all, in a manner that would take advantage of the multiple roles I could play.

This involved more planning—and more practicing—than people sometimes realize. With Air, I found that I constantly had to be prepared. As soon as I picked up one instrument, I had to start preparing mentally for the next one. I couldn't wait, because there were physical challenges in the switch that could give me trouble if I wasn't ready. If I wasn't prepared, my embouchure could become too set, too habituated to the demands of whichever instrument, and then I'd have to struggle to adjust.

Switching instruments is very difficult in a trio. Great instructors often possess certain secrets when it comes to doubling instruments for color in show bands. But the stakes are completely different when you're part of a large ensemble. You play one passage on oboe and then later play another on clarinet, but you only use them in the moment. You're not standing up there exposed for ten or fifteen minutes straight, the only woodwind on the bandstand. You're not faced with having to explore all the highs and lows, all the types of articulation, implicit in any given instrument before shifting to another. To get up there and have to switch horns in the middle of a piece, playing with musicians who are on fire, relentlessly pushing you—that's another story.

Even as Air became my primary canvas as a composer, I kept exploring in other directions. I had an idea for a larger ensemble that would combine multiple basses, flutes, and voices. I'd been listening to instrumental music from Burundi. They used an instrument that functioned like a bass, but it was made from a cut-out tree. It looked like a canoe. And when the musicians struck the hollow trunks with mallets, it made the most beguiling sound. That was the thing that impacted me the most at the time: that particular sound. I was after that. I can't get that sound with a single bass, I told myself.

In October 1974, my group X-75 had its premiere concert at the N.A.M.E. Gallery on West Lake Street in the Loop downtown. I played a number of times at that art gallery, both with Air and with X-75. That year I'd been awarded a two-thousand-dollar grant from the National Endowment for the Arts to develop a "composition for woodwinds string bass choir." The texture of X-75 was unique: the basic conception was a combination of wordless vocals with multiple reeds, flutes (including piccolo and bass flute), and basses (including piccolo bass).

When I was finally able to record some of this music in January 1979 for an album released by Arista/Novus, I was forced to adjust the original palette to a certain extent. When I started writing for this ensemble five years earlier, I used five or six basses. But the producers didn't want to pay for the musicians who were still in Chicago to come to New York for the session, so I had to reorchestrate it for four. Back in Chicago, I would also use the poet Ajule Rutlin along with Amina Claudine Myers (or Gloria Brooks) on vocals. The pairing of voices— Ajule reciting and Amina singing simultaneously—was central to the texture. But I wasn't able to use Ajule for the recording in New York. So I asked the poet and critic Thulani Davis, who became a close friend and collaborator once I moved to New York, to provide liner notes in poetic form for the album. It was meant to be a sort of spoken-word postlude, as it were—a dis-

X-75 in performance at the N.A.M.E. Gallery in Chicago, 1974

placement of the word from the moment of performance to its aftermath.

I gave Thulani the music and asked her to respond to it, to fashion something that would go along with it. She wrote poetic responses to each side of the record:

> *at the turning of the day*
> *in these winters / in the city's bottomless streets*
> *it seems sometimes we live behind god's back*
> *we / the life-blood*
> *of forgotten places / unhallowed ground*
> *sometimes in these valleys*
> *turning the corner of canyons*
> *now filled with blinding light streams*
> *caught alone between this rock & a known hard place*
> *sometimes in an utter solitude*
> *a chorale / a sweetness / makes us whole & never lost*
> *a high string calls back*
> *that sorrow song that had no words*
> *a song the old folks knew sighs like a violin*
> *the lowest bass notes all agree*
> *there is no sadness / there is only a pause*
> *without introduction or explanation*
> *a plucking / a motion / this music*
> *clips the heartbeat & eases*
> *eases like the smoothest dude on the block*
> *into the street / into where we live*

Like the entire project, the liner notes were an experiment. You grab something and see what works. Can I use this? Can I use that? This way of working—putting together whatever you can put together—lies at the heart of Black art. That's what it's always been and what it still is. And it will keep working that way until it gets where it's going to go.

It's ridiculous to try to prevent people from experiment-ing. It's wrongheaded to try to curtail this exploratory urge by

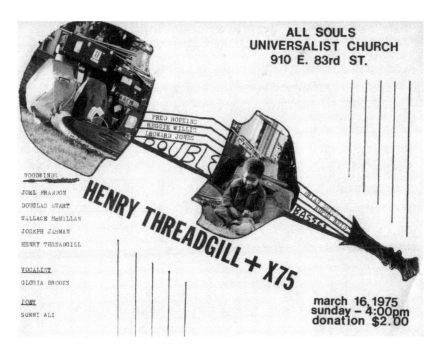

Concert flyer for X-75, 1975

hemming people in according to some narrow definition of a received "tradition." We can't stand in the way of young people coming behind us and tell them that they can't use this or that. They'll use whatever they can, because ultimately the music *is* that resourcefulness—that impulse to tinker with an art that is provisional, always in the process of finding its form.

If you look at a book on the history of Western classical music, there's centuries of background you can read about. Black music in America is relatively young. It's still just the beginning. And it's too soon to get upset and start making grand declarations about what you like and don't like in terms of the directions the music is taking. You don't have to like it all. What you have to recognize is that it's not the end of the line. In another hundred years, assuming we're still here, imagine how much more artistic information will have accumulated from Black music. And it's not going to be the twelve-bar blues from now until the end of time.

All of us left the country in 1974. We kept in touch, and we knew Air would come back together when we were all in the same place again. But we took a sabbatical from the trio. Steve spent an extended period back in Europe, mainly in Spain. Fred and I took shorter trips: he went to Canada for a little while, and I decided to explore South America.

I had always been curious about Brazil. In elementary school it was the country I chose for my presentations in geography class: I was fascinated by the Amazon. But I didn't have enough money to get there. I made my way to Miami and realized that tickets to Rio were simply too expensive. I ended up deciding to go to Venezuela instead—the flights were much more affordable. My initial plan was to find work there and earn enough to pay my way to Rio. But I ended up staying in Caracas.

I didn't really have a plan when I went: I just packed up and tried to find a flight. I took all my instruments with me: my alto, my tenor, my baritone, my flute, my bass flute, my clarinet, and my piccolo. It made for quite a pile.

When I showed up at the immigration desk at the Simon Bolivar International Airport in Caracas, the authorities held me up. I've always had a thing for hats, and I remember I was wearing some flamboyant headgear on the flight. Between that and all the black cases, the customs agents didn't know what to do with me. They seemed to be convinced I was a drug smuggler or a particularly brazen gun runner.

They detained me for a long time. I opened up all the instrument cases and showed them that there was no contraband inside. "Why do you need so many?" one of the agents questioned. I tried to explain that I played all these instruments and might want to use them in different circumstances. They forced me to prove to them that I could play the horns. So I sat there in the detention area, playing arpeggios and flourishes on one instrument after another for all the guards. At last I convinced them to let me into the country.

When I arrived in Venezuela, I didn't speak any Spanish at all—I didn't even know what *sí* meant! I found a taxi and asked to be taken to a "hotel." (Fortunately that word is a cognate, so the driver understood.) Signaling with my hand, I made him understand that I wanted to be taken to a place to stay that wouldn't be too expensive: not too *high*, not too *low*, but *right in the middle*. The taxi driver laughed when he figured out what I meant. He took me to a moderately priced place in the middle of town.

I had one contact in Caracas: an architect who was a friend of a Swedish woman I'd met at the consulate in Chicago who was into the arts. It was a tenuous connection, but it was all I had to go on. The architect didn't know I was coming to town, because I hadn't even been planning to stay long in Caracas. I decided to introduce myself and ask him for help. The next morning I got a map of the city and made my way to his house. A servant or assistant answered the door and, after some awkward back-and-forth in his broken English and my nonexistent Spanish, he got me to understand that the architect was out of town and wouldn't be back for a few days.

I went back to the hotel room and considered what to do. I only had a little money with me; I wasn't going to be able to stay in a hotel more than a few days. I was intending to find work. I'm a professional musician, I told myself. I should be able to find a gig to get by, one way or another. But how was I going to do that in a city where I didn't know anyone and didn't speak the language?

I sat down and went through the telephone book, copying addresses that I thought might prove useful: nightclubs, theaters, music studios, schools, radio and television stations. The first place I decided to go was the television station. I took my alto and got in another taxi.

My approach was bold. What did I have to lose? The television station was up on a hill surrounded by a fence. I walked up to the guard at the gate and presented myself. The guy said something in Spanish. Of course I had no idea what he was saying, but I just barreled ahead.

"*Hola*," I said—in the course of my Venezuelan adventure, I had already learned one useful word!—"My name is Henry Threadgill. I'm here to play."

The guard stared at me befuddled for a few seconds and, not knowing what to do, went into his booth and called up to the station. He must have told them there was some crackpot African American who'd shown up out of the blue at the gate with a saxophone case.

They sent a lady down to talk to me. She could speak some English, so we were able to have a conversation. When she understood my request, she looked mystified, too. She told me that the orchestra wasn't there that day. But she suggested I go to the national radio station. She gave me the address and the name of someone to ask for, and I got back in the taxi and headed over there.

The radio station was in a building with a bunch of recording studios. I spoke with one of the main disc jockeys there. He was on the air when I went in, so they had me wait a few minutes until he emerged from the broadcast booth.

When I finally got to speak to him, I explained, "I came down here to play music. I'm hoping to sit in with some of the local bands."

"Really?" he said. The deejay didn't know much about the Chicago scene and hadn't heard of the AACM. But he traveled to New York all the time and so he knew the jazz and salsa scenes. His reference points were the big names in New York: Coltrane, Ornette, Miles, Eddie Palmieri, Willie Colón. But at least it gave him some sense of context—some general understanding of where I was coming from. And he spoke English fluently.

"Come on in the booth," he said, beckoning me in. "I'm going to put you on the radio right now."

I thought, What the hell. Here's my shot.

The guy made a big deal out of it on the air. How this jazz musician had come on a pilgrimage to our country, driven by his desire to play Venezuelan music. Nothing like this had ever happened before. Listeners started calling in, asking me about my career and who I'd played with, and about the scene in Chicago. Suddenly I was the featured guest for the afternoon.

The lead trumpet player from the Venezuela Symphony Orchestra was one of the listeners who called into the show. He was accomplished and well connected, not to mention fabulously wealthy, and he volunteered to take me to his mansion up in the hills. As we drove there, he told me he had hosted Cannonball Adderley when he was in town. His place was palatial, with servants hovering everywhere and bronze busts of Liszt and Beethoven in the drawing room. It was pleasant to be coddled, but after a few days I started to feel like some sort of exotic plaything. The trumpeter hosted a cocktail party to show me off to his friends. And the mansion was in an isolated location some distance outside of central Caracas.

After a few days of luxurious imprisonment, I tried the

architect again. It occurred to me that he might be back in town. I took a taxi back down to his place, and this time he was home. Luckily he spoke English well, too. When I told him the Swedish woman had told me to get in touch with him, he told me he'd be honored to host me while I was in town.

He had an atelier outside of Caracas. A few European students were there studying with him. But there was an extra room in the basement. He told me I could stay there as long as I needed to. So I took another taxi and went to get all my instruments.

The atelier was in a sort of suburb of Caracas, separated from the city proper by a sprawling graveyard. It was a fabulous, light-drenched studio. I had my own space where I could practice and write without bothering the architects, and there was a cook whenever I got hungry. I just set up there and used it as a sort of base. At night I would take off and walk through the graveyard into the city. The architects thought I was crazy, walking through the graveyard in the middle of the night. But it didn't bother me—it was the most direct route, and I figured I wouldn't have any trouble on the road or anything.

It might seem unbelievable that the airport customs agents thought I was a drug runner because of my instrument cases. But I've encountered that kind of thing more than once. It obviously made no sense: what smuggler would be stupid enough to try to travel internationally while lugging contraband around in conspicuous instrument cases? Still, the impulse to racial profiling has a way of overwhelming common sense.

In the early 1970s, before I decided to relocate to New York, I made occasional trips there to play gigs. Once I was driving to a concert in Montclair, New Jersey, with Leroy Jenkins, Wadada, and the producer Kunle Mwanga, and the cops pulled us over. One of them was a rookie. He was clearly nervous; he had his hand on his pistol as they approached our car, as though he expected us to open fire at any moment. They told us to step out of our vehicle and asked us to open the trunk. When they saw our instrument cases, they immediately lost it. The two police officers both drew their guns and ordered us to put our hands on the car while they checked out what they assumed was our stash. A trumpet case: undoubtably suspicious. A clarinet case: inexplicably oblong. But then they saw Leroy's violin case and went completely nuts. It was like something in a cartoon. Did they think we were Al Capone's henchmen packing a tommy gun?

Laughable, yes. But it was dangerous, too. Wadada was incensed, and we were trying to keep him calm because we could see he was on the verge of losing his temper. "Be cool," I whispered. "This cat could shoot us in a minute." Finally we convinced them to arrest us and take us down to the station. "Look, officers, if you suspect us of being involved in some illegal activity, why don't you just take us in?"

Once they got there, they opened the cases in the trunk and discovered to their great surprise that we were professional musicians. And then of course they whipped out the usual blather: "Oh, it was simply a mistake. They fit the description of suspects who were being sought at the time." That sentence can be molded to fit any circumstance. We always seem to fit the description.

Caracas was dripping with oil money in those days. The nightclub scene was jumping with exceptional musicians. I started hanging out with a few guys, getting gigs playing in different bands around town. There was Rolando Briceño, the alto saxophonist and flute player, and another flute player, named Pepe. The three of us would play dates as the reed section. We worked with all kinds of bands and composers, including Vytas Brenner, who was developing a sort of fusion of progressive rock, Latin music, and traditional Venezuelan music. We were playing in all sorts of contexts: Colombian cumbia bands, salsa bands, and all kinds of way-out stuff.

I got a chance to play with some indigenous musicians up in the mountains at one point. We were in a recording studio, and they had to cart all this dirt into the room. The whole floor of the place was covered in a layer of dirt, because these indigenous musicians played this instrument using hollow bamboo pipes of different sizes. They'd toss these bamboo pipes up into the air and then slam them into the earth to make this thudding percussive sound. The different-sized pipes would give different pitches, somewhat like organ pipes. The musicians played together in this amazing way, with a group of them tossing the bamboo up and down to create this intricate rhythmic pattern. And then we played music Vytas composed to fit with what they were doing. I wish I had some of the recordings I made with Rolando and Pepe and Vytas. I don't think any of the work I did was credited.

After a couple of months in Caracas, I knew most of the musicians on the scene and I was working steadily. But as a foreigner, I was getting systematically underpaid on gigs in comparison to the locals. My friends went on my behalf to the musicians' union in Caracas and demanded that I be admitted. It was the only way to guarantee pay equity. To be paid union wages, though, I also had to be a legal resident with a work permit, rather than just a tourist who was hanging around. So I had to petition the government, too. They agreed, but said that I could only get residency status and work papers if I left the country temporarily and applied from abroad before I re-entered.

I still didn't have much money. Where could I afford to go for a little while that wouldn't be too far away? The easiest solution seemed to be somewhere in the Caribbean. I ended up flipping a coin between Haiti and Trinidad. And the coin toss decided it: I went to Trinidad.

I didn't have any contacts at all in Trinidad. I just went there, hoping to be able to support myself by playing, just as I'd been doing in Venezuela.

Waiting for my flight at the airport in Caracas, I met a young guy from one of the richest families in the country. His name was Eduardo. He was going to Trinidad to study English. He latched on to me in the airport lounge. He was sitting there with a cassette player, singing along to American pop songs. It was so annoying listening to him warble along to these tunes that I asked him to turn it down. When he realized I was American, he started asking me to help him with the lyrics. "What is he singing here, please?"

It was some sappy pop song. I couldn't even make out what the singer was saying. I finally went along with it. "Let me hear that thing," I said, and took the cassette player.

Once we got into that routine, with me helping him decipher English song lyrics, he stayed glued to my side. He was young and he'd never been out of the country; I think he was anxious about the trip. He insisted on changing our seat assignments so we could be next to each other for the flight.

When we arrived at Piarco International Airport outside Port of Spain, we came down the airstairs onto the tarmac and there was a huge white Cadillac limousine waiting for Eduardo. There was a chauffeur in a suit with a little black hat who ran over to get his bags. I was ready to take my leave, but Eduardo exclaimed, "No, you can't go! Please, stay with me!" And he insisted on giving me a ride. So the chauffeur loaded my instruments into the limo. Eduardo took me to lunch and then to the hotel where he was staying—the best hotel on the island. It was buzzing, because there was an international tennis tournament going on.

This hotel was completely over the top. I took one look at it and said, "Oh, no, I can't afford to stay here. This isn't a five-star hotel. This is more like a nineteen-star hotel!"

But Eduardo wouldn't be denied. He dragged me with him to the front desk. I didn't have much money, so I went along with it for the time being, just in case it was going to lead to a free place to stay. A suite had been reserved for him. "He's with me," Eduardo declared to the desk clerk. And that did it. The valets took my stuff up, too. So I moved in with Eduardo for a while. The suite was certainly spacious enough: there were multiple bedrooms, and it was so big that we could have been staying there without even running into each other.

I agreed to keep helping him with his English. He was taking classes at night and I would walk him from the hotel to his school in Port of Spain. He was scared to go out at night. I would drop him off and then head to the clubs and try to sit in.

It was fine as a temporary arrangement, but I knew I needed to extricate myself at some point soon. Life as Eduardo's sidekick and tutor quickly got to be suffocating.

I was sitting in the hotel bar one evening and I started talking to a guy there who turned out to have a lot of connections with folks in the music scene in Port of Spain. He started giving me names. He told me I should get in touch with André Tanker, the famous guitarist. His music was a sort of folk-jazz hybrid, but he had started using a lot of Caribbean percussion and was writing songs about Black consciousness. I called up Tanker and we started hanging out. It finally led to a way out of Eduardo's orbit: I went to stay with Tanker.

André Tanker introduced me to everybody who was anybody in Port of Spain. He hooked me up with these steelpan bands: I did shows as the only saxophone—me on tenor with a fifty-member steel band behind me! It was enormous fun. I played all over the island with different groups. André even got me a job playing with the legendary calypsonian Mighty Sparrow. And I started writing calypsos myself. I played with a few traditional jazz big bands, but more often with André in different ensembles and with the steel bands.

André also had close ties to the theater and poetry scenes in Port of Spain. He had worked extensively with the poet and playwright Derek Walcott, who was running the Trinidad Theatre Workshop then. André had composed music for a performance of Walcott's play *Ti-Jean and His Brothers* for the New York Shakespeare Festival in Central Park in 1972. The workshop was a vibrant scene, with musicians, dancers, actors, and writers working together on various projects.

I fell into that atmosphere and started playing for things

at the workshop. Unfortunately, it didn't last long, however, because André was going with the company to do some summer residency or tour in the United States. I didn't want to tag along—I was focused on finding out what was going on in Trinidad, and I was still intending to head back to Venezuela. Derek Walcott and his wife offered to let me stay in their house on Tobago. I was tempted. But then I got an offer to do a commission in Cambridge, Massachusetts. I decided it was a sign that it was time to go back to the States.

I barely made it out of Trinidad. It was hurricane season, and a storm came through just as I was about to leave town. I made it onto the last plane leaving Port of Spain. I didn't even have a ticket: I was out on the tarmac with all my instruments in the midst of this throng of folks trying to flee the oncoming storm. People were yelling at one another and begging the authorities to let them on a plane. But there was only time for this last one. I was pressed from all sides in the crowd, trying to hold on to my instruments, and somehow I found myself propelled by the tide of the last passengers and the crowd behind them up the stairs, step by step, and onto the plane just before the doors shut. The stewardesses didn't even care about tickets and seat assignments; they just wanted to close the door and get the hell out of there.

It was the scariest flight I've ever been on. The storm almost swept us up like a twig in its turbulence. I don't know how the pilot kept the plane from falling apart. You could hear it straining at the seams. And the plane didn't seem to be moving on its own power; the storm was carrying us in what felt like a single *woosh*.

At last the clouds cleared and we could see an island below. The passengers were clamoring to land. But the pilot announced that it was Cuba and that we wouldn't be able to land there. He was going to try to make it to Barbados. I'll never forget the tone in his voice over the intercom. "As soon as we touch down safely," he promised, "the drinks are on me." And he wasn't kidding. When we made it to Barbados, everyone headed straight for the airport bar, including a gaggle of priests and nuns on board.

The commission came from Don Sanders, who was directing a show at the American Repertory Theater in Cambridge. The show was written by Arnold Weinstein, the self-described "theater poet" who had collaborated with a wide range of composers, including William Bolcom, Philip Glass, and David Amram. It was only when I got to Massachusetts that I found out what they wanted me to compose for the show: country-western songs. Had I known, I'm not sure I would have left Port of Spain. It took me back to my days on the military base in Kansas, when it seemed like that was the only kind of music on the radio.

They put me up and I spent a couple of months at the end of the summer working on the music. I remember that I got in the habit of having lunch in this little place on Massachusetts Avenue going toward Boston. I happened to go in there one day and noticed a jukebox against the wall. I went over to put something on while I was eating and realized that all they had was country-western music. I needed to reimmerse myself in that world, so I'd go there every day and put on that soundtrack before I headed to my office in the theater to write.

While I was in Cambridge, I also studied at the Longy School of Music with a woman who taught woodwinds there. She was an oboist, but she was savvy about technique in general. I was still working on doubling: strategies for switching among my various instruments. Working with Air, I'd realized that I needed more help with it.

It was something I'd been struggling with for a few years, ever since the period when I was studying flute at the American Conservatory and shuttling between blues gigs and the AACM big band. In terms of the way you hold your mouth, there's a world of difference between playing a wind instrument like a flute and playing a reed instrument like an alto or a clarinet.

You've got your muscles going one way, and then you want them to go another way. You need to develop an embouchure that can float quickly from one posture to another. It wasn't a simple fix. I had to break down my embouchure and reconstruct it to achieve that flexibility.

Some of these sorts of things you can learn on your own through practice or by asking other musicians. But not everything. Not everybody is so generous with the secrets of the guild.

Even as I had started working with Air, Steve McCall and I were also playing with Muhal's sextet. Once we did a bill opposite Yusef Lateef, whom I'd never met before. I was particularly interested to watch his set because I knew he was so proficient at moving among various reeds and flutes in the course of a concert.

At the end of the evening, I introduced myself to Lateef and asked him how he managed it. "I've been having some trouble working on some things on the flute," I ventured. He cut me off. "Well, you'll just have to keep working on it."

I stared at him. I was so shocked by his brusque response that I said something: "That's not very sensitive to a young musician. I just wanted to ask if you had any advice."

Lateef met my gaze without flinching. "I think you'll just have to keep working on it." And that was that. So much for backstage solidarity.

But it was also a lesson. Not everybody is or can be a teacher. And not every occasion is a pedagogical opportunity. The tradition gets passed down that way, too: in the blank spots, in recalcitrance or refusal, in what goes unsaid. Sometimes the lesson you need is to have someone refuse to give you a lesson. No, youngblood, no. It's not going to be handed to you on a platter.

The first time I toured in Europe was with Muhal's group, at the Berlin Jazz Festival in November 1973. I'll never forget that occasion. It was quite a program: the acts included Miles Davis, B.B. King, Odetta, and Louis Jordan. Duke Ellington played with a sextet a couple of days before we did. That was the last time I saw him before he passed. The day before us, it was Keith Jarrett with his quartet with Dewey Redman, Charlie Haden, and Paul Motian. Jarrett had a reputation for being a bit of a prima donna with audiences at times, if he felt that they weren't being respectful enough. He got peeved that someone was coughing or sneezing or something. He stopped the band, got up, and chided the audience. The Germans weren't having it that night, though: they started whistling and stomping, and they drowned him out with their jeers. They were riled up, and they wouldn't stop. Jarrett didn't seem to know what to do.

One of the other acts on the program that week was Rahsaan Roland Kirk. And Rahsaan saved the day. He went out and spoke to the audience, and he got them to calm down. It was astonishing: it was all about the tone of his voice. Rahsaan could bring peace anywhere.

I never played with Rahsaan, but we were close. He made me look silly with my problems with doubling instruments. Meanwhile, he would play three horns simultaneously! He was a man of prodigious talents. Once I saw him perform at the Jazz Showcase in Chicago, and after the show I went backstage to say hello. It was crowded in the green room; there were a bunch of other musicians, and some fans and journalists hanging out. I opened the door and walked two steps into this loud room, and Rahsaan—who was sitting in a chair back in the corner on the far side—looked up and exclaimed, "Threadgill, is that you?" The whole place got quiet. Everybody was trying to figure out how in the hell this blind man identified me from across a noisy room before I'd even said anything. Obviously his hearing was preternatural, but Rahsaan had some sixth or seventh sense, too. Even through a crowd, he could tell it was you because of the way you disturbed the air.

Sometimes in the evenings in Trinidad, the steel bands would start up. People would be out on their porches and verandas, maybe sipping an end-of-the-day rum, and the pan bands would pick up somewhere in the distance. We'd come out into the street and walk toward the sound. We'd just take our rum with us— there was no reason not to, it was an impulse triggered by the lure of the music. A crowd would gradually congregate as people walked from different directions toward the yard where the band was.

But occasionally there would be competing bands, and the crowd might be enticed by the sound of a second band coming from another direction that seemed to be killing it even more than the first band. It was as though the tide could shift. We were like a huge rolling mass, a pedestrian wave that could be pulled toward this other, more insistent gravitational force.

This tug-of-war lingered in the night air as the sun set. Eventually the most powerful band would capture the largest crowd. There might be false starts, and stragglers peeling off in various directions. But in time the best band would pull in the largest audience. When we finally reached the yard—when we finally came in view of the steel band, which itself was a crowd, of course, a pulsing conglomerate of men striking metal in a mesmerizing dance—it felt like the music went to an entirely different level because the accumulating energy of the arrivants fed the sound, made the music swell along with the congregation.

I've always wanted to do something like that: to have a marching band that would work the streets in New York that way. The closest I got was a concert I did in August 1985 down by the World Trade Center at the sandy landfill that became Battery Park. I had a bunch of musicians from various iterations of my band the Sextett—Pheeroan akLaff, Ted Daniel, Craig Harris—play as we walked to the "beach" there, picking up a crowd as we went.

It was fun, but I had wanted to do something much bigger, something that would happen regularly and really become part of the fabric of the city like the steel bands. I had choreographed a big piece where I was going to have musicians moving in different directions across a large area downtown. I also wanted to get the Fire Department involved, because I was hoping to use their

. . . in August 1985 down by the
World Trade Center
at the sandy landfill that became
Battery Park . . .

fire bells. The idea was that it would eventually converge at one spot, but I wanted to drive the audience—to herd the crowd by having the musicians come at them, move among them, and urge them along in a particular direction. The fire trucks would come out once the crowd had converged at the final location.

I didn't want to announce it as a performance that people could choose to attend or not. Instead I wanted it to be a sort of public action. I intended to catch people by surprise and just sweep them up in the momentum. All of a sudden you'd hear this music a few blocks away. And over time, as you followed it, you'd begin to get a sense of the gathering crowd around you—that you were getting drawn into a mass movement. All of this had to be planned, since it involved calculating pedestrian foot traffic and figuring out how to attract and move crowds. It was almost akin to the logistics of military troop maneuvers. It would require the same sort of precise calculation.

It went back to all those years I spent playing in parades in Chicago. But I had something else to bring into the streets. It was going to be a very different sort of parade music with *my* band. That's how I saw it: a gradual accumulation. A music that would gather its own crowd of listeners, amass its own public, corral them, and then move them to a place where all their assembled energy would take the event to another level. Then it wouldn't be about art as some sort of separate sphere, in some codified and commodified space where you could purchase a temporary dash of stimulation. This would be something entirely different: art in life, art *as* life, art as inescapable as gravity: a force that sneaks up on you as you're going about your everyday business and takes you somewhere you didn't know you needed to go.

7

Untitled Tango

Once at Englewood High School my English class was given an assignment to compose a poem. We each had to stand up in front of the class and read what we'd written. One of the girls was the first to go. She stood up at the blackboard and started explaining what she'd tried to do. "This is a poem about—" The teacher cut her off right away. "Stop," he said. "Just read the poem. Don't tell us what it's about." At the time I only heard it as a practical injunction related to what I was going to have to face a few minutes later. But it stuck somewhere in the back of my head, and to me it's a decent summation of the way art works in general. You don't need to know anything about art. You don't need anything to be disclosed in advance. You just need to experience it.

The point isn't that art is universal, except to the extent that all human societies make it in one fashion or another. There are still barriers and ambiguities, aspects of any given instance that some people won't be able to understand or engage with. But you can't explain art. It simply doesn't work that way.

I find that the less I say about my music, the better. If I say anything, it tends to be oblique or oracular: words meant to jar the listener out of the complacency of expectation. Then it's on you to come to the sound curious and open-eared to hear what you find.

———

By the end of 1975, Steve, Fred, and I decided to move to New York. We realized we'd outgrown Chicago. It felt like we'd exhausted the possibilities in the Midwest. The art scene wasn't big enough and varied enough to support what we were doing. We weren't unique in feeling that New York was the next step. We were a small part of a mass migration of creative musicians to the city in the middle of that decade, including a significant component of the AACM (Muhal, Jarman, Braxton, Kalaparusha, Amina Claudine Myers, and Leroy Jenkins, among others) as well as many of our peers from the West Coast (David Murray, Arthur Blythe, Butch Morris, James Newton), from St. Louis (Julius Hemphill, Oliver Lake, Hamiet Bluiett), and elsewhere. To all of us, New York possessed a magnetic attraction, promising broader exposure, new audiences, and funding opportunities. And it wasn't just musicians, either: there were dancers, writers, actors, filmmakers, painters, photographers, all converging on the city around the same time, all driven by the same potential and the lure of cheap studio and performance space. The city was mired in the throes of a severe economic downturn, but that didn't keep us away—if anything, it made the art scene feel more edgy, less predictable.

I'm not sure there's ever been an equivalent anywhere to this mass migration in the history of the arts, in terms of the sheer numbers and the range of disciplines. People sometimes forget that it involved not only artists themselves but also a much broader range of arts professionals, from production technicians to stagehands to graphic designers, editors, and journalists. In Chicago I knew an African American lighting engineer. All those unions were segregated and they wouldn't let him in. So the brother came to New York. And his career took off; later he was the lighting engineer for Natalie Cole.

Air's first official gig in Manhattan took place on a frigid evening in March 1976 at La MaMa Children's Workshop Theatre, one of the offshoots of Ellen Stewart's downtown alterna-

The three of us on the sidewalk in front of La MaMa
Children's Workshop Theatre on East Third Street

tive arts network, a building on East Third Street that Stewart had rented for next to nothing to the drummer Charles "Bobo" Shaw and the trombonist Joseph Bowie. (In the 1980s, it would come to be known as the address of the Nuyorican Poets Café.) By that summer, Air was playing regularly at venues such as the Tin Palace (a restaurant on the Bowery at East Second Street, a block north of the punk and no-wave institution CBGB), Ali's Alley (the ground-floor loft run by the drummer Rashied Ali on Greene Street in SoHo), and Studio Rivbea (which the saxophonist Sam Rivers opened with his wife, Bea, in their loft at 24 Bond Street). Sam was something of an elder statesman on the scene, and his Rivbea Orchestra would meet at his studio to rehearse his venturesome compositions, so his place became a kind of crossroads, the center of the energy swirling around downtown Manhattan. The two blocks on Bond Street running from Broadway to the Bowery were hot as a firecracker, with Rivbea, the Ladies' Fort, CBGB, and the Tin Palace all splayed along a single corridor. Sometimes you'd start the night at one place and end up at another.

The environment at the Tin Palace was extraordinary, just in terms of the concentration of talent in the room: I'd look out at the crowd during an Air concert and see the legendary bebop singers Eddie Jefferson and Betty Carter at one table, the Rolling Stones drummer Charlie Watts at another, and the pianist Cecil Taylor at the bar. People would wander over from the Amato Opera or from CBGB, which were both one block south. The atmosphere at the Tin Palace was a creative cauldron: to my mind, the unique air in that room gave birth to some of the most important groups to emerge in the period, above all the World Saxophone Quartet, which gave its first performance there in 1977.

In late May 1976, along with the majority of the bands on the downtown scene—from Sunny Murray's Untouchable Factor to Wadada Leo Smith's New Dalta Ahkri and Andrew Cyrille's Maono and groups led by Braxton, Lake, Hemphill, Randy Weston, Jimmy Lyons, Ken McIntyre, Dave Burrell, and Marion Brown, among others—Rivers invited Air to perform in the Summer Music Festival at Studio Rivbea, which was recorded by Douglas Records and released as a five-LP anthology titled *Wildflowers* that is probably the best-known document of what came to be known as the "loft jazz" scene. Sam made sure each group received copies of the master recording of its set; Air contributed one track to *Wildflowers* and put out the rest a few years later on our own album *Live Air*.

The label "loft jazz" was misleading because it implied that our music fell into one generic category when in fact the scene was marked by a stunning variety of styles. And the phrase seemed to suggest that our music was somehow forged by the classic, open cast-iron architecture of SoHo and Tribeca, where many artists colonized the cavernous spaces that had been abandoned by industrial manufacturers forced out by the recession. But the music took root in all sorts of formal and informal spaces across downtown Manhattan, from more or less conventional nightclubs to restaurants, cafés, bars, apartments, galleries, and theaters. What made it thrilling was that there were so many places to play. And the audiences came out to support the music—"audiences" in the plural, because different spaces would attract different crowds. Over the next several years, the landscape would shift periodically as spots continued to open and close.

In the spring of 1977, we started playing at a gallery and café on West Broadway called Axis in SoHo, where a young producer named Andrew Plesser started booking a concert series. The scene at Axis in SoHo flourished for more than a year until the influential theater producer Joseph Papp hired Plesser to direct jazz programming at the Public Theater. Founded in March 1978, the New Jazz at the Public series quickly became the pinnacle for the downtown experimental music scene: the institutional space everybody was aiming for. The production was top-notch and the audiences were enthusiastic. At the smaller lofts and galleries, you might get a review in one of the alternative weeklies (*The Village Voice* or *SoHo Weekly News*), but concerts at the

Public Theater were often reviewed in *The New York Times*, *The New Yorker*, and *New York* magazine, as well as all the jazz journals. But there were all sorts of other spaces, too, including a bevy of lofts and studios (Environ, Jazzmania, Ali's Alley, the Ladies' Fort, Studio We, the Brook), alternative art spaces such as the Kitchen, La MaMa, and Franklin Furnace, and the student centers at NYU and Columbia. The only places we weren't really getting into were the more established jazz nightclubs such as the Village Vanguard and the Village Gate, which tended to privilege an older generation of musicians. Even so, the Art Ensemble played at the Five Spot in 1975, and I eventually did a lot of work at places like Sweet Basil. We were happy to move around, because every venue represented a chance to attract a new audience. So we ran the gamut.

At the time, you could really hustle in New York. You'd just hear about things—the word would get out that a new place had opened up. There were places where there were concerts, but also an entirely different network of bars and restaurants where we would meet up and socialize. When I first arrived, musicians used to gather at Phebe's Tavern on the Bowery a couple of blocks up from the Tin Palace. You'd go by and have a beer in the afternoon and run into people, and it served as an informal employment clearing house as well. Someone would hook you up to work on a project or ask you to play on a recording date. There were extended discussions about everything that was going on. It served as something like a perpetual salon.

There were places associated with various art forms as well. Sometimes we would hang out at Le Figaro Café, the spot in Greenwich Village at the corner of Bleecker and MacDougal where the poet Ted Joans would hold court. You might see an actor you knew, or a filmmaker. You might find some of the younger writers, such as Ntozake Shange, Jessica Hagedorn, Renée Montagne, and Thulani Davis, at the Old Reliable or DeMonte's in the East Village. I also spent a good deal of time working with the dancers who would convene at Roberta Garrison's loft on the top floor at 61 Crosby Street. And there was

Performing with Roberta Garrison in her loft on the top floor
at 61 Crosby Street. Photo © Jacki Ochs

another scene uptown at Sounds in Motion, the choreographer Dianne McIntyre's studio in Harlem.

In addition to all these smaller, labile gathering spots, Air got into some of the elite theater venues almost immediately. We were invited to perform on a double bill with the Oliver Lake Quartet at Carnegie Recital Hall in September 1976. But we never limited ourselves to one type of space. Even as we got to play in the Public Theater or Town Hall, were also playing in the unofficial hangs like the loft apartment David Murray and Stanley Crouch shared above the Tin Palace, where they occasionally hosted concerts. One of our most stable early gigs was Beefsteak Charlie's Jazz Emporium on Fifth Avenue around Twelfth Street. That was an unusual place to run into Air! We'd play there in the storefront window, visible from the street. But the manager there loved us. There was no pressure to do anything other than what we were doing.

The cosmopolitan atmosphere of New York also launched us into touring circuits beyond anything we'd been able to do hopping around the small cities in the Midwest. We would periodically tour up and down the Northeast Corridor, making stops in all the major cities along the way, from DC Space in Washington and the Foxhole in Philadelphia all the way up to Cambridge and Boston. Air also got taken up by the European festival circuit, and we would make extended trips there almost every year: Willisau, Nickelsdorf, Montreux. We built a large following in Paris, and we'd do two-week stints there at places like La Chapelle des Lombards. It makes a huge difference when you tour that way: not one-night stands, but extended runs. You have a chance to unpack and breathe a little. A band can really develop when you have that much time. It was nice not to have to rush off to the next gig in the next city, especially with all the stuff I was lugging around then. Getting a bass and a drum kit around Europe is cumbersome, but I had a whole menagerie: alto, tenor, baritone, flute, and hubkaphone. I bought this massive blue French trunk where I could put my clothes and all the horns but the baritone. I'd have to cart the trunk around as well as my baritone case and the case where I kept the hubkaphone. I had less mileage on my body then, but I'm not sure how I did it. There were a number of close calls, and some hilarity along the way. I remember one European tour with Fred and Andrew Cyrille in the mid-1980s, after the original Air disbanded, when it seemed like we were running to catch trains in every city we stopped in. A couple of times we must have looked like a clown act from the circus. Once we cut it too close and had to scramble to get all our gear on board. Fred got in a compartment and leaned out the window while Andrew and I frantically handed our bags to him, pushing a luggage cart down the platform as the train started to pull out of the station. We ended up tossing cases in any door or window that was open, just trying to get it all in. By the end of the escapade, Andrew and I were sprinting alongside the train like fools. Finally we hauled ourselves into the last car as the train gathered up speed. Then, after we caught our breath, we had to pick our way through the entire train car by car, retrieving our instruments along the way, to the great bemusement of the other passengers.

There is an expectation that an artist's autobiography will function as a primer, providing "explanations" of the art. But this book is not a listening guide. If anything, it is an extended defiance of that expectation. If it's meant to teach you anything about my music, it starts with the lesson that you need to relinquish that desire for transparency. *Music is about listening.* Nothing I can say can mean anything once you start to listen. It's about the sound, not about the words I might be able to pin up to preface or accompany whatever the sound does to you when it goes in your ears.

If you really need to know, I can tell you—for whatever it's worth—that anything can go into my music. I get ideas from all sorts of sources. It might be going to the theater or looking at a painting or just watching a tree branch outside the window. It might be reading about the muddy intricacies of trench warfare during World War I or poring over *The Book of Five Rings* (Miyamoto Musashi's seventeenth-century book on sword-fighting tactics) or looking at the novels of James Joyce or Heinrich Böll. Anything can seep into the music.

I've always been intensely engaged with the music of other composers. But even if I sometimes glean techniques I can adapt, I tend to get my information on another level. I get more ideas about music by looking at a sculpture or by watching a dance than by listening to other music. I go elsewhere: that's how I get informed. But that doesn't mean the music is *about* any of those other things, or that there's some key source that, if you were aware of it, could unlock the music for you as a listener.

Rather than providing subject matter, these kinds of things shape my music through a kind of loose formal extrapolation. Say I'm reading about trench warfare. It might focus my attention on the way you can have multiple levels of engagement: some things going on above ground and other things happening in the tunnels. As I saw firsthand in Vietnam, tunnels can be hidden mazes—they're networks that give you ways of getting from one place to another without being seen, without exposing yourself. Trenches are territory lines, too: a crude calligraphy of advancing and retreating forces confronting each other across a no-man's-land. And they end up being social spaces, too, where you sleep and eat and smoke and pee and write letters home. You could even say they have their own temporality. A trench is a whole emotional atmosphere with a palette of its own, from apprehension—*Is that a rifle barrel I see poking out from that crevice?*—to silent pools of boredom.

But I'm not thinking about all these things to write music about the historical experience of a soldier in World War I. Instead, the process involves a kind of transposition: how can a piece of music work on multiple levels in a similar way, or suggest that sort of emotional ambiguity? The parallel is subtle—a matter of intuition—rather than straightforward and mechanistic. (In other words, working on multiple levels in music doesn't just mean using a mix of high pitches and low pitches.) The

With Fred and Andrew Cyrille on the platform
of a train station in Europe. Photo © Dany Gignoux

transposition makes me think about musical structure in a different way.

Not everything is everybody's business. The elements that factor into my artistic process are part of that process, but they don't necessarily have anything to do with the impact of the finished artwork on the listener.

As a woodwinds player working in a trio, you're taking a chance. How much music can you play? How do you sustain it? Can you make an evening out of it? From a compositional point of view, does a trio provide a broad enough palette? There was a long tradition of piano trios, of course, but very little precedent for a trio with woodwinds, bass, and drums. As I explained, I knew I wasn't going to try to replicate the herculean feats of Sonny Rollins in that format. So I kept an eye out for other strategies.

One group in particular became a touchstone for me: the Revolutionary Ensemble, with Leroy Jenkins, Sirone, and Jerome Cooper. Leroy and Jerome were both from Chicago and had studied with Captain Dyett at DuSable High School. Jerome had been in school there with Fred. But Leroy was about a dozen years older than the rest of us, and I always thought of him as an AACM elder whom I could ask for advice. He had made the move to New York back in 1970 and had figured out how to find his way in the big city. Even before that, he'd been exploring the trio format, working with Braxton and Wadada. They recorded Braxton's 3 *Compositions of New Jazz* in 1968 before they all moved to Europe. Eventually they called themselves the Creative Construction Company, and when they came to New York they played a famous concert in May 1970 at the Peace Church in Washington Square Park that Ornette Coleman helped them record. Steve had joined the group in Paris, too, and the New York concert featured a larger ensemble, adding Steve on drums, Muhal on piano, and Richard Davis on bass. But at the core of the Creative Construction Company concept was the trio of Leroy, Braxton, and Wadada. The combination of two wind players and a string player was just as unusual as Air's combination of reeds, flute, or hubkaphone with bass and drums. So I had looked at their work very closely. Then Leroy moved into another trio situation with the Revolutionary Ensemble. With its lineup of violin, bass, and drums, the Revolutionary Ensemble was an even closer parallel to Air.

Once we were both in New York, I got in the habit of calling Leroy to ask him for advice. Not so much in terms of the music—I listened to the things he was doing in the trio format, but they weren't direct influences on what I was exploring in my compositions for Air—as about navigating the music business. I'd ask him what he thought about certain possibilities, or about the atmosphere at a loft or club I hadn't had a chance to play in. He pushed me to pay attention to economics. "We were just starting to make some headway, Henry," he'd tell me. "We were just getting to a point where we could demand realistic fees. And now you young guys are going backwards, playing in these places on the cheap."

Although I already thought of myself as a composer, it was Leroy more than anyone else in New York who encouraged me to pursue that side of things deliberately. "We're not going to get anywhere with these one-night gigs," he would declare. "We've got to stretch out."

He started getting grants and commissions. I watched him get funding from the New York State Council on the Arts and the National Endowment for the Arts. And he started writing pieces for big mainstream ensembles, which over the years came to include the Brooklyn Philharmonic, the Kronos Quartet, the New Music Consort, the Albany Symphony, the Cleveland Chamber Symphony, and the Munich Biennale Festival for New Music Theater. He was asked to do composer residencies at universities around the country, including Bennington, the University of Michigan, Carnegie Mellon, and Harvard. He joined foundation panels and served for years on the boards of the Composers' Forum and Meet the Composer.

Leroy dragged me with him into that world. He told me to

Air in concert in Nickelsdorf, Austria, in August 1980.
Photo © Helmut Frühauf

apply for this or that and introduced me to the power brokers in those sorts of spaces. So I give him a lot of credit for pushing me in that direction.

The first couple of Revolutionary Ensemble albums came out on small independent labels such as ESP and India Navigation. But just as we were coming to New York, they got a contract with a major label: A&M Horizon, which released their 1976 record *The People's Republic*. Within the next two years, Air made the same switch, moving from the Japanese label Whynot, which released our first two albums, to Arista Novus, where the producer Steve Backer signed us and put out *Open Air Suit* and *Montreux Suisse Air* in 1978. So I also consulted Leroy about that transition and about the advantages and pitfalls of working with commercial labels.

Over the next decade and a half I kept working with certain independent labels including Nessa in Chicago, About Time in New York, and Black Saint in Tribiano, Italy. But I had an extended period with some of the majors, including Arista, Island, and Columbia. Working with so many different sorts of record companies over the decades has given me what may be a unique perspective on the business.

When the opportunity to go with a big label first arises, musicians find it hard to resist the temptation. The majors offer a lot more money up front and woo you with seductive talk about their investment in marketing and their distribution network. But I came to realize that after the initial honeymoon, those kinds of companies don't keep your music available for any length of time. If your record isn't an immediate hit, it ends up in the cutout bins in a hot minute. Until Mosaic Records did a box set in 2010 of my work on Arista-Novus and Columbia with Air, X-75, the Henry Threadgill Sextett, and Make a Move, most of that music was out of print. A good portion of it hadn't ever been released on CD.

In contrast, the small companies keep your music on the market. The initial run is smaller, but they think in terms of the long game. They have to—that's how they make their money.

Very few people are aware of the weakness with record companies in general: whether independent or commercial, with jazz and experimental music, companies across the board neglect what may be the most important aspect of making a record—postproduction and mixing. They want to put it out immediately. It's an effect of the widespread prejudice against music the record executives think of as "improvised": you made it in the moment, so now it's done. Let's just put it out there. With pop music or classical music, they spend weeks and months after the recording sessions, fine-tuning the production. But not with our music. It makes no sense, because you need to put in the time—and you need some distance on things to gain some perspective on it.

As happy as I was with many of my records, I always felt that every album I made could have sounded fifty times better in terms of the refinement of the sound. When I started working with Pi Recordings in 2001, I remember being struck by their approach. Pi was a small independent label, but they recognized the importance of mixing. They took their time. For instance, with the two volumes of *This Brings Us To* in 2010, we took almost six months to mix those records. They sound good for a reason!

People always ask me about my song titles. "Keep Right On Playing Thru the Mirror Over the Water"—what does that mean? "Salute to the Enema Bandit," "Spotted Dick Is Pudding"—what in the world are you referring to? "To Undertake My Corners Open"? Why are your titles so cryptic? "Just the Facts and Pass the Bucket"? They assume too quickly that titles are always descriptive or programmatic: clues about content. That might be the case for some composers. But I use song titles as another source of stimulation. They might have roots in my artistic process—in the sundry stuff I encountered as I was making the work—but their function isn't to suggest that the music can be reduced to those sources. For the listener, they function as a spark. The language is meant to spur your own thought process as you listen. You don't need to know what I might have been thinking about. Instead you need to start with this material I've thrown on the table in front of you and figure out your own reaction. What now? What does it make you feel? What does it make you think about? Take me out of the equation. You're the equation: your ears, your blood pulse, your own sound world, your own predilections. Now what do we have?

I'm fortunate to have been able to make a number of albums over the years. But I don't think of my discography as the central documentation of my contribution as a composer. My records aren't a monument.

A record is for listening purposes. It is not—and cannot replace—live music, which is a completely different realm of experience. A record session is unstimulated performance. There's no audience. And that makes an enormous difference. As a performer, the stimulation you get from a crowd transforms the music completely, in a way that can't be reproduced in the laboratory atmosphere of a recording studio. The music becomes something else when it's forged in the arena of a live situation through that mysterious exchange that happens with a specific group of listeners who happen to be there for that set on that particular night. What happens there might not be acceptable in the recording studio—things can go out of kilter and then come back into kilter in unpredictable ways that make sense in the room, in that moment, even if they might not work in the documentary calculation of an album. But for me live performance is central to what the music is. It is inherently oriented toward those society situations. It requires that stimulation in the moment, that feedback between the players and the listeners.

An album, on the other hand, is something for people to listen to at their leisure. It might be a document of the repertory at a particular moment: where my music stood at a certain time. The general feel of what the ensemble sounded like. But it represents only a small part of my total production as a composer. In general, with all of my groups, there is much more material that doesn't get recorded than what ends up on my albums. The recorded portion isn't the best—it isn't the culmination. Every record is composed as a deliberate statement, a curated sampling, working within the limitations of the album form. But none of my albums is definitive. What they add up to is nowhere near the whole picture.

Before I left Chicago, I had started seeing someone new: Rrata Christine Jones, a dancer I'd known from the scene around Columbia College. Christine was in Shirley Mordine's company, and she'd also performed with Kim On Wong and was one of the performers in *The Hotel*. Christine actually moved to New York before I did, to dance with the Sun Ra Arkestra. She found a place to stay on Eleventh Street in the East Village, and I joined her there when I made the move in the winter of 1975. A year or so later we moved to Twelfth Street. Christine got involved in the downtown dance scene at Roberta Garrison's studio in SoHo and uptown at Dianne McIntyre's Sounds in Motion, so we ended up working together pretty often.

In 1977 our daughter, Pyeng, was born at St. Vincent's Hospital. And being a parent turned out to be a significant part of my life in the downtown arts scene, because a number of people had children around the same time. We grew close to the singer Jeanne Lee, for example, because her son, Ruomi, and daughter, Cavana, were about Pyeng's age. I think Steve had introduced us, because he knew her from living in Europe at the end of the 1960s. Jeanne lived on Second Avenue around Thirteenth Street. And our kids would hang out all the time. There were others, too, a little farther away: Leroy Jenkins's daughter, Billy Bang's son, William Parker's daughter. These social networks fed into our artistic relationships. Although I never recorded with her, I ended up performing often with Jeanne. A few times it was a straight music gig somewhere like the Tin Palace. But she wrote poetry and did things with dance, too, mixing art forms, so we also performed in lofts like Roberta Garrison's place.

One consequence of all the attention Air was getting was that Fred and Steve started getting asked to play in every unit in town. This was part of the draw of New York, of course. But cats were shameless. You'd hardly have finished a single set and someone would be trying to tear your band up.

In no time, it seemed, Fred was doing shows with David Murray, Don Pullen, Oliver Lake, Michael Gregory Jackson, and Hamiet Bluiett. Steve was on call with Chico Freeman and Butch Morris. By the end of the decade, both of them were playing in Arthur Blythe's *In the Tradition* band. With the blazing young pianist Hilton Ruiz, they started to become something like a house band at the Tin Palace, billing themselves the "Great Rhythm Section" and playing with all kinds of horn players.

In the first few years, I didn't play with other people as much, because I was concentrating on my writing for Air. And I remained determined not to be a sideman. Still, I performed around town and recorded a few albums with old AACM friends and colleagues, including Muhal, Chico, Braxton, Roscoe Mitchell, Amina Claudine Myers, and Frank Walton. As time went by I started to do a few things with other musicians, too: David Murray's octet, Julius Hemphill's big band, and then, in the mid-1980s, James Blood Ulmer's Phalanx. But my priority was always my own composing for my own groups. And I realized almost as soon as we settled in New York that I was going to need to diversify. I still had the X-75 ensemble, which recorded an album for Arista in January 1979. But I also began to consider other compositional possibilities.

A new wing of the scene emerged on West Twenty-third Street at the Squat Theatre, which had been founded in 1977 by a group of radical dissident Hungarian actors, writers, and performance artists. In the summer of 1979, the Squat started hosting music concerts as well. Sun Ra played there regularly over the next couple of years, and the Squat tapped into the downtown jazz scene with shows by Oliver Lake, Ahmed Abdullah, Ted Daniel, Luther Thomas, Frank Lowe, Phillip Wilson, Abdullah Ibrahim, and Leroy Jenkins, among others. The Squat was dependably eclectic. On any given night you might hear a wide range of musicians, including former denizens of Andy Warhol's Factory such as Nico and John Cale and young bands from the punk and no-wave scene, including DNA, Kid Creole and the Coconuts, James Chance and the Contortions, Bill Laswell's Material, and the Lounge Lizards. From the beginning, they also featured blues, with concerts by Luther Allison, Johnny Copeland, Sunnyland Slim, and J. B. Hutto.

I was drawn into the scene because they also brought in my old running mate from Chicago, the guitarist Left Hand Frank Craig. In September 1979, Frank sat in with a group led by the trombonist Joseph Bowie featuring his brothers Lester and Byron as well as Amina, Kelvyn Bell, and Olu Dara, and the combination was such a success that they scheduled a series of "All-Star Blues Jams" shows featuring "the Greats of today's jazz" in November and December. The rhythm section was Melvin Gibbs on electric bass, Martin Aubert on electric guitar, and Steve on drums. Along with Frank, the other guest soloists included the Bowie brothers, Hamiet Bluiett, Ted Daniel, and myself on tenor.

The downtown music journalists were blown away. Robert Christgau at *The Village Voice* was particularly astonished by my unexpected facility with the blues, writing breathlessly that "Henry Threadgill revealed himself as a world-class R&B tenor man." Of course, he had no idea that I'd been playing the blues with Frank in Chicago years before! This was right around the time Air released *Air Lore,* our album featuring some of my old Scott Joplin arrangements from *The Hotel,* so the jazz critics tended to associate me with the downtown experimental jazz world. But for me, the gig with Frank was a breeze—a return to home territory.

The scene at the Squat gave rise to thrilling cross-fertilization. A bunch of the horn players who were often at the Squat, including Joseph Bowie, John Purcell, Pablo Calogero, and I, started playing in a horn section for the combustible singer James Chance in a band he jokingly called James White and the Blacks. We had a lot of fun—and the gigs paid well. James Chance didn't say too much, but onstage he was a lunatic. He would dive into the crowd at the Squat and get beaten up. I'd never seen anybody do something like that. He'd stagger back up to the stage grinning with his shirt ripped and bloody.

I didn't become a regular, but I did play with James White and the Blacks a number of times, both at the Squat and at other clubs like Hurrah, Irving Plaza, and the Pyramid. The band became a minor sensation, as did the other group Joseph Bowie founded around the same time using many of the same personnel, a funk band called Defunkt. I sometimes played with Defunkt, too. And both Joseph and I performed for years in the trumpeter and singer Olu Dara's Okra Orkestra.

At the end of November 1979, a couple of weeks after the first "All-Star" show with Frank, I debuted a new group at the Squat: the Henry Threadgill Sextett. At first the band was me, Joe Bowie, Olu Dara, Fred Hopkins, the cellist Muneer Abdul Fataah, and the drummers Pheeroan akLaff and John Betsch. Muneer and Betsch lived in a loft together on Avenue C around Tenth Street, and that's where we'd rehearse. A few months later, we moved our rehearsals to a bigger loft at 450 West Thirty-first Street that some architects let me use; we would have concerts there, too.

There's a tune called "Ten to One" on *When Was That?* It's an inside joke: I'd always hold rehearsals in the late morning, from ten a.m. to one p.m., so as to avoid conflicting with anybody else's rehearsal schedule. The musicians used to hate that. If anybody complained I'd just say, "Get used to it."

The Sextett in rehearsal on West Thirty-first Street:
Muneer Abdul Fataah, Vincent Chancey, Olu Dara,
Pheeroan akLaff, me, and Fred Hopkins

———

Experimentation is at the heart of the creative process. What sets art and science apart from every other domain of human endeavor is that they are formalized realms for radical experimentation. For taking chances. Areas of activity where conjecture and risk taking are privileged and failures and dead ends are accepted as part of the game. This is the reason there's perpetual tension between musicians and record companies: experimentation doesn't go well with commodification. The same sorts of tensions can arise in science, with the funding of research that seems too theoretical, too far out, too removed from any practical application or patent potential.

To expel myself from my proclivities, sometimes I have to let my mind slip into another world. Then it's hard to fall into habit, into the same old ingrained ways of working. Sometimes I have to destroy my own process to get to something new.

In the winter of 2009 I had a residency at the Copland House in Cortlandt Manor, the town up the Hudson River from New York City where the composer Aaron Copland lived in the last decades of his life. Copland called it his "hideaway." You're up there alone in this beautiful house in the woods. I was reading some of the books I found in his collection there—I came across a copy of *Ulysses* and started rereading that—but I was also just looking out the window. Sometimes that's all it takes.

One day I noticed a vine outside the window in the den that should have been dead. It was December. All the trees were bare. But there was one bush that had a vine coming up through it that had attached itself to the brickwork on the side of the house, and there were a few leaves on it. I started sketching the vine from different angles—just sketching the structure, the three-dimensional distribution of what was in front of me. When I looked at it carefully, I realized how complex it was: some parts of the vine looked dead, and then there were these sections with leaves that seemed like these little residual clumps of stubborn life. A little bit of green that seemed determined to hang on—

wind and snow and ice be damned. Wow, I thought. Look at that.

I didn't have a plan. It just piqued my curiosity.

I would check it out every morning, and then I started to appreciate the ways it was changing. A leaf might fall to the ground during the night. The composition kept altering itself, and there was a rhythm to the changes, even if I couldn't predict exactly what was going to happen when. I woke up one morning and saw that two clumps of leaves had fallen off. They had already lost their color, and the intensity of green of the remaining leaves on the vine seemed heightened in contrast to the brown around it. There was less green left, but that made the color seem even more vivid.

None of this is surprising from a botanical point of view. Changing seasons isn't like flipping a light switch. Nature is filled with peculiar little pockets of resiliency and resignation: some things that seem determined not to die, and others that seem to let themselves go prematurely. But this mundane insight affected my compositional process, because I started playing with contrasts between areas of activity in the music I was writing, too: shifting contrasts between developments in the foreground, the middle ground, and the background of the soundscape. Motifs that lingered "too long" until they came to be highlighted in relief against their surroundings.

This is to say that for me, musical experimentation isn't a matter of finding new content—I was never trying to depict the falling leaves in sound—but is instead a way of finding a formal instigation from an entirely unrelated source through a simple practice of observation. Making myself look elsewhere. It was as though watching that bush provided a way of making my mind go out on a limb.

I knew I wanted to do something different with the Sextett. I started formulating what I wanted the instrumentation to be—I had a certain sound in mind—and then I went after the people I thought would be the right fit.

From the very beginning, I was thinking orchestrally. With Air, it was all shadow and gesture: I was down to the bare minimum. So the Sextett was a chance to bring in some other colors. Still, I knew I didn't want a pianist. I didn't want to write music based on conventional chord changes, and I didn't want to have to worry about out-of-tune pianos at some venue where we might be performing. But most of all, I was wary of the chord voicings on a piano. Even with a sensitive pianist, the accompaniment voicings can make something sound off or wrong. I was already trying to take my music outside of traditional diatonic harmony, and I didn't want a chordal instrument to anchor it. I didn't need a chordal instrument, anyway. What I was after was a contrapuntal music based in the interaction and contrast among single-line voices moving in different directions at the same time.

I didn't think about the structure of the ensemble the way most jazz musicians think about their bands. Most people start with the number of players: a quartet, a quintet. Horns out front, backed up by a rhythm section. But I approached it by thinking about the way an orchestra is set up. There's a brass section, a string section, a wind section, a percussion section. The organization gives the composer a certain range of sounds and timbres to work with and to combine. The melody lines can come from anywhere.

To put it differently, writing for an orchestra is not about the sheer number of musicians on the bandstand. It's all about the combination. That was my focus with the Sextett. At festivals in Europe, sometimes we were followed by a big band, and they'd sound thin in comparison. I remember a festival in Berlin where the drummer Roy Haynes came up to me backstage after our set. "I know that's not a big band you've got," he commented. "But damn, Threadgill—it sure *sounded* big!" I was aiming for a thickness, a density in the sound.

This orchestral approach was the reason I called it a sextet even though there were seven players. People thought it was some sort of gimmick—some sort of wacky, tongue-in-cheek gesture. But the name was a straightforward reflection of the makeup of the band. It had to do with the number of parts, not the number of people. What the drummers were doing in the Sextett was a single sectional part. It simply took two people to play it. I signaled this by adding an extra *t*—Sextett—to emphasize that my version of a sextet had seven players. At first people thought I was being cute. Only the last three albums were credited to the Sextett, starting with *You Know the Number* in 1986. But in my mind, the band's name always had that extra *t*.

As I mentioned, I had previously explored tuning the drums with Steve's kit in Air: you can hear it in *Open Air Suit*, for instance. But with the new group I did it in a more systematic manner. In the Sextett, the two sets of drums were tuned chromatically. Each kit had a bass drum, a floor tom, two upper toms, and the snare drum. One kit was tuned in intervals of a fourth, like the strings of the bass, and the other kit was tuned in fifths, like the cello. We also had two concert bass drums that the drummers used sometimes. This gave me almost all the pitches in the chromatic scale to work with when I wanted to. Sometimes I used the same tunings—so one drum kit would be tuned E-A-D-G, like the strings of the bass—and sometimes I had them tune the drums with other notes. Either way, all the sympathetic vibrations among the percussion and string instruments gave the music a *breadth* that you could hear, even if you didn't know what it was. The drummers could reinforce things going on harmonically in the brass or string sections. Or they could be used to add contrast and depth.

I gave the drummers written parts just like the rest of the musicians. It might have been unusual, but Pheeroan and Betsch didn't have any trouble with it. In fact, they seemed to appreciate it—nobody else was giving them anything as precise as spe-

The Sextett in rehearsal on West Thirty-first Street:
Olu Dara, Fred Hopkins, and me

cific pitches to play. In most jazz ensembles, the drummer is just expected to play time. He might be told to throw in an accent here or there on the melodic statement, or maybe a special figure. But the majority of the time, percussion is taken for granted.

I don't mean that every moment of what the drummers are doing in every piece is written out. They do play time, especially in the parts where there are improvised solos. But once they get accustomed to the way their kits are tuned, both of the drummers can take advantage of the tuning in the way they accompany the other players.

Another important factor for me was the difference in the ways the two drummers played time. I didn't need two people who would play time the same way. John Betsch plays way behind the beat. He has a kind of loping style to his playing. And Pheeroan plays way up toward the top of the beat—almost on top of it, not quite, but almost on top of the beat. That was the reason I chose the two of them. One was ahead and one was behind.

If you have a drummer who plays behind the beat, sometimes when the other instruments play ahead of the pulse it can sound a little bit out of whack. Or if you have a drummer who plays right on top of the beat, everything can feel rushed and tight, and the music can almost seem to clip its own heels or even to run over itself. But when you have that combination between drummers playing with such different senses of time, it makes for a very wide beat. The beat feels spacious and roomy. You can rummage around in it. When the beat is wide, you can put a lot of information into that space and finesse its delivery in microscopic ways. A commodious beat creates an implication of vastness in the music.

I chose all the drummers in the different versions of the Sextett over the years with this consideration in mind. I deliberately looked for players who would be complementary. I tried a number of players in those seats, but it didn't work with everybody because they didn't all gel. We endured a couple of disastrous experiments. I brought in one guy who approached it as though

it were supposed to be a drum battle: who can play the loudest?
We did one concert and everybody else in the band was infuri-
ated. They were ready to kill this cat. After Betsch left, I had
Pheeroan and Reggie Nicholson together for a little while, but I
didn't think the two of them fit together as well in terms of their
time senses. The next pairing that really clicked was Reggie and
Newman Taylor Baker. Newman plays right on the beat, while
Reggie tends to play behind. The two of them in combination
gave the music a beat that felt like it was as big as all outdoors.

I did eventually have a couple of long-term sideman jobs that
were important to me in different ways. They lasted for years,
but most people don't even realize I did them because I never
recorded with these bands.

I knew the baritone saxophonist Pat Patrick a little bit from
Chicago, where he was a longtime member of Sun Ra's Arkestra. Not long after I first arrived in New York, Pat gave me some
work as a substitute in his Baritone Sax Retinue, which featured
seven or eight baritones and a rhythm section. A couple of times
I stood in for Mario Rivera—once, I remember, at the West
Indian Day Parade in Brooklyn—and as time went by Mario
and I became great friends. Through Pat and Mario, I started to
get gigs occasionally in Latin bands. I had experience with the
music from years earlier in Chicago, of course, so it was easy for
me to handle those charts.

It was Rolando Briceño, my old friend from Venezuela, who
connected me with the legendary Cuban bandleader and trumpeter Mario Bauzá. Rolando had moved to New York, and he
was mainly working with Latin bands around the city. Anyone
even tangentially tied to that world knew Bauzá, who is often
credited for having concocted the infectious amalgam of jazz and
mambo associated with Machito and his Afro-Cubans, which
he cofounded in 1939. Bauzá was arguably the most important
relay between jazz and Cuban musicians. He played with Chick
Webb and Cab Calloway, in whose trumpet section he met a

young firebrand named Dizzy Gillespie. He introduced Dizzy to Chano Pozo, the influential percussionist, and over the coming decades the Machito band served as a crucial crossroads, a launching pad for musicians, like Tito Puente, who went on to become major figures in their own right.

Bauzá had left the Machito band in the mid-1970s and fell out of view for a while, but in the late 1980s he enjoyed a resurgence. I played regularly with his band for a number of years in the second half of the decade, along with Rolando and musicians such as the trombonist Conrad Herwig, the baritone saxophonist Pablo Calogero, and the drummer Bobby Sanabria. I held the second alto chair, and I also played a lot of flute. His charts were amazing: subtle and sophisticated. I would just stand there in rehearsals and stare at his writing, trying to absorb as much as I could.

When I took solos, Bauzá insisted that I should play the way I played. He didn't want me to try to fit into some clichéd sort of pseudo-Latin style. He was funny. He'd tell me, "I don't want to hear all that shit. I've heard that. Charlie Parker did all that decades ago. Don't you bring that up in here." He wanted me to play outside. I'd play an unusual figure and he'd ask me, "Why do you do that?" He was curious about things I'd do—musical choices I'd make. He wanted to understand what I was doing. And then he wanted me to keep doing it.

Bauzá would get impatient with some of the more conventional players in the band. I'd have to lower my gaze when they were taking a solo so he wouldn't be able to catch my eye and call on me. Sometimes he'd get bored with a solo—"All they do is play those same patterns and shit," he'd grumble to me afterwards—and want to cut somebody off. He'd look over my way and try to signal me to interrupt them. I'd just keep my head glued to the chart. No, I'd think to myself, I don't need to make any enemies here tonight.

In an even more unlikely turn of events, I also ended up playing for a while with the great bebop trumpeter Howard McGhee, who also had a comeback period in the late 1970s. It was the trumpeter Tommy Turrentine who got me in that band. Tommy was one of the most generous spirits on the scene. The tenor saxophonist Clifford Jordan was the same way: always making connections, always recommending people for jobs. Everybody loved Tommy. He recommended me to McGhee, and I became a regular playing baritone in the band, which for years was featured at the Sunday-afternoon Jazz Vespers at St. Peter's Lutheran Church on Lexington Avenue.

The music was straight-ahead bebop. And most of the other musicians were older players from that generation. I didn't have any interest in soloing in that context. There was no way I was going to stand up there like another bebop clone, noodling those same old lines—*scoobie-doobie-doobie!*—over those same old changes. I wouldn't have been able to look myself in the mirror.

But Howard McGhee would always put me on the spot. I think his motivation was similar to Bauzá's: he was interested to hear what I'd do, because he knew I wouldn't play by the rules. He made it clear that he didn't expect me to mimic bebop. All I had to do was make my music fit. And I knew how that music moved, just as I understood the basic forms and cadences of Latin music in the Bauzá band. So I could go as far out as I wanted, because I knew how to bring it back in.

It got awkward at times, because it was obvious that the other guys in the band couldn't stand the way I played. They came close to saying it openly to McGhee: "You shouldn't let that joker solo." I know they said it backstage to him, even if they didn't say it in front of my face.

And I agreed with them completely! I didn't want to take a solo. It was annoying to put on the straitjacket of those chords changes and to try to wriggle myself out of them.

But Howard would always point to me. The other guys would roll their eyes.

Working with both of them, I wondered what they saw in me. But they clearly appreciated me. Both Bauzá and McGhee used to invite me over to dinners and parties at their houses. Nobody else from the band—just me.

Even though I didn't enjoy being a fish out of water, I learned a great deal from both of them, too. I remember being impressed by how well Howard McGhee knew his craft. His arrangements were pristine. I would listen to the way he made things work, both musically as a player and as a bandleader. You can always learn something. You watch somebody build a house. You might not want to build that same particular house. But you observe the process, you check the technique. You see how to do it correctly. The attention to detail. You pick up little things you might use in your own way later when you build your own place.

You can learn from negative examples as well as positive ones. Once someone asked Charlie Parker, "Why do you agree to play with those guys who can't play?" Bird's answer was matter-of-fact: "So I know what not to play."

I remember sitting in and observing a recording session at some point in New York. It was a marathon session, and I noticed the brass players getting tired. I came to realize that when you're playing demanding music, it's the brass players' lips that are going to give out first. So you watch the trumpeters and trombonists for signs of fatigue, not the pianists or the drummers or the reed players. You might think that the brass players are the powerhouses in the ensemble, these big, rough, and rugged physical players, but in fact they're the most fragile component of the group. As a result, I got into the habit of making my recording sessions shorter than anyone else's. I don't want my brass players to succumb to fatigue. I'd rather stop a little early and come back the next day, or the following week. Those are the kinds of lessons you learn over time.

With Bauzá and McGhee, I also observed their leadership styles—again, not to imitate them, but just for clues about the ways they took care of their business. They were leaders. People gravitated to them. And in different ways, they were both masters of handling the people around them, from the musicians in their ensembles to club owners, sound engineers, booking agents, record producers, journalists, and fans. Sometimes you have to act up to get what you need. Sometimes you have to put your foot down. Other times you need to back off, to give some-one some space.

In addition to the artistic and business responsibilities, being a bandleader is a massive psychological undertaking, because you're dealing with all sorts of complex emotions and relation-ships that are changing all the time, in the heat of the moment, in the throes of the art form. If you're going to keep your musi-cians in check and unmedicated, you have to learn how to deal with that aspect as well. It requires thoughtfulness and ingenu-ity as well as charisma and authority.

The truly great bandleaders—whether Duke Ellington or Fritz Reiner or Sun Ra—are all masters of psychology. The guys in the band might be in a foul mood, squabbling and conten-tious, but Duke knew how to walk in the room in a way that would neutralize the tension, or even sublimate it in a way that would only add to the unified force of the music once they were on the bandstand.

You can't take lessons in any of this—and you have to find your own style that works in your own situation. But watching the best in the business, you learn to keep an ear open for these hints about the backstage arts.

My song titles are not clues to some secret meaning. If I call a tune "Untitled Tango," it's not necessarily a generic description. It's an elliptical prompt. It's meant to prime your responsiveness to the music, not to shut it down or resolve it. Maybe shards of Spanish flit into your head. Maybe you know you know your Gardel and Goyeneche and maybe not. But the title insinuates a set of parameters and associations that affect the way you hear the music.

Titles just come to me. Sometimes the way it happens is sud-den, like a bolt of lightning, but sometimes the words only come into view gradually. I was up in Boston playing a show when my last daughter, Nhumengula, was born. I had been thinking about what we were going to call her, but the name was only coming to me in bits and pieces. Then I got that phone call and it all came together. It can be like that with the music, too. Often it comes in scrambled fragments and they have to be worked out. The title changes because I haven't finished the music, so the language morphs and migrates as I work. Sometimes I come up with something, and then I realize it isn't right. That's fool's gold, Henry, I tell myself. You've got to be patient. And then the right phrase comes.

In terms of my approach to song titles, I tried to say it all in my liner notes to my 1993 album *Song Out of My Trees*:

> *The process of talking about and defining*
> *music literally is one of monumental proportion.*
> *Yet this tradition does have a long and uneven*
> *history and many precedents. [Enter Me]*
> *To me this proposition is like trying to define*
> *apples with pears, or solving the problem of*
> *"if you want to kill the dog, why do you feed it."*

> *Finally there is an area or aspect of music*
> *which is oblique and in a world that we can't touch.*
> *For instance, as an example there are very* high *pitches*
> *that dogs respond to that humans can't hear and we*
> *know this, but we're outside of that reality. The* high
> *pitch instance somewhat correlates to things that are*
> *at play in music that we can't define, agree on or measure.*

> *In spite of all that was said I will say what I*
> *can in relation to the music contained in this disc.*
> *What I have done is assembled*
> *as much information about the*
> *background fabric as Star material.*
> *This concerns intent and descriptive*
> *information about the bigger picture*
> *(Heads or Tails), coming about or into*
> *realization in stages.*

The rest requires the listener's imagination
& participation, thinking, feeling, etc. . . .
In this larger musical picture and equation
Heads and Tails is becoming clearer
in position and perspective.

In the life of any artist, there are possibilities that open up—new collaborations, new areas of exploration. Not all of them bear fruit. You try something and it doesn't work out. You move in a particular direction and find out it's a dead end. But sometimes even the things that seem not to work end up affecting you on another level.

One weekend in February 1980, the Sextett played a series of shows at the Tin Palace. The pianist Cecil Taylor was at the bar, as he often was. And he turned up a couple of days in a row. Clearly he appreciated what we were doing.

Still I was surprised when he came up after the last set and asked me, Muneer, and Fred to play with him. He wasn't trying to break up the band or steal my sidemen. This would be something separate.

We didn't need time to deliberate, of course. So the next week the three of us started rehearsing with Cecil Taylor at his loft downtown on Chambers Street.

His unit was in a transitional period, with a combination of some of his old stalwart companions like the saxophonist Jimmy Lyons and more recent arrivals such as the trumpeter Raphe Malik and the violinist Ramsey Ameen. His previous band had featured Ronald Shannon Jackson on drums, but this new group included two percussionists, Sunny Murray and Jerome Cooper. With Air and the Sextett I played all my saxes, but Cecil specifically asked me to play tenor with his group. So the lineup was alto, tenor, trumpet, violin, cello, piano, bass, and two drums.

We rehearsed and rehearsed all spring in preparation for a date he had lined up in July 1980 at the nightclub Fat Tuesday's on Third Avenue at Seventeenth Street. We played four nights

Jimmy Lyons, Cecil Taylor, Ramsey Ameen, Muneer Abdul Fataah, me, and Jerome Cooper rehearsing at Cecil's loft on Chambers Street, 1980. Photo © Anthony Barboza

there. One night was supposed to be recorded, but the sound technician messed it up. The explanation we received was that he was so entranced by the music that he forgot to press Record.

And that was the end of my Cecil Taylor experience. It wasn't that he broke up the band or said he was unhappy with what we were doing. There just weren't any other gigs. So we stopped rehearsing.

All in all, it only lasted about five months, and it didn't lead to anything concrete in the sense of a recording or even a concert review. Most people don't even realize that I was briefly in the Cecil Taylor Unit. But I did learn a great deal nevertheless.

I found it extremely challenging to try to play Cecil's music, first of all. I wasn't really a "free" player. My music might defy conventional diatonic harmony, but I didn't tend just to blow. So it forced me to figure out a way to integrate myself on an improvisational level into what he was doing in the rehearsals. It took me a little while, but I found a way in.

Cecil's way of working was completely different from anything I'd experienced before. He would dictate all of these notes orally to each member of the group. Just a list of notes. He'd say, "Okay, tenor, you've got C, F-sharp, A, D, E, E-flat. Violin, you've got A, F-sharp, B, B-flat, F, G." It went on and on. Everybody would be scribbling down their list of notes: just the letters, not notes on musical staves.

Procedurally, it was interesting, if a bit bewildering. It felt like you were transcribing a run-on sentence without any punctuation. The first thing that was confusing was that you didn't have any rhythms. You had this long string of letters, but you weren't sure where the commas should be—how the musical syntax was supposed to operate. And you didn't know anything about what usually would be considered harmony: how and when your notes are supposed to fit with everyone else's notes.

Then Cecil would say, "Okay, let's play." And that's where the real problems started.

He didn't count off anything. No indication of tempo or dynamics. And it wouldn't have made any difference if he'd

counted it off, anyway. You didn't know when you were supposed to play the first note, or for how long. Or when to transition to the second note. Or their relative values: should the first
note be an eighth note and the second note a whole note? Cecil
would start playing, but the rest of the band didn't necessarily
come in at the same time. So how were you supposed to know
when to play?

In our rehearsals, I would stand next to Jimmy Lyons. I figured that the best solution was to follow the master. And Jimmy
would stand there looking up at the ceiling, spaced out. He was
so mellow, it kept me from panicking. The horn parts were different. The tenor and alto parts seemed to be related: my list
of notes was similar to his. So I proceeded by shadowing him.
I watched the way he interpreted his notes—when he came in,
how he strung them together, how he handled dynamics. I didn't
try to copy him. It wouldn't have been possible even if I'd wanted
to, because I didn't know what he was going to do. It was more
that watching him gave me a sense of how to speak in this unfamiliar language.

The other unexpected issue in playing with Cecil was that
the concerts were an entirely different universe. Cecil had shown
us all this stuff—we'd studiously written down our lists of
notes. In the dressing room, he'd tell us the order of the tunes.
"All right, we're going to play one, two, and then three," he'd
instruct us. But then we'd go on the bandstand, and Cecil would
start playing number two! He would just dive in without saying anything or even looking at us. Having rehearsed them so
thoroughly, I knew what the pieces sounded like by the time we
got to the show. So in the first set we played at Fat Tuesday's, I
was completely befuddled; I was standing there wondering why
what we were playing didn't sound like the piece I remembered
rehearsing.

Again I looked over to Jimmy Lyons. And Jimmy was just
sitting there looking up at the ceiling, unperturbed. I was determined that I wouldn't make a move until he made a move. But

when Jimmy finally started playing, I realized he was already in the third piece, when I thought we were in number two!

The first night I was just trying to keep my head above water. But I finally realized that the structure was modular with regard to both the individual pieces and the entire set. We could start anywhere. The pieces could be moved around. To play Cecil's music, you had to get to a place where you could let the pieces reconfigure themselves as you went along. The main thing was to make it work rhythmically. So I tried to take my cues off what Jimmy was doing and to make my notes fit somehow with his.

It was disconcerting in the moment, but the experience with Cecil impacted the way I came to think about my own bands. It's important to keep your people a little bit off balance. Familiarity is deadly. You need to challenge and surprise your musicians to get something fresh out of them—to push them to go beyond what they think their limits are. I don't do it quite the way Cecil did, but sometimes I do switch things up on my bands: tell them at the last minute before a show to play the pieces in a different order, or revise an arrangement on the fly at a rehearsal.

I once heard an interview with the bassist William Parker where he recounted an episode that took place when another horn player came into Cecil's band. Perplexed by the lack of clarity, the horn player got frustrated and told Cecil, "I can't play all these notes, man. I don't know how to make this work." Cecil responded, "Well, just play the ones you like."

As peculiar as it might sound, that dictum was true to the philosophy. The system was flexible that way. It took me some time to be able to hear it. It was a sound world of its own. You had to enter into it and follow its rules of gravity.

Some of the things I learned in situations like this came into my writing for Air. The album titled *1-OQA+19* I recorded with Muhal in December 1977 pushed me compositionally in some directions I explored in the music I was writing for *Open Air*

Suit, which Air recorded just a couple of months later, in February 1978. I don't mean it was imitative: the Air record doesn't sound anything like Muhal's record. But I learned something from experiencing the way Muhal was composing with long melodic lines in tunes such as his great "Charlie in the Parker." It was a remarkably fertile way of working; I mined that approach for a long time. Similarly I tried to adapt Cecil's use of modular cells in the long tune I wrote for the next Air album, *Air Mail*, which we recorded in December 1980. The tracks on our album were all dedications: Steve wrote "B.K." for his girlfriend at the time, Bobby Kingsley, and Fred wrote a tune called "R.B." in honor of the great bassist Ronnie Boykins. My own contribution was titled "C.T., J.L." in acknowledgment of what I'd learned from Cecil and Jimmy. I didn't do it the way Cecil would have—I didn't try to replicate the sound world he'd introduced me to. But I adapted his way of using a modular structure: a composition based in discrete, interchangeable cells.

Once a journalist asked me about the title of my tune "Jenkins Boys, Again, Wish Somebody Die, It's Hot" from the record *Carry the Day*. "What difference would it make if I told you?" I replied. I can fill in the background, sure. The title alludes to something my great-grandfather said. In the cotton fields the only way you could get a day off is when a white person would die. Then everybody would get a break for the funeral. Working in the fields on sweltering summer days, Peyton Robinson told me, folks would look at each other and say, "I wish somebody'd die." It was a code: I can't take this shit anymore, it meant. Not a solution, but a way of acknowledging a shared predicament. Slyly veiled hostility, an aspiration for release, passed softly to the person next to you along the row of cotton. The overseer would be standing there but he didn't know what you were talking about.

And in Illinois, whenever it got really hot my Grandma Gertrude used to proclaim: "That's the Jenkins boys." It was what they used to call a heat wave so vivid you could see it hovering like figures on the horizon.

So those different histories—those experiences, those ways of seeing the world, those ways of speaking—are knotted together in the title of the tune. But what does it help you to know that? The song's not a description of that. Listen to it. It's not an ethnographic portrait of labor on the plantation, or a family memoir.

I think that ultimately the listener gets more when the stimulation is *not* explained. Then you have to take it in as you listen, letting the language resonate with the way you hear the music. It's when you don't know exactly what it means or where it comes from that its full implications come into play. Stifling heat. Airlessness. Murderous thoughts, muttered low. A certain lingering menace. *Them boys again.*

In the way they play off each other, the combination of language and music might suggest the desire to get free of something. And in fact, for me, that was the real mathematical problem in that particular composition. That's what inspired it, that compositional question: How do I exit here? Or better: How do I break away from the situation? There has to be a situation—the song sets up a situation—and then I have to extricate myself.

8

Thriving at Sixes and Sevens

The Sextett recorded six albums in the 1980s and came to be recognized as one of the pivotal units to emerge in the decade. Those years were a constant maelstrom of creative activity, as I was branching out as a composer, writing for multiple ensembles simultaneously and trying to juggle it all with family life in New York. Even as the Sextett garnered attention and accolades, I still sometimes found myself frustrated with the assumptions that circulated among jazz journalists about my music. No matter what I said in interviews, there was a predilection among critics to take my song and album titles as programmatic announcements of the thematic content of the music. Because I had a few titles like "Cremation," "Higher Places," and "Soft Suicide at the Baths," some critics inferred that the first three Sextett records were maudlin and death-obsessed. I found it reductive and disappointing. I wanted to tell them to stop looking at the names—just listen to the music! There were all sorts of other things going on.

Threadgill has developed a penchant for writing "funeral marches" or "dirges," some journalists declared. I've never written a dirge in my life! All too often, the rush to affix a pseudo-generic label is nothing more than an excuse not to listen—to confront the ways the music hits you.

Meanwhile the critics missed some of the things I thought were real advancements in my development as a composer. For instance, no one seemed to notice that I extended the work I'd done with ragtime form in my Joplin arrangements for Air into an entire area of exploration with the Sextett. People came up with all sorts of fanciful interpretations of the title of the last Sextett record, *Rag, Bush and All*, but it was first of all a not-so-subtle clue about what I was trying to do formally. If you pay attention to the structure of the tunes, you hear immediately that "Off the Rag" and "Sweet Holy Rag" are written in ragtime form. They maintain the multi-movement structure characteristic of ragtime music, with harmonic and tempo changes in the successive sections. I tried to figure out how to update this venerable music for the 1980s—how to compose a neo-ragtime, as it were. No one had ever tried to do something similar. But the record and concert reviews I saw seemed to miss it entirely. What the hell, I thought. Finally I do what everyone seems to want me to do: indicate the genre directly in the song title. And no one seems to get it.

I admit that death was on my mind in those years, but not as subject matter. Instead I was thinking of it as an entrepreneurial opportunity. Just as I tried to found a marching band a few years later, in the early 1980s I was interested in trying to form a funeral band.

People died all the time, I figured. Why not write original music for funerals? It could be a perfect arrangement for regular commission work. I wanted to set up several ensembles based at different funeral parlors in the New York metropolitan area. I would serve as the music director, writing pieces for different configurations according to the needs and resources of the bereaved.

To me it wasn't a prank. It would have been a great responsibility: What music is more serious than a requiem?

I made an effort to contact funeral homes in the area, but I couldn't get it off the ground. It struck people as a peculiar idea. I tried to make the case that the notion of commissioned compositions for significant occasions of mourning actually has a long history in Western classical music, going back to Bach's funeral cantatas and the famous requiems by Mozart, Berlioz, and others. I might have been able to pull it off if I'd been able to get the backing of some major figures, such as a prominent priest or minister. That would have confirmed the legitimacy of the proposal.

The closest I was able to get were a couple of commissioned pieces for friends and acquaintances who were getting married. I did one for a friend's wedding at St. Peter's Church.

A few years later, he and his wife got divorced, and he jokingly called me out for it. "I blame you, Henry!" he laughed. "You didn't make that music strong enough."

I reminded him that when he requested that I write music for his wedding, I'd asked him, "How long do you want to stay with this woman?" As I told him then, if he wanted the marriage to last for forty years, then it was going to cost more than if he only intended it to endure for five.

"What can I say, man?" I told him now with a shrug. "It was a cheap commission. I could only give you what you paid for!"

Over the course of the decade the sound of the Sextett was transmogrified as people came and left. As often happens, some of the most promising configurations were never documented on record, including the first version of the band with Joseph Bowie on trombone and Muneer Abdul Fataah on five-string cello. When Joe departed I replaced him for a while with Vincent Chancey on French horn, but by the time the independent label About Time brought the Sextett into the studio to record *When Was That?* in late September 1981, I'd gone back to a trombonist, bringing in Craig Harris. That band also featured Brian Smith on piccolo bass, after Muneer had left and moved to Europe.

I told Brian I was only going to be able to use him temporarily. I knew I needed a cello in the ensemble, and I'd already found the perfect player. One of the first gigs the Sextett played was at Fordham University, and I heard a young cellist named Diedre Murray who was there with Marvin "Hannibal" Peterson and

The Sextett: Craig Harris, Fred Hopkins, Olu Dara,
me, Diedre Murray, John Betsch, and Pheeroan akLaff.
Photo © Anthony Barboza

Richard Davis. She was phenomenal, and I knew she would be perfect in the Sextett, so I told her to let me know as soon as she was available. She was eager to join us, but right around then she strained a muscle and had to stop playing for a number of months to let it heal.

Once she was able to perform, Diedre proved to be indispensable to the sound of the Sextett. She was a giant. Most people had no idea what to do with her. Other musicians would have her play free, or treat her like a sort of bass player. But I wrote parts for her that allowed her to explore the full range of what the cello could do. Writing for Diedre caused me to fall in love with the possibilities of the instrument and is the main reason I've kept coming back to it in multiple different contexts over the decades, from the track "Refined Poverty" on my 1995 album *Makin' a Move*, which featured my alto sax along with no fewer than three cellos, all the way through to the role of Christopher Hoffman in my current band Zooid. Sometimes I'd use Diedre down at the bottom of the texture, but I took advantage of the fact that the cello could function as the lead melodic instrument as well. Almost immediately, she and Fred were thick as thieves, and they developed an intuitive rapport. In the early 1990s, they recorded a couple of gorgeous cello-bass duo albums together on their own.

I didn't need booking agents for things in the New York area or in the usual spots in cities in the Northeast. But with both Air and the Sextett, we did start using agents to help with the more extended European tours, when it wasn't a matter of a single summer festival but instead a more complex multicountry tour. Beyond the music and the musicians, handling the business side of touring could sometimes turn into an entire job in itself. Like the other middlemen who populated the music business, agents could be infinitely useful, but they could also be crooks.

At some point toward the end of 1982, Steve left the trio for good. It was almost impossible to find another drummer who

could contribute what he gave to Air. His playing was unortho-
dox in a way that created space: rather than lock us into a propulsive momentum, it gave Fred and me room to operate. With
the Sextett, as I explained, I had to employ two drummers with
different time senses to get something like a similar effect. Eventually Fred and I were able to keep the Air aesthetic going with
Pheeroan akLaff in a trio we called New Air for a number of
years in the middle of the decade. Later we found other ways to
play together in the trio format without attempting to replicate
or extend what Air had been: for instance, when we played with
Andrew Cyrille, we didn't even use the name, and we played
entirely different compositions.

When Steve first left, we initially tried to replace him. One of
the drummers we brought in was Thurman Barker. Fred, Thurman, and I went on a European tour, in a set of concerts that
packaged Air with the South African pianist Abdullah Ibrahim.
The tour ended abruptly because I found out that our agent had
been cheating us. She was double-contracting us. It was a nefarious technique that agents would use in those days: they'd sign
one contract with the venue and a separate representation contract with the musicians. All the agent needed to do was negoti-
ate a higher fee with the club or theater and keep the difference.

Our agent didn't tell us she was doing this, of course. She
thought she could get away with it—and she probably had gotten away with it many times in the past. But this time we found
out, and we confronted her backstage. We were in the middle of
a major series of shows, and we were still scheduled to play in
other places, including a number of cities in Italy, ending up in
Sicily. But Fred, Thurman, and I were so incensed that we pulled
out of the tour right then and there and headed back to New
York.

I thought that saga was over. Needless to say, we didn't work
with that agent again. And I've been much more wary ever since.
But sometime later I went with the Sextett to play at the Willisau
Festival in Switzerland. We were in the wings, getting ready to
go on. And these burly guys approached us and threatened us.

They just shoved their way backstage and walked right up to me. There were four or five of them; they were all wearing dark suits, and it looked like they had guns holstered under their jackets.

One of them got up in my face. "You don't cancel in Sicily," he said to me in thickly accented English. "You don't cancel. *We* cancel."

I was stunned speechless. At first I had no idea who they were or what the guy was talking about. I just held up my hands and looked blankly at him. I certainly wasn't going to say anything that might provoke these fools to violence.

The flustered stagehands had called security, and the guards arrived quickly to escort the intruders out of the theater. The confrontation ended peacefully and the men left. All this happened in the wings backstage, so in the meantime the concert had continued and neither the audience nor the band onstage had any inkling there had been a disturbance.

Only as they started to leave did I make the connection to the tour when Air had backed out of playing in Sicily.

"You remember what I said," the one who'd approached me snarled as he turned away. "*We* cancel."

In the fall of 1983 I premiered work for two new ensembles, both of which became important facets of my growing portfolio as a composer. They originated with two commissions from Carnegie Recital Hall in November and December. One was for a flute quartet that featured me, James Newton, Lloyd McNeill, and Frank Wess. When we performed at the Public Theater and elsewhere over the coming years, the group was sometimes listed under James's name. But it was something James and I came up with together—our little contribution to the efflorescence of single-instrument groups in the era, such as the World Saxophone Quartet, the Baritone Sax Retinue, Max Roach's percussion ensemble M'Boom, and Stanley Cowell's Piano Choir. When we were finally able to record an album for Black Saint in 1990—with Pedro Eustache and Melecio Magdaluyo filling out the foursome, because neither Wess nor McNeill was able to make the date—James and I split the composer credits: we did three of his tunes and three of mine.

The first commission from Carnegie was for a group of my own that received far less notice than the Sextett because we never had an opportunity to record. But I composed a huge amount of music for it, and I consider it equally pivotal in my development. I called it the Windstring Ensemble.

As I strove to diversify my arenas of activity, I kept an eye out for opportunities to compose for different sorts of ensembles. There were always calls for submissions for string quartets, since they were such a central format in the history of Western classical music. I was tempted to give it a shot. The problem was, I never really liked the string quartet. I can appreciate the classics of the genre—I love the Bartók pieces, for example, and Debussy's 1893 String Quartet in G minor, the only one he wrote—but it's simply not my favorite instrumentation. I realize it may sound ironic from someone who's worked so often with groups of multiple flutes and basses, but to my ear there's simply too much sameness to the texture of a string quartet.

I decided to try to morph the string quartet into something else. I was thinking of the woodwind quintet as a model. As a mix of instruments, it always struck me as more promising because it was a hybrid, a combination of wind instruments (oboe, clarinet, bassoon, and flute) and an interloper from the brass section (the French horn).

At first I tried to write for a quintet that would combine my saxophone or flute with a modified string quartet of violin, viola, cello, and bass. But it didn't work: it was too oppositional. No, this isn't it, I thought.

It dawned on me that I might be able to replace the bass with a tuba. That would give me another wind instrument that would balance the mix between the sections of the group. The Windstring Ensemble started out with Diedre Murray in the cello chair. (Later I used Akua Dixon, another fabulously talented player.) I asked Leroy Jenkins to play viola, and got Akbar

Flute Force Four in concert in Verona, Italy: Pedro Eustache,
me, James Newton, and Melecio Magdaluyo.
Photo © Elena Carminati

Ali and later Patmore Lewis on violin. On tuba, I called on Bob Stewart, who'd made a name for himself working with Arthur Blythe and others on the downtown scene.

As I conceived it, the use of a tuba wasn't a matter of trying to return to the prominence of that instrument in early New Orleans jazz and parade music. It originated as a solution to a textural problem. The tuba is a mysterious instrument. It can blend with strings—it has a tonality that fits comfortably with cello and violin in a harmonic structure. But then it can also take on more of a brass role, and even provide a sort of percussive undercurrent when you need it to. I didn't think of the tuba primarily as the foundation of a rhythm section, in the conventional way it's used in marching bands—*oom-pah, oom-pah*—but instead as an instrument capable of darting around among the sections and thereby linking the parts of the ensemble. The tuba has what I'd describe as a quicker response time than the bass: it can jump right into a new section and fit. It can move in and out among the other instruments like a ghost. But it can take center stage, too. As with Diedre's cello in the Sextett, the tuba in the Windstring charts often takes on the lead melodic part, too. It has remarkable dynamic range, and it could add all kinds of things to the fabric if you used it up toward the top of the register.

Once Bob Stewart departed, I started using Marcus Rojas on tuba. Marcus learned how to improvise in the context of the Windstring Ensemble. This proved crucial in my development, because it introduced a shift in my sound world that later became a direction I was compelled to pursue. When I made the shift from the Sextett toward my next primary ensemble, Very Very Circus, the new group featured Marcus and Edwin Rodriguez on tubas in an extension of this component of the Windstring sound.

My most peripatetic year was 1984. That year the Sextett was almost like Louis Armstrong and His All-Stars: a touring band.

It was chaotic at times, but we thrived in the chaos. The year before, when we recorded *Just the Facts and Pass the Bucket*, Rasul Siddik had replaced Olu Dara in the trumpet seat, but otherwise the personnel remained the same: me, Craig, Diedre, Fred, Betsch, and Pheeroan.

In January we started with a tour of England. The idea was for it to serve as a launching pad for our first trip to South Asia. But the plan almost blew up in our faces when a club owner in London ran out with all our money just as we were supposed to be leaving for India. We had been playing for a few nights, and the guy was supposed to pay us at the end of the engagement before we left town. But he disappeared. We didn't have time to try to wait for the police to track him down. Instead we simply got on the plane to Bombay and hoped for the best.

We were scheduled to play at the famous Yatra Festival as part of a formidable lineup including Don Cherry, Woody Shaw, Ronnie Scott, Daniel Humair, and Zakir Hussain. In the airport, we ran into the broadcaster and journalist Phil Schaap, who was being brought in to serve as a sort of master of ceremonies. He and Diedre were old buddies from New York, and they spent the bus ride into the city chatting and catching up. The other group that arrived with us on the plane from England was the clarinet-ist and saxophonist Bob Wilber's Bechet Legacy Band, a septet whose specialty was music associated with the legendary New Orleans soprano saxophonist Sidney Bechet.

We got to the hotel and a festival representative gave a speech to the two bands in the lobby before we went up to our rooms. There were strict instructions about what we should and shouldn't eat and drink. "Don't even brush your teeth with the water out of the tap in the bathroom," the man warned. "Your bodies are not familiar with the organisms in the water here." They had special jugs of water you were supposed to use for drinking and for things like rinsing your toothbrush. Having spent time in South America, I knew that these sorts of warnings could be serious, and so I took note and made sure the band did as well.

That very first day, after we dropped off our luggage, they

took us on a tour of some other sections of the city to do some shopping and sightseeing. When we got back that evening, there were several ambulances parked out in front of the hotel. We exchanged glances—obviously something had happened.

We walked into the lobby and were stunned to see them bringing Bob Wilber's entire band out on ambulance gurneys, one after the other.

One of the hotel staff members explained to us that they hadn't heeded the tour representative's stern warning. Instead they wandered out into Bombay and decided to sample some fragrant street food.

It scared the shit out of Phil. In fact, he demanded they put him right back on the next plane to New York. "Oh, no, I can't do this," he declared, and hurried up to repack his suitcase. He left the same day—for years we would tease him about it whenever we'd see him in New York. "Hey, Phil! What's up? You got the runs?"

While we were in England, my back injury had been acting up again. It got so bad that I could barely walk. The doctors in London gave me some strong painkillers that didn't address the underlying problem but at least allowed me to manage to get around.

The main venue of the Yatra Festival was Brabourne Stadium in Bombay. But we also toured the major cities around the country. When the Sextet played in New Delhi, they told us that Indira Gandhi was going to be in the audience. We were honored and even a little awed.

Brabourne is an expansive cricket stadium, and the concerts attracted huge crowds of jazz fans knowledgeable about the music. Yatra was well established in Bombay by that point. The festival had been founded in 1978, when the US State Department helped to fund the participation of a number of the American artists, including Sonny Rollins, Clark Terry, Joe Williams, and Don Ellis.

In Delhi, however, we played in a smaller, ornate theater, and the atmosphere was more restrained. Indira Gandhi was in a prominent seat toward the front of the orchestra. The Delhi audience was sophisticated, but they may not have been exposed to as much of the contemporary jazz scene from the United States. By the time we got there, we were hot. The Sextett could blow the lid off a joint when we got going, and that evening we didn't hold back.

When we finished, the theater remained utterly silent. I had never had that happen before. It lingered long enough to become disconcerting. The band was looking at me for a cue. But I didn't know what to do. So we stood there awkwardly for a few moments in the stillness.

Then Gandhi suddenly leapt to her feet and started clapping furiously. And then the whole place erupted in cheers and applause. It was as though they were waiting for her approval. After the pause, the eruption was overwhelming: the ovation seemed to go on and on.

The band was introduced to Gandhi very briefly after the concert. We didn't have a conversation with her. But somehow she found out about my back problem. And she took it upon herself to intervene.

Someone showed up at the hotel and informed me that the prime minister was hoping to be of assistance with my back condition. She had them take me to the greatest orthopedic surgeon in the country, a man named Dr. Patel who apparently had served as the personal physician of the Shah of Iran. He was a great opera lover and traveled periodically to attend events in New York, Paris, and Milan.

Dr. Patel had an astonishing studio with all sorts of gleaming machines and devices. I'd go there for sessions and he'd strap me up in these contraptions that would stretch my spine. Miraculously, the treatments eased my pain and helped wean me off the sedatives the doctors in London had given me. I still had a slight limp, and Dr. Patel sent for a sculptor who carved a special cane for me.

Another mysterious thing happened in the hotel. During that trip, I had taken to wearing a tea cozy on my head. I like hats, and I would make them out of all sorts of things. I was especially fond of this plush tea cozy that fit around my head like the belly of a kettle. Nobody needed to know it was a tea cozy. It looked like some sort of cross between a turban and a Russian ushanka.

I came into the hotel wearing the tea cozy hat and a beautiful blue suit from Austria with chains going across the chest, limping slightly on my custom-made cane. The staff in the hotel lobby seemed particularly struck by my appearance. They stood out as well: they were all strikingly tall men with big mustaches. When they saw me, they stopped what they were doing—they dropped the bags and packages they were carrying for other guests and approached me, forming a sort of honor guard. It was a strange little spur-of-the-moment ceremony: they even bowed to me as I passed through.

I was taken aback. "Who are these people?" I asked a woman at the front desk.

"They're from the Land of the Kings," she told me.

"Why did they stop what they were doing and line up for me?"

"They think you're one of them."

This didn't strike me as particularly likely. But it was clearly a gesture of respect. "But isn't the Land of the Kings in Egypt?" I asked the desk attendant.

"Yes, that's one Land of the Kings. But there's another one here: Rajasthan." She explained that it was a region to the east of Delhi, known for its bright colors and cultural festivals.

I said, "But don't they realize I'm just an American musician?"

"It is a gesture of respect. Don't say anything," she counseled. Not that I was planning to—what could I have told them?

I never figured out exactly what they saw in me. But it continued every time I came through the lobby. Although I was intrigued by the unexplained homage, I was embarrassed to be singled out each and every time I showed up. It got to the point where I was tempted to try to sneak out a back exit so I wouldn't cause a commotion.

When we came back at the end of January, we ended up having to leave Rasul Siddik in India. For some reason his passport ended up in John Betsch's pocket, but Betsch didn't realize it until we were back in the States. So we found ourselves at passport control in the Bombay airport, looking everywhere for Rasul's papers. They wouldn't let him leave the country. Fortunately I was able to give him the number of some contacts we'd made there, and he ended up staying a couple more weeks while he was waiting to get a replacement passport. He had a ball.

Rasul made it back in time to participate in the other big escapade of the year: the first Great American Music Tour. Why not do a cross-country tour? I thought. An old-fashioned version that would let the Sextett play for audiences among parts of the American population that would never have a chance to see us otherwise? It didn't need to be a big, expensive promotion. We could do it on our own.

And so I just went ahead and did it. I trekked out to a place in Asbury Park, New Jersey, and rented a brand-new Pace Arrow motor home with the latest aeronautical design for five thousand dollars for two months.

A couple of days before we were scheduled to depart, I picked up the rig and drove it over into the city. I found a space in the truck parking lot behind the Manhattan Plaza apartment complex in Midtown. That very same night the motor home got stolen. We became a major national news story before we even left town.

How do you steal a thirty-seven-foot-long motor home? The police detectives couldn't prove anything, but they suspected that one of the attendants in the parking lot must have been in on it. It was audacious. Somebody had brought a tow truck large enough to transport the Pace Arrow. They had set down skids to brace it as they winched the motor home up onto the tow truck.

The operation left skid marks on the asphalt, and it tore up the sidewalk in a couple of places because the motor home was so enormous. The detectives concluded that the thieves had taken the Pace Arrow to New Jersey to a chop shop.

Fortunately I had gotten insurance with the rental. The company was miffed. But they had to give me a replacement. They didn't give me the same model—the Pace Arrow was new, but they gave me a used one that was larger but not quite as spiffy as the first. But finally we made it out of the city in the replacement motor home, traveling the country from late March until the end of May 1984.

We drove thousands of miles, from Michigan to Massachusetts, Georgia to Illinois, Texas to New Mexico, and all the way up into Saskatchewan, Canada. We hit a few major clubs in big cities: we played the Great American Music Hall in San Francisco, the Caravan of Dreams in Fort Worth, and the Jazz Showcase in Chicago, and we ended up back in New York for a four-day run at Sweet Basil. But for the most part we aimed at an entirely different slice of performance venues across the country: undergraduate student centers at big state universities, municipal art museums, community cultural centers, schoolhouses. I lined up the big dates in advance, but we also found places to play as we went. The idea was that even if a town might not have been able to afford to bring me under normal circumstances, if we were coming through anyway we might be able to find a way to arrange a show on short notice almost anywhere. If an organization couldn't put us up in a hotel, no problem: we were traveling with our own hotel. We'd just collect a nominal cover charge and that would be the band's fee.

It was easy to make it work. And it was refreshing to play different sorts of places in circumstances where the music was the main thing rather than the business. At one point we were driving through a state park. It happened to be a beautiful day, and we decided to stop and play right there, outside in the open air. People in the park heard us playing and wandered over, curious. The music changed drastically across the course of the trip.

That transformation can happen in any situation where you have extended time to play together. But something about the shifting array of unusual environments pushed the process even further. We radically modified the arrangements of some of the older pieces.

The motor home was a self-contained world. We each had our own bed. There was a shower, a television, a table where we could play cards, and a cooking area with a refrigerator and stove. We kept our instruments and gear on a rack on top, covered with a tarp. Gas was cheap at the time, and there were places you could stop and clean the vehicle, empty the septic system, and change the propane tank. We were basically traveling with the truck drivers. How often do you get to have a conversation with a trucker at a rest stop? I got a lot of material just being in their company, listening to them, getting a sense of the pace and flavor of their itinerant lives. I started contemplating doing an album that I was thinking about calling *King of the Road*.

As for driving, our rule was that there was always one person at the wheel and another sitting in the front passenger seat to keep the driver company. Six of us could drive, and we agreed to take three-hour shifts. This meant that even if we kept driving nonstop, everyone would have eighteen hours of down time between shifts.

Craig Harris couldn't make the trip, and so I had to find another trombonist. Craig recommended a friend of his. So there was one new addition to the group that had just been in India: the inimitable Henry Mitchell.

This is another of the great gaps in my recorded discography: the version of the Sextett with Henry Mitchell. He was something else. Trombonists are renowned for their physical capacities—for the sheer amount of air they can force through the horn—but Henry was operating on another plane. It sounded like the instrument was about to explode when he played it. Some players have a lightness to the way they flick their wrists as they move the slide, but not Henry: his playing was agitated and effortful, as though the trombone were some sort of hot, sweaty beast he had to wrangle physically in order to squeeze out the music. It was visually riveting to watch him engage in a noisy struggle with the horn every time he took a solo. Henry never needed to use a microphone. He could project his sound into any corner of any room.

When I first brought him into the band, he told me he was worried that he wasn't going to be able to handle the music. "This stuff is hard, man," he told me.

"Forget that," I said. "Forget about any kind of theory. Don't worry about how it's supposed to be way out and all that stuff people say. You can play this music. Find your own way into it. Just use your ears and play."

Henry was the only one of us who didn't have a license. The sole problem with Henry was that he swore he knew how to drive, even if it was obvious that he had no clue. He didn't even know how to start the vehicle. But he was bold and weirdly determined to take his turn behind the wheel. We had to be constantly vigilant to make sure he didn't find a way to start trying to drive.

We learned this because one night in Iowa he somehow cajoled someone into letting him have a turn, and we ended up off the highway in a cornfield. After that taste of pandemonium, our one rule of the road was never to let the trombonist drive the motor home.

Henry was from Harlem, but he was country in the particular way that people from the city can be. It's a hard phenomenon to describe unless you've witnessed it, but there's definitely such a thing as an urban rube. Although we tend to think of cities as cosmopolitan places, that conscribed experience can lead to a special brand of parochialism.

One time Henry got in an argument with Pheeroan. We were driving along the highway looking at the view—I think we were passing through some section of Colorado where the beauty of the landscape was especially stunning. Henry broke the silence.

"Hey, Pheeroan, did you see that herd of rabbits?" he asked.

"What the hell are you talking about, Henry?" the drummer said. "Man, those were deer!"

We all heard Henry, because the motor home was close quarters and we were all awake and looking out the windows. The rest of us exchanged looks of disbelief. A herd of rabbits?

Diedre muttered under her breath, "What in the world is with this cat?"

I couldn't even quite bring myself to chuckle—it was hilarious, of course, but his innocence also seemed to come from so far beyond any common frame of reference that it was hard to know how to respond.

The truly astonishing thing was that Henry was stubborn about his assertion. He doubled down on it. We were all sitting there staring at him and it didn't faze him at all.

"Stop fooling around, Pheeroan," Henry replied with conviction. "I know a rabbit when I see one."

In the month between our return from England and the Great American Music Tour in February 1984, I played another concert with the Windstring Ensemble at Carnegie Recital Hall. Even as I was galavanting around the world with the Sextett, it was important to me to maintain this other strain of my output. It sounds counterintuitive, but it was the way I worked through the decade: not one ensemble following the other in succession, but instead a constant interweaving of different realms of activity. Logistically it was a lot to juggle, but I found it productive compositionally to force myself to shift my focus from one sound world to another.

That summer, once we returned from the cross-country excursion, I started getting commissions to compose music for multimedia theater productions that pulled me into an entirely new wing of the downtown scene. I reconnected with my old

collaborator the director Donald Sanders from Columbia College in Chicago, who asked me to do the music for two shows
he was developing for the Public Theater. The first, in July 1984,
was called 33 *Scenes on the Possibility of Human Happiness*. It
was a theatrical piece without dialogue constructed as a series of
tableaux ("Eight Ladies at Dinner," "Banquet," "The Painter,"
"Marriage in the Country," "Fireworks," "The Foolish Virgins,"
"Five Foot Soldiers," etc.) that both evoked and sent up the aesthetic paradigms of a series of famous eighteenth-century paint-
ings. Don recruited the actors from the New York Art Theater
Institute, an experimental troupe located on Fourteenth Street
east of Union Square.

Since there was no script, the commentary was delivered
through the combination of the performers' movements; the
costumes by Don's wife, the designer Vanessa James, which
often updated period costumes in raucous ways, using the arti-
facts of contemporary consumer culture (in one scene depicting
Louis XIV as he posed to have his portrait painted as Hercu-
les, Vanessa dressed the actor in baggy trash bags to ridicule the
king's insufferable pomposity; in another, a new mother wears
a dress fashioned from a shower curtain as she takes her baby
to be christened), and my music. I composed each "scene" as a
vignette in which the musical elements told the story. I worked
with a quintet drawn mostly from the Sextett: me on alto sax,
Jason Hwang on violin, Rasul Siddik on trumpet, Fred on bass,
and Reggie Nicholson on drums. But the writing was a very different sort of challenge, because of the way the music had to
be charged with narrative implication and radically varied from
vignette to vignette.

The following year, Don and I collaborated on another
theater piece, *Thomas Cole, A Waking Dream*, which he
described as an "unsung jazz/performance art cantata." The
show was a reflection on the life and art of Thomas Cole, the
early-nineteenth-century visionary painter associated with the
Hudson River school. This time there was a script, although
it was spoken by the fourteen actors rather than orchestrated

(thus "unsung"). Again the sets and costumes by Vanessa and my music were integral to the construction of the show's dreamy historical mood. This time I used an octet: me, Joseph Jarman on reeds, Ray Anderson on trombone, Rasul, Diedre, Fred, Reggie, and Thurman Barker. As with *33 Scenes*, this was all new music, although in the case of the second show I did later adjust the arrangement of one tune, "Theme for Thomas Cole," to include on the Sextett's 1986 album *You Know the Number*.

When the Sextett stopped in Chicago to play at the Jazz Showcase, the band stayed at my place. I held on to my apartment in the city until the year of the Great American Music Tour. I would occasionally go back, both to see my family and because on some level I still felt rooted there. I'm not sure why, but passing through town with the Sextett made me realize that I didn't live there anymore.

While I was in town I saw my grandmother, and it occurred to me to look for a box I'd left in her basement years earlier with some of my first compositions. There was a piece titled "Gray," a tune for the octet at Wilson Junior College that I wrote after hearing Coltrane's "Giant Steps." My composition wasn't anything like Coltrane's famously virtuosic workout, but it was my attempt to synthesize what I was learning from what Coltrane was doing, those rapid harmonic changes every two beats. I had written another piece in 6/8 meter called "Richard XV" that the guys at Wilson liked to play. I remember there were also things I was learning from listening to the arrangements of Gerald Wilson that I was trying to incorporate into my compositions, little effects and strategies. I'd also kept some of the music I'd written for the sanctified church. I was curious to look at those scores again.

The box was still there, but it was empty. My grandmother told me that some of my mischievous little cousins had gotten into it at some point. To them it was scrap paper: building materials for paper airplanes, stuff to light on fire with a magnifying glass. Or a coloring book, a doodling pad. It had all been repur-posed and discarded by the time I came back for it.

I'd left the box in her basement in August 1967, during that month I had at home before I was deployed. The other thing that I'd put in there, it occurred to me, was the arrangement of patriotic songs that got me sent off to Vietnam. I'm not much inclined to nostalgia. And that arrangement wasn't particularly brilliant. But I did feel a slight pang of regret when I found the box empty. I would have liked to have found those scores, if only as a memento—as proof of the potency of art, a reminder that music can get you killed.

The day we departed for the Great American Music Tour, the Sextett gathered by a studio I had on Thirteenth Street, where the band would often rehearse. Henry Mitchell was the last to arrive. The rest of the group was starting to get peeved. We were scheduled to arrive at our first gig—in Michigan, I think—at a particular day and time, and nobody wanted to start off a cross-country tour by being late.

Finally I saw him coming down the block. It looked like he had taken the subway downtown from Harlem. "Here comes the brother now," I told the others.

Henry had his trombone on a strap over his shoulder. But he had a lot of other stuff, too. He had these two big black bags he was more or less dragging down the street. As he got closer, we realized that they were plastic garbage bags he seemed to be using to transport his clothes and personal effects.

"It's my luggage!" he announced, unperturbed by our glares.

There wasn't much to say. So that was how he traveled. Any-where we stopped at a hotel, Henry would drag in these two great big garbage bags.

His resistance to the constraints of conventional luggage almost led to a major fight in Los Angeles. We played at a museum, and it turned out that the saxophonist Julius Hemp-hill was in town. The next evening he asked Fred and Pheeroan to play a set with him in a loft. So they did a set, and then the Sextett played, too. We ended up spending the night there, so we brought our things in from the motor home.

The next day we were leaving to head up the coast to Santa Cruz and San Francisco. So in the morning we brought all our stuff outside to load it back on the motor home. But in the process of bringing out our baggage and equipment cases, one of the people who was helping us must have gotten confused. It was garbage-collection day, and there were a bunch of trash bags on the sidewalk right next to where we were packing up. Somebody mistook Henry's "luggage" for regular garbage bags and it ended up getting left behind, piled with the other trash.

Henry was furious. He didn't notice his stuff was missing until hours later, but he acted like it was our fault. "You left my stuff on the street on purpose!"

Fortunately he did have a sense of humor about it. We teased him a little bit, and I bought him some new clothes—and a suitcase.

We nearly drove the motor home into a tornado in Texas. We had just performed at the Caravan of Dreams in Fort Worth. The next morning, we woke up early to pick up some clothes we'd left at the cleaners before we drove to New Mexico, where we were scheduled to give a concert a couple of days later.

There's a particular metallic smell that comes into the air when a tornado is approaching. I had experienced a few in Illinois as a child, and so I recognized it immediately. It was one of the key warning signs. Another was that the raindrops that were starting to fall were unusually big. As we came out of the hotel, the rain plunked down on the street like coins being dropped on the asphalt.

I convened the Sextett and told them that we needed to leave immediately. "Forget the laundry," I told them. "We've got to get out of here right now."

None of them had been in a tornado, and at first they were

skeptical. But they could hear the urgency in my voice. I knew better than to fool around with a tornado.

We loaded up the Pace Arrow quickly and started out of town. Betsch was driving. Even as we began to leave, some of them started suggesting that we should go back to the hotel or take shelter somewhere else in town.

"We're not going back," I said. I told them tornados were unpredictable—they could tear a building apart until nothing was left but twigs and broken glass, or pick it up and carry it off to deposit the pieces miles away. Eventually they stopped arguing. But I could tell they were all antsy and frightened.

There was a pickup truck coming toward us on the highway with a horse trailer hitched behind it. And while we were all sitting there looking out the window as the rain lashed the windshield, the tornado picked up the tailer, ripped it off the back of the truck and tossed it off the side of the road. That scared the hell out of everyone. Some of them just wanted to get off the highway. "We're out here totally exposed!" they pleaded. "We've got to take shelter."

"No," I said. "We're going through this." I planted myself right behind Betsch at the wheel. "Press it to the floor and keep it to the floor."

At the top of an incline, we stopped at a deserted service station because we realized the tarps holding down our gear on top of the motor home were coming loose. Pheeroan went out to try to secure them. The wind was vicious: it ripped off the screen door as soon as we opened it.

After he had been outside a few minutes, we started to get worried. I looked in the rearview mirrors and eventually saw Pheeroan hanging off the other side of the motor home, holding on for dear life. Fred took a rope, tied one end to the side ladder and the other to his waist, and went up himself to rescue Pheeroan and fix the tarps.

Once they were safely back inside, we roared off down the hill away from the service station. The storm had gotten worse—we couldn't see the funnel of the tornado, but we could feel its fury. Coming down the hill, it nearly got us. I was up front with Betsch. He was gripping the wheel tightly and pressing the accelerator, but it didn't seem to have any effect on our speed. For a few seconds, we didn't seem to be in contact with the ground anymore. It felt like we were hydroplaning, but without the water—the tornado briefly lifted us up into the air! It was terrifying. Finally we bumped back down.

We outran the storm, driving as fast as we dared straight to Abilene, about a hundred and fifty miles west. Once we got there and felt safe enough to stop, someone went to get something to eat from the kitchen at the back of the motor home and we realized the wind had ripped the refrigerator out of the back wall. We opened the fridge and there was nothing left: we were looking straight out into the street. We had to take a detour across the border into Mexico, where we found a repair shop that had the parts we needed.

The episode did teach us a lesson. We were seasoned tornado veterans after that.

Later, we nearly ran into another one. We didn't notice it coming at first. We had stopped at a big hardware store to buy a new rain tarp. The band members were arguing about the best way to attach it. Henry Mitchell wanted to take charge because he claimed to be an expert with knots. The others didn't believe him and an argument broke out.

I was just standing there listening to them quarrel like a bunch of little kids. There was a woman walking by in the parking lot. As she hurried to her own car, she paused for a moment to interrupt our bickering: "You boys can keep up that shit if you want to, but when that tornado gets here it ain't going to matter."

She pointed to the hills in the distance, and we saw there was a storm gathering. Within five seconds, the Sextett was working in coordinated silence—we got that gear tied down and got the hell out of there. I had never seen knots tied so quickly.

———

Around 1986, I received another invitation for the Sextett to play in Sicily. This was yet another incarnation: the ensemble featured on my albums *You Know the Number* and *Easily Slip into Another World*. Frank Lacy had replaced Henry Mitchell in the trombone chair, and Reggie Nicholson joined us after John Betsch decided to leave.

I was working with another booking agent at that point, and I told him about the confrontation with the menacing guys back-stage in Willisau. He told me not to worry.

"It's not the same people," he explained. "There's a new god-father in charge." The only catch, he added, was that I shouldn't expect to be paid. The rumor was that they hosted you gra-ciously but then stiffed you on your artist's fee.

According to my agent, the request came directly from some-one he identified as the godfather's son, who was a fan of my music. The son was something of an arts connoisseur. He had restored the oldest opera house in Sicily to its former splendor, and he had also helped to repair a famous church that had been damaged by bombing during the war.

"This guy specifically asked for you, Henry," the agent said. "I think you should do it."

So we went. It wasn't just a single gig. This was an extended stay on the island. They offered to put us up for a couple of weeks and sponsor concerts in multiple towns.

We scheduled it at the end of a multicountry European tour, and we flew to Palermo from Rome. I had my instruments with me, but my suitcases had been misplaced during the train jour-ney to Italy and I arrived in Sicily with nothing aside from the clothes I was wearing, a black ski suit and boots.

The godfather's son was there to meet us at the airport. He was appalled when I told him my bags had been lost. "You got a-nothing?" he asked, his face twisted in commiseration as though my sartorial bereavement were a crime against humanity. He had a charming Italian accent. "You ain't a-got no clothes?"

We stood there by the baggage claim as he scrutinized me in my single ski suit.

"No, no, no. *Impossibile*. This cannot a-be."

He had the driver take us to the hotel, and we dropped everyone else off. As the rest of the band went up to their rooms, he turned and said, "Now you come with me."

At the time, Palermo boasted some of the most talented designers in Europe. I wasn't sure what to expect—and I was thinking, "How in the world am I going to afford a shopping spree?" But I'm the guest, I figured. And so I followed along.

The hotel was downtown, a few blocks from the fashion district. The first place he took me was a clothing store that was so manifestly beyond my means that I was afraid to walk in the door. It was like a gilded palace, the sort of place where they would bring you a glass of sparkling water with a lime twist or an espresso while you browsed because they knew how much money you were about to lay down.

He led me over to the pants department, and I saw these white corduroy trousers—I had never seen a pair of white corduroys in my life. They had this extraordinary, improbably soft texture, almost like they were made out of cashmere or alpaca.

I couldn't help myself from touching them, but then I looked at the price. When I saw what they cost, I gasped, quickly flipped the tag back over, and turned away. It hurt my eyes even to look at that number.

But he had seen me gravitating over to them. He followed me and picked up the pants and put them on the counter.

"Why don't you a-try these on?" he cooed. "These remind me of you, Henry. Why don't you see how they feel?"

I didn't want to be impolite—I'd learned from previous experience that refusals could be unwise in Sicily. So I took them to the changing room.

When I emerged, he said, "Ah, *sì*. That's a-you, I tell you. That's a-you."

I couldn't argue. They were exquisite. I didn't know what to say, so I just nodded and went back to the dressing room to change back into my ski suit. I thought I'd try to leave them on the hanger in there.

But he followed me again and grabbed them and put them over his arm. Even worse, he smiled at me and walked back over to the rack where I'd gotten them.

"You can't have just one pair of pants, Henry."

He picked out another pair—this one was some kind of purple-blue color, almost a midnight blue. I was about to faint. And then he picked up some tan ones, too. In my head, I was calculating how many months of salary they represented. How am I going to get myself out of this one? I wondered.

Whirling around, he gave his pile of gorgeous pickings to the nearest shop attendant and summoned me to follow him to another section of the store.

"You don't have any shirts or nothing!" he exclaimed. I realized he was having fun, picking out clothes for the musician he'd brought to town. There was nothing to do but play along for the time being, even if I knew there was going to be a painful reckoning soon enough.

He took me to the shirt department and started having me measured for these butter-smooth silk shirts. They were outrageous, in these eye-popping colors, some solids and some tasteful prints.

I stood there paralyzed with anxiety as he picked items off hangers for me to try on. "This one looks just a-like you, Henry. Try this one."

He tossed two more to me. "You can't a-wear one shirt, can you? Every day? No, no."

Finally all our choices were gathered by the main counter. The in-house tailors were already making the necessary alterations right there as we continued to shop. Meanwhile, the godfather's son lit a Cuban cigar and chatted nonchalantly with the store clerks, smiling and laughing. He handed me a cigar, too. I couldn't really follow what they were saying, but I tried to stand there with my cigar and give an appearance of being entirely in my element. Other attendants were packing up the items that were ready to go in elaborate boxes with ribbons.

It occurred to me that no money was changing hands.

We lingered there for a while as everything was prepared. He made arrangements to have a few things delivered to the hotel. And then we just walked out the door, smoking our cigars, with shopping bags full of swag.

What the hell just happened? I asked myself. I didn't have much time to think about it, because he wasn't done. He took me down the street to another store, where we got an entire set of underwear and T-shirts. The excursion ended up taking all afternoon, as he seemed tickled to keep coming up with other things I needed.

At one point we exited another posh boutique and he seemed to remember the dilemma of my footwear.

"You can't a wear those boots with nice clothes, Henry," he scolded. Weathering the onslaught of his extravagance, who was I to argue? "Come on, we'll a-go across the street."

He led me over to a shoe store and we spent a moment gazing at the wares displayed in the window as we savored our cigars. Everything was handcrafted by master cobblers. I noticed one pair of ankle boots and I couldn't keep my eyes from widening slightly. I tried not to look—I really made an effort to convey complete and utter indifference—but these boots were just singing to me. "*Indossaci*," they purred. I didn't even speak the language but I knew what they were saying: "Put us on."

Again he noticed me looking. "Why don't we a-go in and a-try some things on?"

I had never seen, much less touched or worn, boots like these. The leather was so supple it must have come from a baby calf. The cobblers must have committed unspeakable crimes to produce something this sumptuous, I said to myself. But he insisted that I try them on—and then picked out a couple of other pairs that he thought would complement our choices in apparel.

It went on and on. The shoe store reminded him that I didn't have any socks. Our growing collection of shopping bags led him to realize that I didn't possess any luggage. My first day in Palermo, and here I was refurbished by the godfather's son himself.

———

I started to get a sense of the son's influence on the island when we had a problem with our driver. We were traveling by bus all over Sicily to play concerts, and the roads could be treacherous. It was a big tour bus, and the driver was taking these hairpin turns in the hills as though he were in a Formula 1 race car. I asked him to slow down. "Hey, man, ease up," I said. "You're going to get us killed." But he kept acting like a daredevil.

Finally he took another turn too fast and we almost tipped right off the side of a cliff. We all screamed and clung to our seats. I was pissed. So the next time the son called me at the hotel to ask how the shows had been going, I told him what had happened.

"He did what?" he said calmly, asking me to repeat the story. "And you told him not to do that?"

"Yes," I said. "I asked him nicely to slow down. We weren't in a hurry. There was no need to risk our lives."

The next morning we got up and came downstairs to the lobby to get ready for that night's show, and a guy I didn't recognize ran up and grabbed my bags. I resisted—I didn't recognize him, and I thought he was trying to steal them. "Hey! Who are you?"

"Oh, *scusi, scusi, signore*, I am your new driver," he explained. "Please don't touch anything. I'll carry everything to the bus. Just let me know if you need anything."

We never saw the first driver again. He simply vanished. We supposed the son had fired him. As artists, after dealing with so much flak on so many tours around the world, it was a pleasure to have a protector for a change. The band and I joked about it that night at dinner. "Now *that's* an impresario," we laughed.

My booking agent had described my benefactor's father as "the godfather," but I went to Sicily assuming that term was at least partly a euphemism. I took it for granted that the man was powerful and wealthy, but I wasn't sure exactly what those words meant in context.

I met the old man a few days later after an incident in the hotel dining room. I had come down to eat lunch alone. I couldn't say much in Italian, but I could improvise my way around a menu. The waiter had gotten my order wrong, and then he insisted that I pay for dishes that I hadn't even asked for. The waiter wouldn't admit that he'd misunderstood.

I got annoyed at his haughty attitude. "I am not paying for food I didn't order!" I said loudly. I took my napkin and threw it down on the table. It was enough to cause a scene. Everybody in the restaurant looked over. I got up from the table and walked out.

A little later, one of the hotel staff came up to my room and tried politely to present a bill. "I didn't order this," I declared. "I'm not paying for shit."

This left us at something of an impasse. But later that afternoon, the son called the hotel to check in on the band. He asked to be connected to my room. "Henry, what a-happened?" he asked. I recounted the episode. It was no big deal—a misunderstanding over a lunch bill. "Okay," he told me. "We'll be there tomorrow."

The next day he called me and told me to meet him in the lobby. I came down and watched as these black limousines pulled up. A squad of men got out. They were carrying guns— not concealing weapons under their clothes, but openly carrying pistols and machine guns. They stationed themselves around the main floor.

This was the advance team. They cleared all the tourists out of the lobby and set up a big leather couch in the center of the lounge area. The entire hotel staff was standing there lined up at attention, looking petrified.

Then another limousine pulled up. A guard opened the rear door and the old man emerged. His son was in the car with him. They gingerly made their way in, and when the old man was ready to sit down, he simply lowered himself in the vicinity of the couch and the henchmen quickly pushed it up under him. They put a humidor by the couch next to him. The old man reached in and took out a cigar. Another guy was there to light it when he was ready.

The son beckoned me over and he and I sat in chairs in front of the old man. He looked first at me and then at his son. They spoke in Sicilian—the only words I could make out in English were the first two: "Ask Henry . . ."

The son had a grave look on his face as he translated. He said, "Henry, my father would like to know who it was."

I realized that the situation was much more dangerous than I had grasped.

"Hey, you know," I wavered, "it wasn't really such a big deal, he just—"

"No. My father wants to know who was the offender."

The poor guy was standing over to the side with the rest of the restaurant staff. We could almost hear his knees knocking from across the room. Finally he stepped forward feebly, pleading for forgiveness.

The mood was so ominous that I thought they might summarily execute him, as insane as that sounds. It was truly frightening. They didn't kill him, fortunately—at least not as far as I knew. But he did have to leave the hotel. They dismissed him right then and there. The guy scurried out, tears streaming down his face. I felt horrible.

Then they had the hotel manager come over and apologize. The father and son just stared at him as he sputtered excuses. Finally the father said something softly. The manager turned to face me and started offering his apologies to me, too.

"It's all right," I said. "I understand . . ." I wanted to get it over with as quickly as possible.

"No, it's not all right," the son corrected me. And the manager continued. Finally he told me, "We will not accept any of your money for as long as you're staying with us. In the restaurant, in the gift shop, please help yourself to whatever you want. You don't pay for anything in the hotel." It was a pitiful scene.

I told the band what had happened and we were very careful after that. We didn't want to be responsible for getting anyone knocked off.

Father and son would summon me to lunch every couple of days. The godfather's stomach was bad, so all he would have was a bowl of clear broth with a little bread in it and a half-glass of white wine mixed with water. He told me to order whatever I wanted, and then he asked me for reports. The son served as interpreter.

"Henry, my father would like to know how things went in Trapani and Marsala. Were you a-treated well? Did you have any problems?"

I'm certainly not going to tattle on anyone, I told myself. Let's keep everything nice and easy.

"Oh, we had a wonderful time," I replied, keeping my descriptions as sunny and bland as I could. "The audiences were wonderful."

The concerts were a lot of fun, it was true—and people in the small towns around the island really seemed to appreciate the music. Occasionally there was some static, of course. In one town, the concert was supposed to take place in the union hall, and when we showed up the union was holding a meeting. I don't know why they needed to do it right before our set. It went on and on and we had to scramble to set up for our show.

But what I'd seen had placed my petty annoyances into perspective. So the next time I met the godfather and his son for lunch, I made sure to emphasize how gracious the union had been in accommodating us.

We enjoyed the somewhat sinister hospitality of the godfather's son one last time on our final evening in Sicily. He asked me if I needed anything in preparation for the final show in Palermo. I told him that because the concert was scheduled to start late, at ten p.m. or so, I was slightly concerned that the band wouldn't be able to find a place to eat afterwards. "Won't everything be closed?"

"Don't worry about that," he reassured me. "We'll keep a restaurant open for you."

And he did. It was a sophisticated place, of course, and the Sextett were the only late-night diners. As soon as we settled in, the waiters started wheeling out these carts piled full of delicacies: antipasti and cheese and olives, oysters and crayfish, salmon. They brought out a 1945 brandy from Spain—"You must celebrate end of tour!" the maître d' proclaimed—and an assortment of cognacs and various liqueurs, along with a selection of the Cuban cigars that seemed to be omnipresent in Sicily.

Once we were ready, they asked us what we wanted to eat. No menus. Whatever we wanted. When Frank Lacy said he thought he might like some lamb, the waiter asked, "How would you like to have it prepared?" They took a few of us into the walk-in refrigerator in the kitchen to show us what they had available, and they had all sorts of meat, fowl, fish—almost anything you could possibly want.

At the end of the meal, another waiter approached and asked, "What would you like for dessert?" I remember I gave him a detailed order—I actually did have a taste for something specific.

"I'd like to have some dark chocolate," I told him, "melted and mixed with some kirsch liqueur and grapefruit in a frying pan with butter, and then poured over vanilla ice cream."

"Certainly, sir," he replied, as though it were the most commonplace request imaginable.

I wonder what happened to the godfather's son. I went back to Sicily six or seven years later with Very Very Circus—just for a single show in Palermo, not an extended stay—and I heard there was a new godfather. I suppose that's the way that sort of power operates.

In any case, he certainly sent me off in style. I left Sicily sharp as hell. When we landed in Rome, I was informed that my lost luggage had been located. So I even got my old clothes back, along with an entirely new set of the finest duds. Everybody in the band was teasing me for months about my white corduroy pants. But that didn't keep me from wearing them!

In December 1987 I got my first major commission for chamber orchestra from the Brooklyn Academy of Music. *Run Silent, Run Deep, Run Loud, Run High* was an evening-length, four-part composition for twenty-eight musicians (vocals, strings, percussion, and my alto), conducted by Hale Smith. The piece combined elements of Western classical music with jazz and other non-Western influences, and I used a number of the exceptional musicians I'd crossed paths with over the years, including Leroy Jenkins, Akbar Ali, Jason Hwang, Diedre Murray, Fred Hopkins, Abdul Wadud, Andy Bey, Avery Brooks, Jo Jo Morris, Asha Puthli, and Amina Claudine Myers. I needed players who were impeccable readers but who also could improvise: as the sole horn, I thought of my own role as something like an onstage "activator" or "cantor" whose interjections repeatedly compelled the music into passages of collective improvisation.

The four percussionists (Thurman Barker, Bryan Carrott, Eli Fountain, and Warren Smith) play a prominent role—I'd always thought of percussion to be criminally underutilized in the American orchestral repertoire, and I wanted to try to explore the endless melodic and textural possibilities the percussion section can bring if it isn't used solely for color and emphasis. I used my own libretto for the vocal score, but *Run Silent* isn't a narrative or character-driven piece—instead I used the vocalists as another orchestral section, and asked the singers not only to sing the settings of the lyrics but also to perform various nonlinguistic effects and sounds as part of the sonic fabric.

Rather than explicative, the text is deliberately opaque in its lyricism—"Black box riding up the river. / Inside a beacon that guides without a keeper. / Never having passed this way before"— and used to set the mood rather than to tell a story. The underlying theme of the piece is "creation, and the natural unity and common evolution of all life—and all music," as I put it in the program note. The title is partly an allusion to the 1958 Hollywood film *Run Silent, Run Deep* starring Burt Lancaster and Clark Gable, a drama about World War II submarine battles in the Bungo Channel south of Japan. Submarines sometimes make recourse to a stealth mode they call "silent running," in which they try to evade enemy sonar by moving at a low speed and shutting down as many mechanical systems as possible. The piece explores the implications of adapting this strategy for composition: in addition to whatever was happening on the surface of the music, could you have other things going on in the depths, major moves that were almost inaudible until they revealed themselves?

For the concert, I wore a custom-made black silk suit covered with silver-and-gold concentric designs. It was an idea I'd been playing with for some time—it was also behind the ballad "Silver and Gold Baby, Silver and Gold" that I composed for the Sextett album *You Know the Number* the year before. I had those designs hand-painted onto the suit with a special luminescent pigment. When the light hit me, it looked as though I was standing in these bright circles, like a planet with glowing rings. There was a matching scrim with circle patterns behind the orchestra, too. The lights slowly came up over the course of the four movements, bringing the halos of light into view.

Since *Run Silent*, I've gotten a steady stream of commissions over the years, including my *Mix for Orchestra* in 1993 for the Brooklyn Philharmonic Orchestra conducted by Dennis Russell Davies, with the drummer Max Roach as featured soloist, and other pieces commissioned more recently by groups including Petr Kotik's S.E.M. Ensemble, the Young Salzburg Philharmonic Orchestra, the American Composers Orchestra, Aggregation Orb, the Modern Ancient Brown Foundation, and the Kronos Quartet.

Even as I've moved into this world, I've remained frustrated with the prejudices and limitations of the classical concert scene in the United States. For years, when AACM composers such as

Leroy Jenkins, Jason Hwang, and me in the painted suit
onstage at the Brooklyn Academy of Music, December 1987.
Photo © Michael Wilderman

Roscoe Mitchell, George Lewis, Leroy Jenkins, and I did anything in a more mainstream orchestral setting, critics tended
to attack us for stepping out of the venues traditionally associated with jazz. The point of the reviews seemed to be less about
the music than about making sure we stayed in our lane. When
Max Roach performed *Mix for Orchestra*, one of the reviewers
sneered that it might have been "better served" if it had been
performed in a nightclub. It's disrespectful, like telling someone
he isn't "allowed" to speak another language even when he's
speaking it fluently right in front of you. The prejudice has even
impacted African American composers who primarily work in
the classical realm and are hardly associated with jazz at all,
from William Grant Still and Florence Price to George Walker
and T. J. Anderson.

Even as hordes of students are studying jazz improvisation
in high schools and colleges across the country, the American
classical orchestra remains associated with a blinkered conception of the European concert tradition. The problem isn't just a
matter of overt racism—it's not something that can be addressed
simply by imposing blind audition policies, so that a trickle
of musicians of color might be able to get into the traditional
orchestras. We need to rethink the orchestra as an institution
altogether. It would mean thinking creatively about training:
What tools should a player in an orchestra have to be able to
play the full range of American concert music? Shouldn't she be
able to improvise? Shouldn't she be able to play my music as well
as that of Elliott Carter, Eddie Palmieri, Aaron Copland, John
Cage, Wadada Leo Smith, and Harry Partch? The most exciting
groups thinking in this direction are the independent ensembles
and experimental collectives: Bang on a Can, Wet Ink, Alarm
Will Sound, the International Contemporary Ensemble. But
their versatility shouldn't be the exception—it should provide
the template for rethinking the American orchestra.

It's time for a new paradigm. In this respect, I still marvel
at the foresight and bravery of the founders of the AACM, who
were so far ahead of the game. It's all bound up in that word

"advancement." It's a much bigger word than I appreciated at first. Advancement doesn't just mean adding one of us (whichever "us") to the mix and continuing to do things the same way. Advancement might not only mean addition—it might require some subtraction, too, or a completely different method of calculation. It's like Abbey Lincoln sings: "I've got some people in me . . ." I've got more than just some people in me. I've got some ideas in me, too. And we're still developing: anything that's put in front of us can be digested and refashioned into something entirely new, something entirely unexpected. We need a vision of the American orchestra as a vehicle for advancement on a level that can keep up with the breadth of the American composer's appetite.

In the fall of 1984, I produced a set of concerts with the Windstring Ensemble at the New York Art Theater Institute that took the "wordless theater" idea I'd been exploring with Don Sanders in a different direction. I called them the Live Music Imagination Series.

Each piece was the soundtrack for an "imaginary script" in a different medium. The first, titled *When Life Is Cheap and Death Is Taken for Granted*, was presented as a soundtrack for a film. Then there was music for a radio play, *Bed Ghosts . . . or, I'll Be All Over You Like a Cheap Suit*. And I wrote a third score to accompany a fictional TV show called *The Android That Terminated Hugh-Pinkston Sells and Committed Suicide*. I also planned a fourth one, a dance in which the choreography was based in the gestural vocabulary of semaphore, but I never got to perform it.

For these concerts, in addition to myself, the Windstring Ensemble included Tony Underwood on tuba, Akua Dixon on cello, Leroy Jenkins on viola, and Patmore Lewis on violin. I also brought in a couple of guest soloists: Olu Dara played with the group for the imaginary TV show, and the guitarist Jean-Paul Bourelly joined us for the film.

These pieces demanded an unusual sort of audience partici-pation, since the performance didn't provide what was supposed to be the primary medium. There was no film, in other words: as a listener, you were asked to imagine the film only by listening to the instrumental music of its purported soundtrack. It was programmatic music without a program.

Even though I didn't provide it to the audience, I did outline the plots of each of these works in great detail as part of my com-positional process. So I had a clear sense of the ways the music needed to suggest the narrative development. *The Android That Terminated Hugh-Pinkston Sells and Committed Suicide,* for example, was a sort of science-fiction space odyssey. The story centered around the fate of a band in an intergalactic circus that traveled from planet to planet, entertaining audiences. They returned from one extended tour to find that Earth had been infiltrated by androids that had insinuated themselves into all areas of human society. As in the film *Blade Runner,* the androids were such lifelike replicants that it was impossible to discern the difference between human and machine. But the band realized that the artificial intelligence behind the androids had one telling flaw: the machines couldn't understand why humans committed suicide. They just didn't get that aspect of the human psyche. It made no sense to them. So the story concluded with the robots deciding to commit collective suicide in order to understand what would drive humans to take their own lives—at that point, of course, it became clear who was an android. I later adapted the tune "100 Year Old Game" on the 1997 Make a Move album *Where's Your Cup?* from this performance: in the original imag-inary script, suicide is the "game" that's been around such a long time.

One of the pieces in the Live Music Imagination Series was semi-autobiographical. The radio play, *Bed Ghosts . . . or, I'll Be All Over You Like a Cheap Suit,* was a reflection on my experiences working as an orderly at the University of Chicago Hospital in

1965 and early 1966. There were all sorts of crazy shenanigans going on in that place. I nearly lost my mind. As I explained, my main responsibility was to deliver human specimens from one place to another. I knew where all the labs were and who handled what tests—I learned how to make myself indispensable. But my unfettered access to the underbelly of the institution meant that I witnessed all sorts of shady dealings: illicit assignations, drug deals, all sorts of wild stuff.

Beyond all the kooky characters I encountered in the institution, working there saddled me with a severe phobia about germs and contamination. It all started when I was delivering some urine samples to some lab or other and mistakenly strode into the X-ray room.

The technicians looked up at me, surprised. "What are you doing here? And why aren't you wearing protective gear?"

I realized that they were all wearing lead protective coverings to protect them from the radiation. I'd just waltzed in wearing my usual scrubs.

I was petrified. I dropped the urine samples—the bottles shattered on the floor—and backed out. The technicians just stared at me.

After that happened, I developed an irrational fear that I had been exposed to radiation. The peril seemed to be everywhere. In my head it expanded into a general fear of contamination: any space, any surface could lead to infection or exposure.

As I went around the hospital on my rounds, I started having powerful compulsions to bathe. I would shower multiple times a day and scrub myself raw. I got a reputation among my colleagues: Threadgill, the one who's prone to strip down anywhere and everywhere and start washing himself. When I couldn't find a shower, I'd just use a sink. Nurses would come into unoccupied rooms and find me standing there half naked washing myself fanatically in a disturbing sort of St. Vitus' dance. Then I began to store changes of clothes in various rooms around the hospital, like a squirrel burying nuts for the winter. I hid bars of soap and industrial-strength cleansers in cabinets in various rooms.

I'd rush in and grab my supplies whenever the impulse came over me.

I've been wearing these scrubs for a whole hour, I'd think to myself. They could have picked up any number of germs as I interacted with patients and collected samples. I have to get out of these clothes right now! I'd duck into a room where I'd left a store of supplies. Once I was wheeling a patient somewhere on a gurney and the urge came over me so forcefully that I just left him lying there in the hallway while I fled to do one of my ritual cleanses.

It got so bad that I threatened to quit. "I'm sick," I announced. "I have radiation poisoning, I know it. I can't come in to work anymore." But I had made myself so essential to the everyday functioning of the hospital that my bosses panicked. They pleaded with me to stay. They gave me a raise. They put up with my obsessions.

Bed Ghosts was a hallucinatory account of that time in my life—a deep dive into my close shave with insanity. Looking back twenty years later, it occurred to me that some of the things I thought were so dire weren't such a big deal after all. Working on the piece gave me a chance to look back at my own foibles and laugh at myself for once.

The music journalist Howard Mandel saw the performance at the New York Art Theater Institute, and he told me, "You know, Henry, you should do one of those for real."

Howard offered to try to find a way to produce *Bed Ghosts* as an actual radio play that would combine a script with my soundtrack for the Windstring Ensemble. Another friend, the actor Bob Wisdom, was married to a woman who worked for a satellite radio company. It turns out that they had funding and were interested in producing new radio broadcasts. They offered to support the production and then to distribute it on satellite radio. I knew a couple of people who worked at WNYC, the public radio station, and they were able to arrange for us to use the studio for free to record the session. I got a commission from Improvisers Unlimited to allow me to finalize the score and to come up with the script. I had to change the music somewhat, of course, now that it actually had to accompany a radio play, rather than suggest by implication an "imaginary" story that wasn't being provided. Howard ended up producing it for a show he hosted on public radio in Chicago, introducing the broadcast with a short interview with me about the Live Music Imagination Series.

The voices were performed by the actors Bob Wisdom and Alva Rogers and the singers David Garland and Cassandra Wilson. I tried to take it seriously as a radio play, which is a genre with its own illustrious history: it's all about being able to deliver a line, to make the listener imagine an entire situation with just the sound of your voice. Finally I approached my friend the writer Thulani Davis for help with the script. I spent a couple of long brainstorming sessions with her and Howard, telling them stories from my time in the hospital. Thulani found the material quite humorous, and she worked with me to bring out the warped surrealism of my orderly days. In the end she convinced me to tone it down a little. What really happened in those hallways was far more outrageous than what we ended up with.

When I think back to all the antics on display during my time working at the hospital, it occurs to me that from another perspective that foolishness shouldn't have flustered me at all. In fact, I'd spent a good part of my early childhood being subjected to what were more or less a series of madcap scientific experiments.

I mentioned that I was close to my grandfather, Luther Pierce, who would often take me on Sunday mornings to the Maxwell Street Market, where I first heard Howlin' Wolf. Grandpa Pierce passed away in 1956—in other words, a half-decade before his father-in-law, Peyton Robinson. But I lived with my grandfather until then, and he was quite an exceptional character in his own right.

Although he worked in a steel mill, my grandfather had the chutzpah to consider himself an expert in any domain under the sun. Why pay someone else to do something you could figure out how to do it yourself? He was resourceful—or reckless—to a degree I have never encountered in any other human being. And with a household full of kids and young adults, he had ample opportunity to demonstrate his breadth of knowledge.

As kids, we knew we were in trouble when we saw him put on a uniform. He had the official duds for every profession, which he seemed to be convinced qualified him to practice it.

He had a barber's smock and hand clippers, even if he didn't actually have any clue about cutting hair. He'd wrap the barber cloth so tight around your neck that you thought you were going to pass out even before he launched his assault with the shears.

Often he'd be smoking a cigar while he clipped your hair, and invariably some of the hot ash would fall and catch you on the neck. If you reacted with the slightest twitch at being burned, you would bump his wrist and he would take out a chunk of your hair by mistake.

This was your fault, of course.

"Keep still!" he'd growl. "Look what you made me do, boy! You messed up your head! Let me see if I can fix it."

He insisted on preparing the hair of my youngest aunt before her high school graduation and fouled it up so extravagantly that she refused to go. She was distraught. My mother was supposed to accompany her to the ceremony, but I heard later that she'd just given my aunt a headscarf and told her they'd skip it. They walked the streets until it was time to come home, so my grandfather wouldn't know they'd been too embarrassed to have her seen in public.

Grandpa Pierce was Mr. Everything. The carpenter. The plumber when the pipes under the kitchen sink would leak or when the flapper valve on the toilet broke. The electrician,

replacing the frayed cord on a lamp. The on-call exterminator—
always a key role in Chicago, the bedbug capital of the world.
When I was little, before we moved to Englewood, I slept in the
same bed with my sister Carol and my cousin Michael, and I
remember that my grandfather would periodically surprise us
in the middle of the night with bedbug raids. The adults would
rush into our bedroom in the dark, hustle us out of bed, gather
all the sheets and light them on fire with kerosene. And then
scrub us down with a cleanser. It was traumatizing.

He was the self-appointed family cobbler as well. In elementary school I had a favorite pair of brogans, and I remember hiding them under the pile of shoes in the hallway so he wouldn't
notice that the soles were starting to wear thin. But he would
check periodically, and he found them.

"Those shoes are fine, Grandpa," I told him. "Please don't
fix them." But he ordered me to get his tools. He had a set: a
special shoemaker's hammer, an awl and leatherwork needles,
pliers, a shoe stand. But he didn't know how to use them. The
replacement sole was too big, so he used my shoe as a mold and
trimmed the sole around it with a pocket knife. It left a jagged
edge, but he paid it no mind. He ripped off the old sole with the
pliers and tried to attach the new one with leather stitches. In
some sections he had trouble forcing the needle through, so he
nailed it on with tacks.

He looked at his handiwork approvingly. "There we go." I
was nearly in tears.

I put them on but I could hardly take a single step: a few of
the tacks were sticking up inside the shoe. It was like walking
on nails. I was wincing in pain but he ignored it and sent me off.

I had an excruciating day at school, and on the way home I
made up my mind to tear the new soles off. I stood on the curb
and gradually wrenched the uppers free.

I was hoping that it would force him to admit that he didn't
know what he was doing and take them to a real cobbler. But
when I got home looking like a clown with both soles flapping,
he was unfazed.

"Oh, your shoes came loose, huh?" he observed. "I guess I didn't use enough tacks. Bring me my stuff."

My grandfather considered himself a professional tailor as well. One Sunday morning when I was five or six, he summoned my cousin Michael and me and declared, "It's about time you boys started wearing a shirt and tie to church." He grabbed a couple of old shirts and jackets that had belonged to my teenage uncles and proceeded to make the necessary alterations himself. The sleeves were way too long—he'd just grab a pair of scissors and cut them where he thought our wrists would be. To take up our trousers, all he required was some safety pins. Then he'd grab a necktie and try to tie it in a way to make the dress shirt look like it fit us, scrunching up the fabric behind our necks so it almost appeared presentable in the front.

However ridiculous we ended up looking, once he was satisfied he'd simply declare the job done and dismiss us to face the public humiliation of Sunday school.

"You look good to me," he'd say. "Now get out of here." My mother and grandmother would appraise his bespoke tailoring with resignation and try to make the best of it.

The worst was when he played doctor. One person would catch a cold and the whole family would come down with it. My grandfather would line up the kids in the hallway.

"Come take your medicine," he'd call. And we'd all try to hide or flee. As soon as anybody in the house started sniffling, the kids would scatter before he could organize a mass treatment session.

He had the usual folk remedies—castor oil, bitter apple, ginger, comfrey root, goldenseal, elm bark—but he had a stash of all sorts of other stuff. He would invent his own concoctions. In Englewood he had sacks and jars of ingredients in a trunk in the basement. Sometimes they were harmless, or even beneficial— herb-based tinctures and liquids made of plants like black jack or juniper steeped in alcohol—but sometimes they were positively frightening. He'd invent the most appalling combinations as though they were accepted medical treatments. A case of whooping cough?—A teaspoon of sugar with a drop of gasoline in it.

At the same time, my grandfather was the most generous person I knew. He and I both loved ice cream, and in the summer after a shopping excursion to the Maxwell Street Market he'd take me for a treat. But he got serious when something needed fixing.

The most amazing thing about it was his nerve. I think he would have been capable of performing open-heart surgery on one of us had he considered it necessary. Whatever it took, he was ready to do it: nothing was out of bounds. I loved that about him. And I suspect that a little of his spirit of radical experimentation rubbed off on me.

In the midst of all my other activity in the 1980s, in the latter part of the decade I inaugurated yet another group: the Society Situation Dance Band. Like the marching band and the funeral band, it started as another of my entrepreneurial brainstorms— but this one gained some traction, and we played regularly for a number of years both in New York and in Europe. With the Society Situation Dance Band, the decision not to document it on record was entirely deliberate.

It was conceived as a large orchestra of about sixteen to eighteen pieces. In terms of instrumentation the Dance Band was structured somewhat like the Sextett, with a string section (violin, cello), a brass section (trumpet, trombone, saxophone), and a percussion section, and there were some old mainstays from various iterations of the Sextett: Craig Harris, Rasul Siddik, Reggie Nicholson, Ted Daniel. But I often also called on other old associates from the AACM (Leroy Jenkins, Amina Claudine Myers, John Stubblefield) and elsewhere (Rolando Briceño). And I brought in other instruments as well, including tuba and accordion. This was a period in which I was gravitating toward a new sound that would culminate in my next band, Very Very Circus, and some of the players I used in the new ensemble (such as

A lighthearted moment with Jason Hwang, Brandon Ross,
Leroy Jenkins, Rolando Briceño, and the
Society Situation Dance Band on the tour bus in Germany

Brandon Ross and Tony Cedras) also appeared with the Dance Band. And I always used singers: Amina, David Peaston, Sherry Scott, Drew Richards, Aster Aweke. The music I wrote for the Society Situation Dance Band was party music, and the singers always got people up and grooving.

When Grandpa Pierce died, I tried to claim the collection of herbs and chemicals he had in his trunk in the basement. My mother and grandmother rushed downstairs to confiscate it before I could get my hands on it. I was offended. "They took my stuff!" I muttered, glaring at them as they locked the stash away. I considered it my inheritance—the keys to the kingdom.

Even before elementary school, I had been pursuing my own experiments. I wasn't interested in being a handyman around the house. No, I had greater ambitions. I thought of it as laboratory research, even if there was more than a dash of fiction in my notion of science.

As far back as I remember, I had two major objectives. I wanted to be able to fly. And I wanted to be able to turn myself invisible.

I was convinced that there had to be a formula—some potion you could brew that would grant your body those powers. I remember an episode of *Flash Gordon* where Dr. Zarkov invents a "light machine" that turns Flash temporarily invisible. Taking advantage of his newfound power, Flash infiltrates and defeats the henchmen of Ming the Merciless. It must be possible to make that happen in real life, I told myself. I just needed the right machine or the right chemicals.

I spent hours and hours in a concerted effort to find the magic mix. I didn't study books or anything—I just tried different combinations—but I took it very seriously. I observed the things my grandfather used, and I adopted some of the same ingredients. And I also accumulated a secret cache of materials of my own. When my mother would take me to people's houses, I'd go in their medicine cabinets and take things. I especially kept an eye out for hazardous products with the skull and crossbones symbol; to my mind that was a guarantee that the stuff would have an effect. I didn't consider this stealing. I was conducting experiments. And like my grandfather, I had no qualms about using my friends and relatives as test subjects.

At first I was focused on an invisibility formula. I convinced my sister and cousin to try my potions. I would give them a teaspoon of my latest mix and wait to see if it had any effect. I even carried around a little notebook, and I would stand there and observe them after they'd swallowed it. I don't know how I convinced them, but for some reason they'd acquiesce to my experiments. They were always game. They made faces when the liquids were pungent or bitter—"What is this stuff, Henry?" they'd complain—but they still drank it.

My invisibility experiments came to an abrupt conclusion after my mother took me to a party at someone's house and I got caught trying to make a baby disappear. I was playing with some of the kids in the people's kitchen. I went and found some bottles in the medicine cabinet, and I poured a few drops of various things into a basin I filled with warm milk. We were supposed to be keeping an eye on someone's baby and it was there in the kitchen, too, in a bassinet, placidly observing us. I thought I'd see if I could make the baby disappear by dipping it into the milk potion. Everything was going smoothly—the baby didn't even cry when I picked her up—but just as I was putting her in the milk, one of the adults came in and saw me.

"He's trying to kill the baby!" she screamed. The rest of the adults ran in. I tried to explain that the baby was fine. I wasn't going to hurt the baby—it was just an experiment. But they wouldn't listen. "Get that boy out of here," they told my mother. "And don't ever bring him to anything again!" I got banished.

My mother was furious. "I don't know what I'm going to do with you, Henry." She said she hoped I had learned my lesson. But the spectacular failure of my invisibility bath simply made me turn my attention to flight.

I did have the good sense to stay away from the chemicals

for the time being. I concentrated instead on inventing a flying machine. I would take cardboard boxes and balloons and scraps of wood and fabric and try to construct something that would allow a human body to achieve liftoff and stay airborne. All I knew about the physics of flight was what I could guess from observing birds and planes and making paper airplanes and whirligigs. But like my grandfather I was endowed with unshakable self-confidence.

I spent months trying out different contraptions. My mother and grandmother thought I was making costumes. But I would build these wearable technologies and then test them out on my sister and my cousin, telling them to jump off the couch or a table to see if my inventions would keep them aloft.

This stage of my career as a mad scientist culminated at another neighborhood party. It may have even been the very first time my mother was allowed to bring me somewhere again. A bunch of children were playing in the back room and I started building a flying machine, tying together some sheets to make wings and attaching them to a sort of harness. I remember there was an umbrella on top, too.

The other kids were captivated. "What's that you're making, Henry?" they asked.

"You'll see," I told them, focused on my design.

When I was finished, I put it on one of the little girls and instructed her to jump out the window. I was standing there with a pencil and paper, ready to observe the test run. All the other kids were watching, engrossed by the drama.

But the girl called my bluff. "Why do I have to jump, Henry? If this thing works, why don't you do it yourself?"

"I have to take notes," I explained.

But her objection set off a mutiny among the others. "Yeah, Henry, she's right!" they exclaimed. "One of us can take notes. If this thing works so well, why don't you show us?"

So I had to jump myself.

Although I would have preferred to maintain the objectivity of the observer, I had convinced myself that my flying contraption was going to work. Once I saw that the girl wasn't going to do it, I didn't hesitate.

We were in a second-floor apartment. I put on my invention, clambered up onto the windowsill, and leapt out. The paraphernalia didn't do much to slow my descent, of course. I plummeted into the branches of a big tree outside the window and then down onto a garage in the alley behind the apartment building. It's a good thing that garage was there, because it arrested my fall somewhat and probably saved me from breaking my neck.

I cut my leg on the tree and hit my head when I bounced off the garage. I ended up on the ground, lying on my back in the remains of my contraption. I could see the kids crowded at the window, looking down at me.

"Mrs. Threadgill, Mrs. Threadgill!" one of them yelled. "Henry jumped out the window trying to fly and killed himself!"

I got lucky. I was scraped and bruised, but I didn't even break any bones. To the parents in the neighborhood, the escapade was further evidence that that Threadgill boy had a screw loose. Once we were home and I was bandaged up, my mother just sat by the bed and gave me an imploring look, posing for the first time the question that became the refrain of my childhood. "Henry, why do you have to be so *extreme*?"

I didn't say anything. How could I have explained it? Where did these impulses come from? Even lying there in pain, though, I knew that I wasn't going to give them up. And in fact, I never abandoned those aspirations. In the back of my head, I'm still trying to figure it out. I may have stopped mixing potions, but I haven't dropped those dreams.

The Society Situation Dance Band first performed in a Russian club in the basement of a building in the West Village. Somebody asked me to play for a party or reception and I took the opportunity to inaugurate this new outfit, putting together a book of original arrangements. Then we started getting gigs in the Puck Building, SOB's, and other places downtown.

I didn't want fixed versions of any tunes. I didn't want to hear the usual whining from audience members or critics: "Why didn't they play it the way they did it on the record?" I didn't want to be worried about hits—about which track might get radio play. I only wanted to put myself in a position where I could employ a large group of talented musicians, pay them well, and have the freedom to write the way I wanted to compose without any of those sorts of pressures. Some of the tunes I wrote for the Society Situation Dance Band have great names—"Dance Goes Dance," "Everybody Will Hang by the Leg," "Spin in the Wind"—but I didn't always announce them in concert; I didn't want people getting hung up on that aspect, either.

The concept is explained in the name: I wanted to make a music not for contemplation in the salon or entertainment in the nightclub, but expressly for social dancing. I grew up going to dances and shows with live music, and I wanted to invent that space for a contemporary dance-based creative music. I have no problem with Lindy Hops and tango milongas, but my aim wasn't to commemorate a classical style—nor was I trying to concoct some sort of pop-music crossover. I wanted to forge that sort of social situation in a new way, on my own musical terms.

The point was to create an atmosphere where bodies in motion were the main thing—where there was room to move and where the audience could jump up and let it all hang out. There are bharata natyam dance academies in Chennai where the drummers arrive at seven o'clock in the morning. By the time the dancers show up, the musicians have been warming up for a couple of hours and the space is hot—activated, charged with potential. There's something unpredictable about a hot room like that, where there's no time frame, no way to know exactly how things might develop and how long they might last. What might have been only a brief moment on a record can dilate in a live-performance situation: the musicians might decide to extend it, or develop it, sometimes reacting to what they see the dancers reacting to. What I wanted was a room like that, full of heat and grime and turbulence.

9

To Undertake My Corners Open

When the Sextett toured India in 1984, we had been scheduled to perform in Goa, the small state on the southwestern coast of the country. But our concert there was canceled. I didn't have a chance to go to Goa until the beginning of the following decade, when I was invited back to the Yatra Festival with my next band, Very Very Circus. With its unique architecture of forts and Catholic churches, the product of more than four centuries as a Portuguese colony, Goa felt noticeably different from the other places I'd been in South Asia. After the bustle and crush of Bombay and Delhi, Goa seemed placid, almost like a tropical island, sheltered from the rest of the peninsula by the looming mountain range of the Western Ghats.

The festival was right on the beach—we watched the sun descend under the horizon behind the crowd as we played our set. We were rocking that night, but the crowd's reaction to our music still took me by surprise. They had folding chairs and the audience started out seated. But they responded physically to the music to a degree that I'd never witnessed in any concert I'd ever given. You would have thought we were in a Holy Roller church. People stood up and were dancing in the aisles—not just a couple of free spirits, but what looked like a majority of the crowd. Some were running up to the edge of the bandstand and spinning around in circles or falling on the ground like they were catching the spirit. I suppose the only way to describe it is to say that they *were* catching the spirit. I'd seen congregants transported to the point of possession and speaking in tongues in evangelical churches in Chicago, and I'd seen my share of frenzied thrashing and slam dancing in the punk scene in New York. But I'd never seen one of my ensembles provoke quite this degree of collective delirium.

It was so extreme that it freaked out the band. They didn't stop playing, but their eyes got wide and they kept shooting me anxious looks. I kept going and tried to convey the message that we should just hold steady in the tumult we'd unleashed. I ignored the pandemonium in the crowd and concentrated on the music. I didn't know what else to do. We had taken the crowd to this plateau—now the only option was to try to sustain it.

When we finished our last tune, the audience erupted in a raucous ovation, and I exchanged glances with the band. Clearly there was something special about this place.

By that point night had fallen like an opaque shroud over the coast. There was no moon and it was almost pitch black. The concert organizers had guides waiting backstage with lanterns to lead us up to the bungalows where we were staying a little ways inland from the beach.

Still tingling with the adrenaline of the set, I decided to take a little time for myself and told the guides that I'd walk to my bungalow on my own. It was only a few minutes away. But I misjudged how disorienting the darkness had become. Once I moved into the jungle, away from the soft glow of the stage, I almost immediately lost my way and found myself enveloped in the foliage. There were trees with leaves as big as my body, and underbrush so thick that it cut off the trickle of light from the beach.

I could barely see my own hand in front of my face. I paused for a moment to catch my breath and let my eyes adjust to the darkness. I stood there trying not to panic.

Suddenly a little old woman stepped out from the bush right in front of me. I was startled, but it happened so quickly that there was nothing to do: I just stared at her. She was a rail-thin old lady, black as coal, with some sort of basket strapped to her back. She walked right up to me as though she was expecting to find me there. The whites of her eyes gleamed as she got in my face, so close I could smell her breath as she exhaled.

She pointed her finger at me and spoke to me in English.

"You belong here," she declared.

And then she turned and melted into the bushes.

I recorded *Rag, Bush and All*, my last album with the Sextett, at the end of 1988. Given the popularity of the music I wrote for the various iterations of that band across the course of the decade, people were dumbfounded that I was going to give it up. They attributed it to what they took to be eccentricity or contrariness. "Threadgill's finally got a popular band, so of course he's going to abandon it," they sniffed disdainfully.

That year I was featured in one of those omnipresent magazine ads for Dewar's White Label Scotch whisky. I would run into people who congratulated me on it as though they thought that that was the pinnacle, that getting a Dewar's Profile meant you'd made it—meant you'd finally "crossed over." Crossed over to what, I wondered. Maximal commercial exploitation? Oblivion? The other side? They didn't look at the ad copy carefully enough. When the people putting together the profile asked me for an emblematic quotation, I pointed them to something I'd said the year before in an interview with the journalist Gene Santoro: "Tradition is a background of ingredients; in itself it's nothing. If you can't make something out of it, the world can do without it." When they asked me why I did what I did, I said, "It was either make money or make music which for me wasn't even a choice." In the photo I'm sitting there with a bemused expression on my face, looking away from the bottle of Scotch, off to the side, my palm cupped to my ear, as though I'm listening for the next thing.

The truth is, when I transition from one ensemble to another, it is the result of an unavoidable process in my development as a composer. I realize I might be unusual that way. I don't just hire new musicians and continue to play the same songbook, fiddling a little with the arrangements. When I change bands, I also change sound worlds—I move into an entirely different universe. And so my music changes accordingly.

With each of my ensembles, I've reached a point where it felt that the possibilities of that situation had been exhausted. It's not an easy transition—on the contrary, it's a struggle, not least because it's a matter of human relationships: close collaborators and friends I've spent significant time with.

I don't choose musicians simply on the basis of technical ability. Of course there's a baseline—they have to be able to keep up with the demands of the music. But what I look for is something deeper. I need players who are capable of a special level of commitment. It's not just a matter of gigging. The allegiance has to go farther than that. It almost requires a sort of abandonment: the musicians have to give themselves over completely to the art. They have to make a significant investment, shaping their lives to prioritize the music, to make space for what happens when we inhabit the compositions and take them somewhere I wouldn't have been able to predict. I'm grateful for that commitment, of course—I deeply respect the sacrifices it requires. And all these factors make me reluctant when it comes time to change bands.

I never want to get rid of people. It's a hassle, and sometimes it hurts my heart. But it's like having a house full of children. You get to a point where you're on top of one another and you just can't take it anymore, and there's only one thing to say: "Some of you all have got to get out of here and go do your own thing. I love you dearly, but it's time for you to go. I need some room."

I can sense when something is over for me. It's never abrupt—the change in mood from Saturday night to Sunday morning. Instead it's gradual and fitful. Usually I feel myself falling into a sort of fog, an aesthetic confusion. I can't figure out how to proceed. The dead end is musical, first of all—a compositional cul-de-sac—but then it sometimes also becomes personal: the collaborative relationship doesn't seem to function any longer.

The Sextett performing at Jazzwoche Burghausen in Austria
in March 1988: Yoron Israel, me, Fred Hopkins, Deidre Murray, Frank Lacy,
Newman Taylor Baker, Rasul Siddik. Photo © Helmut Frühauf

At that point, awkward and unpleasant as it can be, I know I have to step back and regroup.

Not surprisingly, all this artistic turmoil can take a toll on my personal circumstances, too. Eventually my restlessness and dissatisfaction led to the demise of my relationship with Christine. After we separated, I shared an apartment with my friend the cornetist Butch Morris in Chinatown, on Eldridge and Grand. We were both refugees from failed relationships: my daughter Pyeng would come to stay with me part of the week, and Butch's son was there part of the time, too. By the mid-1980s, I was living in Brooklyn, in Fort Greene and Clinton Hill. At the time, it was the hip part of the borough, colonized by waves of musicians. It seemed like you'd run into everybody on the block or in the bodega: Joseph Jarman, Thulani Davis, Lester Bowie, Hannibal Peterson, Pheeroan, Betty Carter, Bill Lee, Charles Tyler. Finally, at the end of the decade I moved back to Manhattan, ending up in the place in the East Village near Tompkins Square Park where I've been ever since.

I've come to realize that the confusion when I'm reaching the end of an ensemble is partly due to the fact that I'm slipping into another sound world. The only way to work through it is to attune myself to that new climate. It's not about the people—it's about the sound. I start hearing something totally different. Sometimes I can keep some of the players, if they fit in the new configuration. But first I have to step back to listen to that sound as it emerges—from somewhere far away, somewhere inside—in order to figure out where I need to go compositionally.

I don't hear melodic content floating in the air: what I tend to hear are textures, combinations of instruments that provide a particular palette. And that's what changes when the sound world morphs. So I have to try to figure out what the mix is— what's making the sounds I'm gravitating toward. Is it an apple falling from the tree? Is it a stampeding elephant? A grocery cart with a loose front wheel? A bazooka?

Generally there's at least one mistake in the recipe at first. It can take some trial and error. I tried French horn for a while in the early years of the Sextett. I had a bass with the Windstring Ensemble before I realized it needed to be a tuba. Or you can hear the heuristic quality in the discrepancies in the sonic palette between the two albums I recorded in 2001 as I was transitioning between my group Make a Move and my new unit, Zooid, one with vibraphone in the mix and the other with oud. Sometimes I find myself guessing as to the identity of the sound source. I can't quite make it out at first.

Still, when the mix isn't right for where the music needs to go compositionally, I usually figure it out pretty quickly. That should have been a glockenspiel, I realize, not a piccolo. It needs to be a field drum, not a tenor drum. Often the ingredient becomes obvious when I start getting down to the concrete task of cooking. It's when I start trying to compose for a certain configuration that I realize that one of the elements just won't work.

Very Very Circus wasn't a departure from the Sextett, much less a rejection of what I'd been doing. I just started hearing something else. As with the previous ensemble, I continued to think about composition orchestrally, in terms of instrument sections. But the makeup shifted in my ear.

No more bass and cello. That was a major shift. I had been working with basses and cellos for the longest time. Now it felt like that was over. At first I thought the new sound was going to involve me playing with a steel band, tubas, and electric guitar. Even all those years after my time in Trinidad, the sound of those tuned fifty-five-gallon industrial steel drums was still ringing in my ears. But after a little experimentation I realized that that mix wasn't going to work. Instead, the new sound needed to revolve around pairings of brass and string instruments: a labile relationship between odd couples of tubas and electric guitars. That's what was going to make this band run.

In building a group, I never start with the individuals. I start with the sound and then I find the people. On trombone I brought in Curtis Fowlkes, and he recommended the drummer

EJ Rodriguez, whom I'd heard play around New York with the Jazz Passengers. EJ left after a few months and I switched to Gene Lake, the son of the saxophonist Oliver Lake, who became the primary drummer with the band over the next few years. I'd met the guitarist Brandon Ross at some point in the late 1970s, when he was playing with the great alto saxophonist Marion Brown in Massachusetts. I paired him with a second guitarist, Masujaa, whom I'd heard with various groups around the city. Marcus Rojas had started working with me in the Windstring Ensemble, as I mentioned, coming in as a replacement for Bob Stewart. So I brought Marcus in for Very Very Circus as well, matching him with another tuba player, Edwin Rodriguez.

I thought of the coupled instruments like the two rails of a train track—one tuba and one guitar on each rail. They could be running along parallel to one another but doing completely different things. And then the wind instruments—my alto sax or flute, and either Curtis Fowlkes's trombone or, later, Mark Taylor's French horn—could either move on both rails at the same time or else bounce from rail to rail. The horns would ride the propulsive drive of those tracks.

People sometimes describe Very Very Circus as my response to Miles Davis's going electric on *Bitches Brew* or to Ornette Coleman's Prime Time band. That's not entirely incorrect, but for me it was first of all about the sound I was going for: the unusual quality of that tuba-guitar combination, and the way the doubling allowed me to have multiple things going on at once.

Why "Very Very"? As usual, people thought I was trying to be clever. Threadgill doth protest too much, methinks. But there was no other option. It seemed obvious to me that "Very Circus" would have been all too demure, all too circumspect. No, "Very Circus" clearly wouldn't do.

Very Very Circus! The ebullience of it—the sheer too-muchness! That's what this sound world was about. When I started to compose for the new ensemble, I remembered all those extended tours across Europe with Air a decade earlier.

In almost every city, we'd come across these traveling circuses. We'd see them in train stations and on the outskirts of town, pitching their tents, or packing up their caravans to head to the next stop. As any kid can tell you, the thrill of the circus has everything to do with how much is going on: lions and tigers and elephants and bears and clowns and acrobats and the flying trapeze, all together under the big top.

The most important question with a circus is always the same: how many rings does it have? How many things can you keep going simultaneously? A single ring is nothing. To draw a crowd, you have to offer a two-ring affair at least, or better, a three-ring show. Then the ringmaster's job is to direct the audience's attention to the attractions in one ring after another. What makes the circus exhilarating is the abundance and variety—there's always another act, always somewhere else to look, always another kick to discover.

You can really hear the multiring setup of the band on a tune like "Breach of Protocol," from our live 1991 album at Koncepts in Oakland. My flute is darting around maniacally in one ring with one tuba-and-guitar pairing, and the French horn is shimmying in another ring with the other. The drummer is in a third ring of his own, but it sounds like he's hopping back and forth between our rings, too: coming over to join one of the subgroupings and then switching to the other. The opposition between the units creates a dynamic tension. Playing this music, I always felt that I was dancing on a live wire—or more precisely, dancing between two electrified wires, thin and taut, strung way up in the air.

In April and May of 1991, I embarked on a second Great American Music Tour, this one with Very Very Circus. It was more formally organized than the tour in 1984. I made the mistake of listening to an agent who convinced me to hire a bus driver and someone to handle the bookings. Even if it saved us the burden of having to do stints behind the wheel, it took away the cama-

Very Very Circus live onstage during the second
Great American Music Tour, 1991: Brandon Ross, Edwin Rodriguez, me,
Larry Bright, Marcus Rojas, Mark Taylor, Masujaa

raderie of the Sextett tour—the feeling that we were out on an adventure together. The second tour was more of a commercial affair. There was much less improvisation along the way than there had been with the Sextett, where we were liable to stop anywhere and start playing. Still, we performed in a wide variety of venues: clubs, theaters, old movie houses, community centers, art galleries, museums, and high schools. This time we started from Northampton, Massachusetts, and made our way through Montreal to an extended set of gigs in the Midwest (Michigan, Ohio, Indiana, Illinois, Minnesota), before heading up to Vancouver and then down the West Coast through Seattle, Oakland, Santa Cruz, and Los Angeles, before swinging back east through New Mexico and Texas. Even with the more formal schedule, we did leave room for other sorts of engagement with folks in towns along the way: in addition to our concerts, we arranged workshops for musicians in eight or nine cities, showing them the way the music was put together and giving local players a chance to read through some of the charts.

One of the few major missteps on the first Great American Music Tour was my failure to arrange a recording session for that version of the Sextett with Henry Mitchell. In 1991, remembering that error, I made sure to schedule a live session for Very Very Circus at the Koncepts Cultural Gallery in Oakland in early May, about halfway through the tour. This was the second iteration of the unit, with French horn rather than trombone. Gene Lake had appeared on the first Very Very Circus album, *Spirit of Nuff . . . Nuff*, which was recorded in November 1990, but he wasn't able to join us for the tour the following spring. So the band on the second Great American Music Tour and the resulting album, *Live at Koncepts*, featured Larry Bright on drums.

By the time we got to Koncepts, we were smoking, energized by the crowds and the dizzying succession of landscapes we were passing through. Playing night after night for weeks on end, you develop not only a deep familiarity with the music—to the point where you know it so well that you can toy with it, stretch it into new shapes like putty—but also a heady level of confidence,

Scenes from the second Great American Music Tour, May 1991

fine-tuned reflexes, and physical stamina. It's an amazing sensation to find yourself together with other artists in that zone, in full awareness of your collective prowess. Standing up there in front of that band, I felt like Hannibal commanding the forces of Carthage in the Second Punic War. We were ruthless. Any place we came through, we knew we were going to tear it up.

When we did the live recording, I remember we were running late as we drove down to California from Washington. It was a brutal turnover: we played a show in Seattle and had to get to Oakland for a show the very next day. David Baker was the engineer. He was always in huge demand because it was an open secret among musicians that he could work magic at the soundboard, especially when conditions weren't ideal. And they certainly weren't that day. David had flown from New York specially to do the show. He had set up a mobile recording unit, and he was ready for us. The tour bus pulled up at Koncepts and we spilled out with our instruments like a crack crew of firemen ready to tackle a five-alarm blaze. We ran into the gallery and went right onstage—the crowd was already in their seats waiting for us. We didn't ever have time for a standard sound check. Instead we simply did a basic line check—to be sure everything was hooked up—and then we hit.

You can hear it on the record. That first track—we open with a tune called "Next," a little inside joke to underline the breathless pace at which we'd been hurtling from one engagement to another—starts up abruptly. The announcer just gives the bare minimum of an introduction: "And now would you please welcome Henry Threadgill and the Very Very Circus . . ." And away we go.

I didn't tell the band about the old woman on the beach. I didn't tell anybody. I didn't know how to explain what had happened. It would have sounded too strange—too implausible. But when we left Goa, I knew I was going to have to go back. I needed to spend more time there to try to figure out what it meant.

The Very Very Circus trip to India in 1992 was arranged in a manner that replicated much of what I'd done with the Sextett eight years earlier. This time, too, we played in various cities across the UK first. But we added an extended series of dates around Europe before we continued to South Asia. This was the trip when I went back to Sicily and heard that there was a new godfather in charge. Marcus Rojas couldn't get away for so long, so I brought Edwin Rodriguez and a new tuba player, Dorian Parreott. (Both Marcus and Dorian would appear on the next Very Very Circus album, the 1993 *Too Much Sugar for a Dime*.) We took on a daunting marathon of almost a month of one-nighters across Europe before we flew to Bombay.

Later the guitarist Brandon Ross teased me about it. "I don't know what you were trying to do to us, Henry," he laughed. "At the time," he added, "I seriously thought you might be trying to kill us. By the time we got to India, we were all in a daze."

The Yatra Festival always included a stellar array of Indian musicians as well as various representatives of the international jazz scene. In 1992, the foreign visitors in Bombay included a Swedish big band and Ornette Coleman's longtime collaborator the tenor saxophonist Dewey Redman. Don Cherry was there again, too. Normally the foreign groups would appear in the afternoon and evening, and the Indian artists would come on at the end of the night. They could go until dawn. I remember seeing that year the legendary Hindustani classical vocalist Bhimsen Joshi. I was backstage when he arrived. Joshi was intense. He showed up and drank an entire fifth of whisky before he went on. And then he sang for three hours without stopping.

At the end of the festival, just before we left the country, my friend A. D. Singh asked me to perform with Very Very Circus at his café called Just Desserts in Bombay. It was at this last-minute gig that I met my wife Senti for the first time. I certainly hadn't gone to South Asia on the tail end of an exhausting tour intending to find myself in a relationship. But when the band and I came into the café to set up and I saw her there across the room, I felt like I recognized her, even before a word was spoken—even though I was sure we'd never met. It was the most peculiar sensation, almost like seeing a ghost.

I couldn't help myself from going up to her right away to introduce myself. I asked if we could speak after I played. Sure, she answered shyly. Senti told me later that she was going through the same inexplicable sensation of recognition. She was so baffled and disconcerted by it that she ended up walking out at the end of the concert without waiting to talk to me.

Our friend A.D. found out what had transpired between us. Sensing how madly intrigued both Senti and I had been, he put us in touch the next day.

When we met, I learned that she was in Bombay studying philosophy and working with the great keyboard player Louiz Banks, singing jingles and doing voiceovers. She had grown up in Nagaland, a tiny state in the northeastern corner of India on the border with Myanmar.

There was something overwhelmingly potent between us— something undeniable. An instant spark that could have electrified the entire city. It was beyond anything I could explain.

It took some time for us to find a way to be together. The wait was torturous—I wrote her letters almost every day from New York. Finally I was able to travel to India again the next year. Through a connection, I got a room at the stately Royal Bombay Yacht Club in Colaba, overlooking the Gateway of India, and Senti spent some time with me there. We felt like spies, lurking undercover in a bygone luxury hotel among the aristocrats and their opulent sailboats. I found it revitalizing to find myself so far off the grid, so far away from my usual haunts on the downtown performance scene in New York. For me Bombay was an oasis: the first time in my life where the primary thing was a relationship. A cozy spot and nothing else: just us.

We decided to get married. It seemed impossible to imagine ourselves on opposite sides of the globe. Right away we both knew: we had stumbled upon something miraculous and rare, here in a place that was home to neither of us: a home in each other. We held the wedding in Bombay, right next to the Hanging Garden, and my good friend the bass player Sanjay "Storms" Swamy served as my best man.

I told Senti about my experience in Goa. We decided to spend some time there and get a feel for the place. When we made the trip down the coast from Bombay we didn't have a plan or a place to go, so we set ourselves up in a hotel on Calangute right on the beach, a couple of miles north of Panaji, the principal city in the area. Along the coast, Goa is basically a string of gorgeous beaches, one postcard picture after another.

After a couple of weeks, we moved into a modest bungalow in a sort of gated community a little farther inland. But by then we had both realized that we wanted to be able to spend significant time in Goa. We started looking for a house.

We gradually met people there and to hear about places that were for sale. We didn't have a real-estate agent—it was an informal, word-of-mouth process. Day after day, we would visit places, but none of them felt right. One was too close to the tourist scene at the beach, another too remote up in the hills. One was too dilapidated, another too lavish.

We met a guy named Xavier who seemed to know everybody in Goa. "I can help you," he offered. "I know this family that's selling their mansion up in the hills. Let me take you to see it."

Xavier took us to view the place and to meet the family. He introduced us to a sophisticated and erudite woman named Ana Marie. Her father had been a colonel in the army, and for decades the whole family had lived in an old Portuguese house with a spacious veranda. It was up in the hills in a town called Moira, a hamlet ringed by a winding river and surrounded by jungle and rice paddies. Xavier came down with Ana Marie to pick us up at our bungalow and drove us up to see the house.

Senti and I were sitting in the back seat on either side of Ana Marie, who gave us a little tour of the area during the fifteen-minute trip from Calangute, pointing out the sights: the Shri Dev Bodgeshwar Sansthan temple in Mapusa, the slightly larger town next to Moira; the fish market; the Sataporio Chapel in the center of Moira. As she was speaking, I looked past her at Senti and I could tell we were both thinking the same thing. It was a feeling of arrival—a certainty, even before we actually saw it, that this house was our destination.

It was something in the air. We pulled up in front of the house, and there was a guy sitting on a bicycle wearing nothing but a loincloth. He stood there perched on the bike and watched us park. When we emerged from the car, he got off and approached us, talking to Xavier but looking at me. Then he picked up the bicycle and rode off.

"What did he say?" I asked Xavier. Senti and I waited expectantly for the translation.

"He said to tell you 'Welcome to the village.'"

We went into the house and had a deal within an hour.

At least at that time, you didn't get a mortgage from a bank to buy property in India. You paid in cash. You either had the money or you didn't. The price included a portion up front, on which taxes had to be paid to the state, and a larger sum exchanged under the table.

It all came together at exactly the right time. I had just done *Philoktetes Variations* at the Kaaitheater in Brussels, which had paid very well. Once I changed the dollars into rupees, I had such an enormous pile of bills that we had to transport it in shopping bags. Xavier took great relish in directing the transport operation as though it were a major military exercise, barking out orders to the crew carrying the bags to the van. He stood there while the loading took place in front of the bank and squinted suspiciously at passersby.

The counting went on forever. Ana Marie was counting. The lawyers were counting. Other family members and friends were recruited to help with the counting. Then there was a flood of forms to sign. We signed papers at the house with Ana Marie. We signed more papers at the bank. We went to register the deed and signed more papers.

And then it was ours. A roomy house in the hills of Goa. Our neighbors in Moira made me an official citizen of the town. I'd been living in New York for almost twenty years, but Goa was the first place I owned a piece of property. Somehow it felt like I'd come home. A real Moiracai.

Having the house in Goa allowed me to establish a new rhythm in my creative life. I didn't give up my apartment in the East Village. But for most of the following decade, we spent at least five months out of the year in India. Usually Senti and I would leave New York in December and stay in Goa until April. While we were away, we would sublet the place in the East Village.

Our daughter, Nhumengula, was born in 1996, and we brought her up as much in Goa as in Manhattan. She would run around the village barefoot on her own. The first time it happened we were worried sick. We ran out into the jungle, calling her name, and started knocking on people's doors. She was fine, of course, just out playing with some of the other little kids. When it happened that first time, my inclination was to try to keep her inside. I locked the gate to try to make sure there was no way she could wander out. But she kept finding ways—she was quite the little escape artist. She figured out how to climb over the wall and slip through openings. Eventually I learned a different style of parenting, at least when we were in Goa. We realized that she needed to run around. To be honest, even as a toddler Nhumi knew her way around the village better than we did. And she was perfectly safe in that environment—everybody in town knew her, and people would keep an eye on one another's kids. That mutual responsibility was taken for granted.

I didn't perform at all when I was in Goa. I didn't want to compete with the local musicians. A few collaborators came and visited for an extended period and I rehearsed with them: the guitarist Brandon Ross, the accordion player Tony Cedras, the bass player Karl Peters. We could practice all night if we wanted to. The house had more space than I knew what to do with: everybody had their own private bedroom. We had a cook and

With Senti on the veranda
of the house in Goa

help, so all our needs were taken care of. You'd wake up in the morning and the staff would bring coffee and ask what time you wanted to have lunch. It was a charmed existence.

I deliberately made myself difficult to reach. When Senti and I first went to Goa and were staying in Calangute, we didn't have an address. The only way to mail something to me was to use the ersatz poste restante system on the beach. You could address a letter to "Henry Threadgill, Calangute Beach, Goa" and it would reach me. The postman would come to the beach and ask people if they knew me. "Oh, yeah, that's the American musician," someone would tell him. "He always has breakfast at the place down the road." They'd leave things for you wherever you were a regular. Even after we got the house, I didn't give anyone my address and I didn't have a telephone. I'd use a fax machine at a copy shop in Mapusa to stay in touch with booking agents and friends in the US.

Once I eradicated the continual buzz of what even then was an overly connected world, I found I could devote time to listening to what was going on in my head. I slowed down and paid attention to my senses: the new spices and colors and sounds around me. I would spend hours reading. I think I read everything Agatha Christie wrote while I was in Goa. Dostoevsky. Books on physics and astronomy. I had a telescope on the veranda and I would spend hours peering at the constellations. And above all, I composed. I got a record deal with Columbia just when I started spending significant time in India. I wrote all the music on my three Columbia albums while I was sequestered there in Moira.

The sources of inspiration were endless. The tune "Laughing Club" on *Where's Your Cup?*, my last Columbia record? That was a real Goan organization. I used to go to watch them sometimes. There was a Laughing Club that used to meet out in a field near Moira early in the morning, right as the sun was coming up. They would gather and start chatting, exchanging greetings and doing these yogalike exercises. Then they would take turns telling funny stories and jokes. And they would just let themselves go. One person would start giggling and another would chortle, and they would kind of egg each other on. They pushed each other to successive heights of amusement simply by watching each other get amused. In a few minutes, it would look like the group had been overcome by a paroxysm of jolliment. By the end of the session, it grew into a sort of communal rapture, with some folks rolling on the ground, hollering and flailing and kicking, so deep in the joy that it took over their limbs.

Eventually the members of the club would laugh each other into submission. It was quite a sight in the early morning: a field full of neighbors lying on the ground, heaving with the remnants of their guffawing, trying to catch their breath.

And then the session would end. People would gradually get up, brush themselves off, and head off to take care of their usual business. I found it remarkable, observing it, how unceremoniously the ritual came to a conclusion. The laughing petered out, and when they were ready, people just drifted off into the day, nodding to each other or exchanging a quick farewell: "See you next week." What a delightful idea, to take the time for therapeutic mirth.

Very Very Circus was both expanding and heading toward its final chapters when we got the house in Goa. Often that's the way it happens in the confusing transitional period when I start hearing a new sound. Things overlap in my ear—I'm no longer sure about what fits with what. My inclination is usually to start getting bigger before I get smaller and hone it down into a new ensemble. My 1994 album *Song Out of My Trees* is filled with me trying out new combinations: a piece for four guitars and piano; a piece with accordion, two cellos, and harpsichord. For the first two Columbia records, *Carry the Day* and *Makin' a Move*, both released in 1995, I used an augmented version of the band, adding other instruments, including the Chinese lute called the pipa, violin, accordion, piano, cello, and classical acoustic guitar. On some tunes I used vocalists, including Senti and Mossa Bildner, as well as Johnny Rudas and Miguel Urbina, two young Venezuelan percussionists recommended by Rolando Briceño who were specialists on the slender drums called the *culo e puya*. I was trying other combinations, too, that didn't always get documented on record. One of my favorites was a group I had in the fall of 1993 that played a series of concerts at the Thread Waxing Space in downtown Manhattan featuring Wu Man on pipa, Amina Claudine Myers on keyboards, Ed Cherry on guitar, Ted Daniel on trumpet, and Reggie Nicholson on drums. That band was killing.

If the title of the second Columbia record seemed to announce that my music was changing as I was changing house—that I was "makin' a move" in more than one sense—that declaration of migration ended up serving as the name of the new band. The impulse to go elsewhere, to follow what I was hearing, was so strong that it felt like the right way to describe the ensemble itself. The third Columbia album, *Where's Your Cup?*, was credited to Henry Threadgill and Make a Move. Here was where I pared things back down after the expansiveness of the Very Very Circus–plus experiments. Rather than the high-wire act of contrasting pairs of tubas and electric guitars, Make a Move offered a very different texture, with my alto sax and flute combined with Brandon Ross on electric or acoustic guitar, Tony Cedras on accordion and harmonium, J.T. Lewis on drums, and Stomu Takeishi on five-string fretless bass.

At first I didn't have a bass player. I knew the new sound required a return to the bass, though. When they came to visit me in Goa, I assigned Brandon and J.T. the responsibility of finding a bassist back in New York. I told them I needed them to find somebody before I returned to New York that spring.

"You'll know if they fit," I assured them. "Just trust your ears. You'll know."

They held informal auditions and checked out bands in the nightclubs. We were communicating by fax—Brandon still has a pile of my faded missives from Mapusa on that flimsy thermal paper you used to have to use. They found a young guy from the Virgin Islands who was promising, but he played stand-up acoustic bass and I had made up my mind that I was going to use electric bass. Then he had to go home to the Caribbean, anyway, so that didn't work out.

Finally they found Stomu. There was something about his sound on the fretless five-string electric bass that they were confident would mesh with the group. Stomu could also play acoustic bass guitar, and I had Brandon play both electric and acoustic guitar, so it gave me multiple options.

Stomu comes from a prestigious musical family in Japan. His brother Satoshi is a brilliant percussionist. The family was known for its lineage of accomplished koto players, and as the eldest Stomu was expected to take up that instrument and continue the tradition. Instead, he left home and came to the States to study bass at the Berklee College of Music in Boston. His rebellion caused a minor scandal back home: beyond the family pressure, people there were shocked by his rejection of the classical instrument. Giving up koto for electric bass is a little bit like going from eating caviar to a steady diet of potato chips. Stomu was a runaway child. It was years before he could go home and reconcile with his folks. Fortunately, both he and his brother were able to get US citizenship through the visa lottery in the 1990s.

When J.T. left the band, I replaced him with the Cuban drummer Dafnis Prieto. Working closely with so many musicians with international backgrounds over the years has made me reflect on the radical differences in musical education in different countries. It was especially striking with Dafnis. I was astounded at his technical ability and physical control. When I compared him with American musicians of his generation, it seemed clear to me that the system he came up in gave him enormous advantages, just in terms of what he could do.

I asked him to tell me what it had been like to study music in Cuba. He said he considered himself fortunate that the state covered everything. Once you made a commitment to a field, the state provided every possible resource to further your development—all you had to do was concentrate on your art.

"So how many days did you go to school?" I asked him.

"What do you mean?" he responded, confused by the question.

"How many days a week did you have classes?"

"Every day," he answered, as though surprised that there could have been another option. "All day, every day."

I peered at him skeptically. "You really studied all day?" I assumed he was exaggerating.

"Yes, all day," he insisted. "Well, some days there were some guys who might not stay in the group rehearsals until midnight— they'd go home early to their dormitory and practice there, or arrange a late-night session with some friends that wasn't part of the official curriculum."

He also told me that in Cuba, whatever instrument you were specializing in, you had to study percussion. It reminded me of my time at the American Conservatory in Chicago, where as a composition student I was required to demonstrate proficiency on piano. The presupposition was not only that the piano repertory was the cornerstone of Western classical music, but also that the foundation of music composition was harmony: counterpoint, voice leading, building up to sonata form and orchestration.

The notion that every student should have a foundation in the study of rhythm was an entirely different philosophy. What if American string players were required to study timpani—or timbales or djembe or gamelan? Putting rhythm at the center of conservatory education would forge a totally different brand of musician, performers with a deep polyrhythmic facility. My experience working closely with musicians from such a wide variety of backgrounds—players trained in India, China, South Africa, Cuba, Venezuela, and Japan—has come to make me question many of our basic assumptions in the United States about what a music education should be. We don't even recognize how parochial we are.

———

Make a Move wasn't just the next step, in my mind. In a way it represented the last step. Even as the mix of sounds changed, with each ensemble up to that point I'd been composing in the major/minor system of diatonic harmony. I kept pushing things farther and farther, and finally with Make a Move I went as far as I could go. I reached the top floor and there seemed to be nowhere else. I was standing on the roof.

I had been trying to figure out a way to move beyond the confines of diatonic harmony for a long time. I knew that eventually I was going to exhaust the possibilities of the conventional approach, and so I spent a lot of time looking for another way to organize sound.

It's easy enough to say that, of course. But it's not so easy to do. It isn't something one can accomplish by divine revelation or by mistake.

The aim wasn't to abandon harmony altogether. I have never done anything "free" in my music—as though one could get away from the question of form. Form isn't predetermined, but it is inescapable: it emerges in anything you do. Whatever you make takes on a shape, it takes on certain patterns, a particular mix of regularities and departures. You can't pretend you can simply ignore the issue of aesthetic form.

What I wanted to find was another way to understand harmonic structure beyond or outside the bounds of diatonic harmony. The only way to figure it out was through dogged, constant research and study. I knew I was going to reach the end of the diatonic. I knew that ship was going to sink. So I was looking for a life vest, so to speak—or for another kind of vessel entirely.

I finally found it in Goa. I spent hours and hours reading about math and physics and astronomy and warfare, studying philosophical treatises, reading books about various musical systems. At first the research felt directionless. I was just reading as much as I could. But gradually I started to get a sense of the direction I needed to go—not an easy solution, some prefabricated model I could simply apply, but instead the area where I needed to focus. The scope of the problem emerged. I began to see how things might be related. As I kept working at it, I started to notice that I could make connections between pieces of the puzzle. Going through tons of material, I slowly took stuff off the table until I just had the few essential ingredients I was going to need.

I had been working and working at it, and one day all of a sudden it came to me. Senti says she remembers hearing me yell from the other room.

"I got it!" I exclaimed. "Senti! I finally got it!" I ran out into the hallway and tried to explain what I'd seen. I couldn't describe it very well at first. I was babbling with excitement.

"Wow, Henry! That's great!" she said, genuinely thrilled to see me reach a point of discovery after struggling after it for so long—even if she might also have suspected that I had finally broken my brain.

My research drew on an eclectic range of sources. But the thing that opened the door for me was studying the music of Edgard Varèse. Going back to my time in college in Chicago, I had always been interested in his music. What was fascinating was that he was thinking about musical organization in innovative ways that didn't emerge from serialism, which was the dominant experimental vocabulary of his time. Varèse didn't follow the twelve-tone model of Schoenberg and Webern and their acolytes. He went his own way.

Varèse spent a great deal of time thinking about development techniques: ways to build and extend musical structures out of initial configurations. He writes about a technique where he flips the intervals between two notes to create harmonic derivations. In the major/minor world of diatonic harmony, one starts with a given tonal center—G major, say—and then the music proceeds through a set of operations in relation to that, moving to the relative minor, modulating up a half step, creating tension and release by resolving back to that center. But this isn't

what Varèse was after. Neither was he simply doing an inver-
sion, where, for instance, you have a C major triad and you can
flip the lowest note in the chord to the top, so that rather than
C-E-G you end up with E-G-C and you're still maintaining that
C major tonal center.

The derivations Varèse was experimenting with aren't the
product of diatonic harmony, the product of extensions or sub-
stitutions of a given tonal chord. Instead, they were solely a matter of the intervals. He called the variations of this procedure
"infolding" and "outfolding."

I took that basic idea and developed it into a way of thinking about harmony that was still based on the foundation of
the twelve tones of the equally tempered octave, but which
approached organization through intervallic relationships rather
than through tonal centers. Here, harmony is chromatic rather
than diatonic.

What brings order is not playing a given chord. In this chromatic language, what brings order is the consistency of the intervals. It starts with a three-note cell—any three notes can be the
core of a harmony. If that first group of notes is, say, C-D-F, then
I derive the harmonic possibilities from that parent cell out of
the intervals it contains. For instance, C to D is a major second.
So if we start with C and move a major second down instead of
up, we end up with B-flat. And that gives us one derivation of
the parent chord: that initial C-D-F gives rise to a second chord,
B-flat-C-F. Likewise, we can take the other internal interval, the
minor third between D and F, and move in the other direction
from the top note of the chord. A minor third up from F is A-flat.
So the initial C-D-F gives rise to another derivation, C-F-A-flat.
And so on. Taking the three intervals present in that initial cell, I
derive all the potential variants, and it gives me a set of intervals
to work with that all contain those same core relationships—
they all share the same DNA.

It sounds complicated, but it's actually not so difficult once
you get the hang of it. It's a language. You just have to learn

how to speak it. When you derive the possibilities from your parent cells, what you end up with is a syntax: a logic of combination in which you can move certain ways but not others. They become rules one has to adhere to in making musical statements. In other words, if I'm writing a melodic phrase in a harmonic space derived in this manner from a given set of intervals, I can only move according to those intervals. I can go anywhere, but I have to use those intervals to get there.

What becomes challenging is that the parent cells can change. I wrote one piece called "It Never Moved" that stuck with the same code throughout the entire tune. But in general, the code is changing throughout the piece, even as often as every measure. And there's no reason that all the musicians in the ensemble have to be using the same parent three-note cells. The guitarist might have one cell and I might give something completely different to the tuba player. Again, what holds it together are the intervals their respective cells have in common. That's what activates the gravitational field. Even if it sounds unfamiliar if you're used to the dissonances and resolutions of voice leading in diatonic harmony, the listener can hear those commonalities between the intervals among the players.

Improvisation is just as important in Zooid as it has been in all my music, but a musician has to be familiar with the intervallic language in order to improvise in accordance with the system. There are places where the musicians can embellish or modify or even discard the information in the score, but they have to know how to resolve things back into the structure, just the way musicians playing the blues or bebop or mambo need to know how to make their solos fit.

If we look at the history of Western music over the past century, the only alternatives to the major/minor system of diatonic harmony have been systems that were made up. The serialism of Schoenberg—organizing the twelve notes of the well-tempered scale into "rows" to avoid the lure of tonal harmony? It's a brilliant invention. Same thing with the more personal systems of Elliott Carter and Ornette Coleman. What is unique about my

Zooid performing at the Village Vanguard, August 2014: Liberty Ellman,
Elliot Humberto Kavee, me, Jose Davila, and Christopher Hoffman.
Photo © John Rogers

intervallic system—and what hasn't been recognized, because generally people still haven't understood what I'm doing in my recent music—is that I didn't invent anything. I just discovered something—a complete world, a chromatic world, with all its rules of gravity already established—already there in the physics of well-tempered harmony. Another dimension, hidden right in front of us. But I haven't published a book about my achievement, so it remains unacknowledged.

As soon as I began to work out the laws of this intervallic language, I realized that I was going to need to find musicians willing to take the time to learn it. I began to incorporate it into my writing for Make a Move at the end of the millennium. In 2001 I started working with Pi Recordings, and my first two albums on the label document the transition. *Everybodys Mouth's a Book* featured the final version of Make a Move, with Brandon Ross, Stomu Takeishi, Dafnis Prieto, and the vibraphonist Bryan Carrott. In the years leading up to that, I'd been figuring out how to use the new language, and so some of the tunes on the record are my first to use it.

The same year, I also put together a new ensemble I called Zooid with a group of musicians I brought together expressly to teach them the language: the guitarist Liberty Ellman, the oud player Tarik Benbrahim, Dana Leong on cello and trombone, José Davila on tuba, and Elliot Kavee on drums. Over the coming decade, when Tarik and then Dana departed, I brought back Stomu on bass guitar and then started working with another cello player, Christopher Hoffman.

The first Zooid album, *Up Popped the Two Lips*, was also recorded in 2001. But that one doesn't feature the new intervallic language. They weren't ready yet. The founding version of Zooid needed to rehearse together for more than a year in order to get to a place where they were all comfortable with the new language, where they could swim in it with assurance.

In biology, a zooid is an organic cell or organized body that moves independently within a living organism. It can function as part of an aggregate or colony, but it operates on its own volition. The name emphasizes the key characteristic of the structure of the ensemble working in the chromatic language: the individual voices are linked as elements in the whole, yet also utterly autonomous.

There are packs of feral dogs in the villages in Goa. If you see them roaming around, rooting through piles of trash, you might think that they're completely wild—creatures driven by pure instinct. But if you take the time to observe them, you realize that the dogs have their own very sophisticated rules of social organization. Everyone knows that dogs are territorial and that they spend an inordinate amount of time marking and remarking their territory. In Goa, there are precise lines of demarcation between the areas of the neighboring packs. If a dog from one group strays even a few feet into another group's space, a fight breaks out.

But the territories might also be described as a demarcation of mutual respect and even collective responsibility. There are women who live in Moira but work in other villages nearby. Some of them finish their shifts late at night. The dogs from our area go over to the other section and walk the women home. And when this is the purpose of the trespassing, there is no static with the pack in the other area. The other dogs let our dogs pass through to accompany the women home, safe and sound.

Social structures can be complicated that way. What on one level seems to be raw antagonism can also be complicity on another level.

The approach to rhythm in Zooid is a different thing entirely from the intervallic harmony. There's a palpable pulse to the

With my longtime friends the painter McArthur Binion and the
photographer Jules Allen at the premiere
of my piece *Brown Black X*
at the Detroit Orchestra Hall, June 2022

music, but no downbeat in a traditional sense. In the scores, the meters can change as often as every bar. So the music doesn't give you regular containers that you can count: one two three four, one two three four.

With the drummer in Zooid, I don't write out the part in as much detail as I sometimes used to do with Air or with the Sextett. I just give the drummer meter. But the drummer doesn't play the same meter the rest of the band is playing, because I don't need him to do that. It would be redundant.

I write music in phrases, not according to regular bar lines. So if a given melodic phrase goes on for, say, twenty-one beats, then that's the unit we're working with. For the drummer, those twenty-one beats might be divided up in a different way from the rest of the band—he might be playing in 7/4 time and then 3/4 and then 11/4, while the rest of the band is playing in 5/4 and then 6/4 and 5/4 and 5/4. When those various units of time are overlaid on top of one another, it creates tension and drive— that's what gives the music its characteristic groove. Everything gets swept up in that forward momentum. But there's still coordination at another level: the whole group can meet up again at the comma at the end of that twenty-one-beat phrase.

In composing for Zooid, I basically think in 1/4 time. Penny to penny, pound to pound. James Brown used to talk about getting back to the one. He'd cajole his band, talking about it, calling for it, demanding it—stretching things out to build anticipation. That's funk in a nutshell: that tantalizing expectation of the downbeat. Here it is—and here it is again. With Zooid, the question is almost the opposite: What if you never get off the one? Everything is always the one.

What I'm really trying to do is eradicate any demarcation of meter entirely. When you sense meter, what you're sensing is division. It disrupts the flow. And the flow is what I'm after. Rather than provide those markers that create expectations, I want to take away all those sharp corners. It makes the ride better. You just get engulfed by that smooth, frictionless groove.

I was always fascinated by the famous closing section of

Ulysses, where Joyce dispenses with conventional punctuation. There are pages and pages of what a junior-high-school grammar teacher would call run-on sentences. But it works. And as a reader, when you realize that it works, it can feel transformative. Magical. There's a thrilling defiance of the conventional rules, a bold transgression of the way things supposedly have to be done. And yet you encounter order and sense anyway—maybe even new or redoubled layers of resonance and meaning, because it isn't done the same old way.

My music with Zooid is modular above all else. Everything can be moved around. Because the intervallic system provides a foundation for everything, the order and arrangement of the parts can be switched without undermining the overall effect.

In every group I've worked with, it has always been the case that new possibilities emerge in rehearsal—not just in terms of the mastery of the material, but also in terms of its modification and extension. Zooid takes that principle to the extreme due to its modular structure. Although my scores are extensive in their detail, I don't want to predetermine everything, because I want to preserve that space for discovery and collaboration in rehearsal. I don't think of rehearsal as simply a matter of playing something repeatedly until you perfect it. Instead, it's a crucial space for collective experimentation. I've always liked the German word for "rehearsal," *Probe,* because it gives a sense of that exploratory, open-ended quality. You don't know what you're going to find. The score is a starting point, not the final product—much less the ideal.

I still use that tactic I learned from Cecil Taylor: I almost always switch things up on my musicians once we get in the room.

"Let's take this section and play it backwards," I'll suggest.

Or: "Instead of starting with part one," I'll tell them, "we'll start with part nine, then move to part two, and then parts five and six." It keeps them on their toes and keeps them from relying on their technical expertise or ingrained habits.

The guitarist James Blood Ulmer once told me something that Ornette Coleman said to him. "Jazz is the teacher," Ornette declared, "and blues is the preacher."

"Yeah, Blood, sure," I responded, smiling at the dictum and then tossing out an addendum of my own. "But time is the reaper."

You can't stop time. There is a momentum in the molecular structure of things. You can't prevent change from happening. You can only try to figure out how to ride with it.

I can't tell yet whether one day I'm going to feel like I've exhausted the intervallic language I've been using for more than two decades now. The basic palette of Zooid has remained more or less constant, although I've been working more and more with expanded versions of the group: Ensemble Double Up, featuring two pianos, and the large group I've taken to referring to as 14 or 15 Kestra: Agg, an "aggregate" combination of Zooid, Ensemble Double Up, and a full brass section. But I don't feel the onset of that stirring toward a transitional period: that sensation of confusion I've gotten in the past when I felt that I'd exhausted a given approach. This sound world still feels boundless: an open area of possibilities to explore.

I remember sitting at the piano in my mother's house when I was young, trying to compose. I wanted to write down five or six voices that could go all over the place yet fit together somehow in some overarching vision. This wasn't for a class—it was just me at home, determined to figure out how to make music. It took me a long time, but I did it. I wrote all these parts and I got it down on the staves in some fashion. I knew even as I was doing it that it was really bad. I didn't have any idea what I was doing. I just wanted to see if I could pull it off.

Twenty workers hustle around a small office and none of them run into each other. They slip past each other in perfect coordination, fulfilling their tasks with maximal efficiency.

There is no hesitation. There are no missteps, no tripping over each other. No wasted time, no procrastination, no dawdling, no standing in line at the coffee maker or the water cooler or the bathroom or the Xerox machine. Everybody does what they need to do at the right moment and never gets in the way of anybody else. The productivity is astonishing. How is it possible?

These are the kinds of things I imagine, sitting and daydreaming. I sit and dream up grand fantasies of orchestration.

Music is something that takes you into a dreamworld. A world where sound is matter and what matters is sound: everything is communicated and digested and comprehended in that form and that form alone. Not translated or approximated into something you can see or smell or taste or say—your senses start and end with what you can hear.

You have to enter that dreamworld in order to create music, as far as I'm concerned, with your neurosis in your side pocket. Your neurosis and your dream, they go hand in hand.

I looked at my composition, sitting there at my mother's piano in the hallway, and it was horrible. An utter mess. An embarrassment.

Henry, you don't know what you're doing, I told myself. You listen to all this music and you think you're going to be a composer. You say you want to have your own band. You claim you're going to be like Sonny, or Monk, or Stravinsky. But you're nowhere near ready yet. You haven't gotten yourself together. And the reason you haven't gotten yourself together, Henry, is that you don't understand the laws of the musical universe.

You are going to have to dedicate yourself to this journey. And it's not going to be a pleasant excursion, a leisurely jaunt into mastery. You're going to have to serve your time. It's going to be painful. You're going to get discouraged. You're going to wonder why you chose this path. At some point you're going to be convinced that you are the original template for the myth of

Sisyphus. You're going to wonder, Why am I still here, still toiling? I've persevered. I've put in the work. I've been up and down the hill over and over again. I've sat at the gate and the gate hasn't opened.

There is no goal. There is no end point—no achievement that if I attained it, I would somehow know that I'd made it. If I'm after something, if I'm aiming at something, if I'm heading somewhere, it's so far out that I can't describe it in words.

The only thing I can call it is freedom. But "freedom" is a funny word—you can't really explain what it means. Total freedom is a mirage. Freedom always comes, only comes, with restrictions. It only arrives through discipline. Through sweat. The intervallic system is the farthest I've gotten in music. What motivates the urge to advance? It's like Icarus: that primordial human desire to defy gravity and take to the air. Then the Wright brothers come along and discover a technology of elevation. A flawed contraption, to be sure, not transcendence. But a little machine that allows for temporary ascent. And further dreaming.

Working with the intervallic series, I'm still making discoveries as a composer. I've figured out how to organize things rhythmically in a way that gives the music a structural coherence not just phrase by phrase but on a much deeper level. And over time, I've learned how to combine interval series: to have multiple sets working simultaneously. At first, working with a single set of intervals, I found that I could put three voices into play at once. Now I can make it work with one or two more sets—so in the large-group pieces, I can get six or even nine voices going at the same time.

At first there were three people in the room, operating independently yet together. Now there can be nine, all doing different things. They all go about their business and nobody bumps into anybody. There are five conversations going on at once and no problem—total clarity.

I've always wanted to be able to do that. And now I think I can.

I'm still there, back at my mother's piano, even if I've slipped into a new sound world. Still there, still working at it. Still wrapped up in dreams, with my neurosis in my pocket—still determined to figure out a way to jump off the roof and fly.

Acknowledgments

The authors would like to thank the many people who helped to make this book possible, including Jules Allen; Anabel Anderson; Anthony Barboza; Daro Behroozi; Fred Brown; Elena Carminati; Cynthia Sesso; Pierre Crepon; Patricia Cruz; Ted Daniel; Jose Davila; Liberty Ellman; Helmut Frühauf; Farah Jasmine Griffin; David Hammons; David Hajdu; Craig Harris; Ray Heckman; Christopher Hoffman; Joseph Jarman; Leonard Jones; Elliot Humberto Kavee; George Lewis; Tommaso Manfredini; Jason Moran; Peter Martin Malijewski; Roscoe Mitchell; Fred Moten; Robert O'Meally; Mary Richardson; John Rogers; Brandon Ross; Adam Shatz; Wadada Leo Smith; Paul Steinbeck; Jacqui Seargeant; Michael Wilderman; and Ben Young.

We are particularly grateful to a number of people who generously lent their time and expertise to support the project. Jacki Ochs was kind enough to retrieve and rescan photo negatives from her archives, with the help of Cameron Haffner at IndieCollect. Thulani Davis and Howard Mandel sent us copies of the script and recording of the radio play, *Bed Ghosts,* as well as other useful historical information about their work with Henry. Hiie Saumaa transcribed many hours of our early conversations as we started to work on the manuscript, and served along with Aidan Levy and Melay Araya as research assistants for Henry's performances at the Tilton and Luhring Augustine galleries in the fall of 2017. Peter Mendelsund and Jules Allen gave critical advice regarding the illustrations, layout, and design. Yulun Wang and Seth Rosner at Pi Recordings provided unstinting moral support as well as practical advice and contact information.

Our agent, Chris Calhoun, has been this book's best friend, championing our collaboration from the beginning and reading drafts along the way. We were fortunate to have the opportunity to bring this book into the world with the help of our superb editor, Erroll McDonald who, with his characteristic grace and perspicacity, helped us craft and revise the narrative into its final form. We also thank the excellent team at Knopf: the copyeditor Patrick Dillon, the designers Linda Huang, John Gall, and Maria Carella, and Michael Tizzano, who helped to coordinate the production.

Above all, we would like to express our gratitude to our respective families, who have supported us through more than a decade of collaboration on this project: Sentienla Toy Threadgill, Nhumi Threadgill, Pyeng Threadgill, Melin Threadgill, Nora Nicolini, Balthazar Edwards, and Ella Edwards. Nora lent her expertise in editing some of the archival photos, and Senti read and reread multiple drafts of the entire book, offering indispensable suggestions about the structure and tone. In our repeated excursions into the upper atmosphere of Henry's life and art, we found solace in knowing that when we came back down to earth, they would always be there to catch us.

Index

Page numbers in *italics* refer to illustrations.

312; recording by, 147; saxophone playing by, 44, 45, 48, 68; *Song For*, 162, 213; Wilson concert band participation of, 58, *59*

jazz: article about, 158–62, *160*, 165–6; association between social events and historical moment, 22, 52; blind spot in jazz education, 174–5; Charlie Parker's influence on love for, 21–2; as door to other doors, 22; jam sessions for, 164; jobs and pickup work in, 177–8, 212; listening to on radio, 5; "Ornette" and not writing, 43; playing with friends from school, 32–3, 46; record shop speakers and listening to, 13–14; redefinition with Bud Powell's performance, 69; as teacher, 379

Jazz at the Philharmonic, 14

Jazz Showcase, 220, 221, 246, 312

Jazz Vespers, 281

Jelinek, Otto, 46, 58, *59*, 61

Jenkins, Leroy: advice from, influence of, and encouragement by, 262–3, 265; chamber orchestra performance of, 326, *328*; Creative Construction Company trio of, 262–3; daughter of, 268; grants, commissions, and composer residencies of, 263; musical advancement of and compositions by, 162; New York, move to by, 252; orchestral compositions by, 329; Paris, move to by and return from, 166, 182; Revolutionary Ensemble trio of, 262–3; Society Situation Dance Band performances of, 338, *339*; Squat Theatre performance of, 270; traveling with and getting stopped by police, 238–9; Windstring Ensemble performances of, 299, 330

"Jenkins Boys, Again, Wish Somebody Die, It's Hot," 290–1

Jewish community and market, 9, 35, 56

Jones, Leonard, 73, 166, 192–4, *193*

Jones, LeRoi (Amiri Baraka), 46, 159, 162

Jones, Rrata Christine, 268, 350

Joplin, Scott, 216–18, 220, 270, 293

Jordan, Clifford, 30, 281

Joyner, Allen (M'Chaka Uba), 32–3, 74, 134–5, 168

jukebox at father's casino, 13

Just the Facts and Pass the Bucket (Sextett), 302

Kaaitheater, Brussels, 208–9, 361

Kansas: American national song medley performance in, 85–8, 89, 313; Church of God in, working at, 82; contract with Army and taking classes in, 82; country-western music in, 82–3; music gigs in Kansas City, 82

Kavee, Elliot Humberto, *373*, *374*

Kennedy-King College, 44 (*See also* Wilson Junior College)

Kenwood, 197, 212–14

King, Martin Luther, Jr., 140

Kingston Mines Theatre Company, 169–70

Kolber, Dieter, 26, 27

Koncepts Cultural Gallery, 353, 355, 357

Lacy, Frank, 317, 325, 349

Ladies' Fort, 254, 256

Lake, Gene, 352, 355

Lake, Oliver, 147, 166, 252, 254–5, 258, 269, 270, 352

La MaMa Children's Workshop Theatre, 252–4, *253*, 256

Land of the Free (MacLeish), 207

Land of the Kings, 305–6

Lashley, Lester, 165, 166, 168, 182, 221

Latin music and bands, 178, 279–80, 281

Laughing Club, 364–5

Lawrence, Claude, *90*

leadership styles of bandleaders, 282–3

Lee, Don L. (Haki Madhubuti), 45–6, 170

Lee, Jeanne, 268–9

Les Brown's Band of Renown, 25, 120

401

Photographic Credits

A Note on the Type

The text of this book was set in Sabon, a typeface designed by Jan Tschichold (1902–1974), the well-known German typographer. Designed in 1966 and based on the original designs by Claude Garamond (ca. 1480–1561), Sabon was named for the punch cutter Jacques Sabon, who brought Garamond's matrices to Frankfurt.

Composed by North Market Street Graphics, Lancaster, Pennsylvania
Printed and bound by Berryville Graphics, Berryville, Virginia
Designed by Maria Carella